Structural Change in the U.S. Automobile Industry

Jeffrey Allen Hunker
Boston Consulting Group

LexingtonBooks
D.C. Heath and Company
Lexington, Massachusetts
Toronto

Library of Congress Cataloging in Publication Data

Hunker, Jeffrey Allen.
  Structural change in the U.S. automobile industry.

  Includes index.
  1. Automobile industry and trade—United States.   I. Title.   II. Title:
Structural change in the US automobile industry.
HD9710.U52H86   1983   338.4'76292'0973   82-48529
ISBN 0-669-06267-7

Published simultaneously in Canada

Printed in the United States of America

International Standard Book Number: 0-669-06267-7

Library of Congress Catalog Card Number: 82-48529

To
G. Farnell Cowan
with my love

Contents

Figures   ix

Tables   xv

Foreword   *Robert A. Leone*   xix

Acknowledgments   xxi

Chapter 1   **Introduction**   1

Structural Change as a Generic Problem   1
Responses to Structural Change   3
Framework for Addressing Structural-
   Change Issues   5
Choice of Methodology   10
The Audience Addressed by This Research   11
Outline of the Research   12

Chapter 2   **The U.S. Automobile Industry, 1965–1980**   15

Forces for Change in the U.S. Industry   15
Strategies of Automotive Companies   23
Financial Issues   54
Implications and Conclusion   57

Chapter 3   **The Global Context of the Auto Industry**   65

Forces for Increasing Industry
   Internationalization   65
Risks in Multinational Strategies   66
The Japanese Auto Industry   69
Conclusion   90

Chapter 4   **Methodology for Analyzing Future
Structural Change**   95

Structure of the Model   95
Structure of the Model within Each Time Period   101
Description of the Market   106
Firm Financial Performance   113

Making Some Assumptions Explicit   119
Model Validation   121
Conclusion   126

Chapter 5   Base Case of the Future of the U.S.
                Automobile Industry   129

Base-Case Scenarios and Strategies   129
Results   136
Financial Performance: Nominal Scenario   140
Financial Performance: Optimistic and
    Pessimistic Scenarios   144
Conclusion   147

Chapter 6   The Role of Japanese Firms in the
                Future U.S. Industry   151

Japanese Profit Maximization   151
Japanese Expansion   163
Japanese Cost Increase   169
Indirect Implications of Quotas and Orderly
    Marketing Agreements   174
Conclusions   175

Chapter 7   Oil Shocks, Energy Policy, and
                Fuel-Economy-Related Issues   179

Background to the Analysis   179
The Risk Exposure of Fuel Economy   184
Trade Policy   198
Energy Policy   202
Conclusions   205

Chapter 8   Other Government-Policy Initiatives   209

Subsidies   209
Extreme Industry Cost Reductions   215
Ford-Chrysler Merger   218
Restrictions on Diesel Engines   220
Conclusions   223

Chapter 9   Implications for Managers and Policymakers   225

Future Risk Exposure of the
    Automobile Industry   225
Implications for Managers and Policymakers   230

Contents

Framework for Dealing with Structural Change   235
Concluding Observations   237

Appendix: Mathematical Description of the Model   239

Index   261

About the Author   265

Figures

2-1	Relative Positioning of Car Models, 1966	47
2-2	Relative Positioning of Car Models, 1975	48
2-3	Relative Positioning of Car Models, 1978	49
4-1	Structure of Model over Time	97
4-2	Structure of Model within Each Time Period	97
4-3	Validation: Operating Income	123
4-4	Validation: Capital Investment	123
4-5	Validation: Fleet Fuel Economy	124
4-6	Validation: General Motors Fleet Average Weight	124
4-7	Validation: Market Sales	125
4-8	Validation: Percent Share Large Basic Cars	125
5-1	Market Sales: Model and Other Forecasts	137
5-2	Average Fleet Fuel Economy, Nominal Scenario, Infinite Supply Elasticity	139
5-3	Capital Investment, Nominal Scenario	140
5-4	Net Income, Nominal Scenario/Infinite Supply Elasticity	141
5-5	Net Income, Nominal Scenario/0.1 Supply Elasticity	143
5-6	Net Income, Nominal Scenario/1.0 Supply Elasticity	143
5-7	Net Income, Optimistic Scenario/Infinite Supply Elasticity	145
5-8	Net Income, Optimistic Scenario/0.1 Supply Elasticity	146
5-9	Net Income, Pessimistic Scenario/Infinite Supply Elasticity	147
5-10	Net Income, Pessimistic Scenario/0.1 Supply Elasticity	148
6-1	Japanese Market Share, Profit Maximization/0.1 Supply Elasticity	153

6-2   Japanese Market Share under Different Levels of
        Future Market Capture, Nominal Scenario/0.1
        Supply Elasticity   154

6-3   Net Income under Japanese Profit Maximization,
        Different Scenarios/0.1 Supply Elasticity   155

6-4   Net Income under Different Levels of Japanese
        Future Market Capture, Nominal Scenario/0.1
        Supply Elasticity   155

6-5   Net Income under Alternative Levels of Japanese
        Future Market Capture, Nominal Scenario/0.1 Supply
        Elasticity   156

6-6   Japanese Market Share under Different Trade
        Policies, Nominal Scenario   157

6-7   Japanese Market Share under Different Trade
        Policies, Optimistic Scenario   158

6-8   Japanese Market Share under Different Trade
        Policies, Pessimistic Scenario   158

6-9   Net Income under Imposition of Quotas,
        Nominal Scenario/0.1 Supply Elasticity   161

6-10   Net Income under Imposition of Tariffs,
        Nominal Scenario/0.1 Supply Elasticity   161

6-11   Net Income under Different Trade Policies, Optimistic
        Scenario/0.1 Supply Elasticity   162

6-12   Net Income under Different Trade Policies,
        Pessimistic Scenario/0.1 Supply Elasticity   162

6-13   Net Income under Different Japanese Behavior,
        Nominal Scenario   164

6-14   Net Income under Different Japanese Behavior,
        Optimistic Scenario   165

6-15   Net Income under Japanese Expansion and
        Imposition of Quotas, Nominal Scenario   166

6-16   Net Income under Japanese Expansion and
        Imposition of Tariffs, Nominal Scenario   166

6-17   Net Income under Japanese Expansion and
        Imposition of Tariffs, Optimistic Scenario   167

6–18   Net Income under Japanese Expansion and
        Imposition of Quotas, Optimistic Scenario   167

6–19   Japanese Market Share under Different Japanese
        Behavior, Nominal Scenario   171

6–20   Japanese Market Share under Different Japanese
        Behavior, Optimistic Scenario   171

6–21   Japanese Market Share under Different Japanese
        Behavior, Pessimistic Scenario   172

6–22   Net Income under Different Japanese Behavior,
        Nominal Scenario   172

6–23   Net Income under Different Japanese Behavior,
        Optimistic Scenario   173

6–24   Net Income under Different Japanese Behavior,
        Pessimistic Scenario   173

7–1   Firm Fuel Economy: Post–1985 Retooling versus No
        Retooling   185

7–2   Capital Investment: Effects of Post–1985 Retooling   186

7–3   Total Sales under Nominal, Oil-Shock, Oil-Price-
        Reduction Scenarios—Effects of North American
        Retooling   187

7–4   Market Share Large Basic Cars under Nominal,
        Oil-Shock, Oil-Price-Reduction Scenarios—
        Effects of North American Retooling   187

7–5   Japanese Market Share under Nominal, Oil-Shock,
        Oil-Price-Reduction Scenarios—Effects of North
        American Retooling   189

7–6   Net Income under Post–1985 Retooling Decision,
        Nominal Scenario/0.1 Supply Elasticity   192

7–7   Net Income under Post–1985 Retooling Decision,
        Pessimistic Scenario/0.1 Supply Elasticity   192

7–8   Net Income under Post–1985 Retooling Decision,
        Oil-Price-Reduction Scenario   193

7–9   Net Income under Post–1985 Retooling Decision,
        Oil-Shock Scenario   193

7–10   Net Income under Post–1985 Retooling—Nominal
        versus Oil-Price-Reduction Scenarios   196

7–11   Net Income under Post–1985 Retooling— Nominal
        versus Oil-Shock Scenarios   196

7–12   Net Income under No Post–1985 Retooling—Nominal
        versus Oil-Price-Reduction Scenarios   197

7–13   Net Income under No Post–1985 Retooling—Nominal
        versus Oil-Shock Scenarios   197

7–14   Japanese Market Share under Different Trade
        Policies, Oil-Shock Scenario/Post–1985 Retooling   199

7–15   Net Income under Imposition of Tariffs, Oil-Shock
        Scenario/Post–1985 Retooling   200

7–16   Net Income under Imposition of Quotas, Oil-Shock
        Scenario/Post–1985 Retooling   201

7–17   Net Income under Different Trade Policies, Oil-
        Shock Scenario/No Retooling   201

7–18   Net Income under Post–1985 Retooling—Oil-Shock/
        Energy-Policy Scenarios   204

7–19   Net Income under No Post–1985 Retooling—Oil-
        Shock/Energy-Policy Scenarios   204

8–1   Net Income with Subsidies, Nominal Scenario   210

8–2   Net Income with Subsidies, Optimistic Scenario   210

8–3   Net Income with Subsidies, Pessimistic Scenario   211

8–4   Amount of Subsidies to U.S. Firms, Different
        Scenarios/0.1 Supply Elasticity   211

8–5   Net Income with Subsidies, Nominal Scenario/
        Infinite Supply Elasticity   212

8–6   Amount of Subsidies to U.S. Firms, Nominal
        Scenario/0.1, Infinite Supply Elasticity   212

8–7   Net Income with Subsidies, Oil-Shock Scenario/
        Post–1985 Retooling   213

8–8   Amount of Subsidies to U.S. Firms, Nominal/
        Oil-Shock Scenarios—0.1 Supply Elasticity   213

8–9   Net Income under Extreme Industry Cost Reductions,
        Pessimistic Scenario/No Post–1985 Retooling   216

8-10   Net Income under Extreme Industry Cost Reductions,
            Nominal Scenario/Infinite Supply Elasticity   217

8-11   Net Income under Extreme Industry Cost Reductions,
            Oil-Shock Scenario/No Post-1985 Retooling   217

8-12   Net Income under Ford-Chrysler Merger, Nominal
            Scenario/No Post-1985 Retooling .   219

8-13   Net Income under Ford-Chrysler Merger, Pessimistic
            Scenario/No Post-1985 Retooling   219

8-14   Net Income under Ford-Chrysler Merger, Nominal
            Scenario/Infinite Supply Elasticity   220

8-15   Net Income under Diesel-Engine Restrictions,
            Nominal Scenario/Post-1985 Retooling   221

8-16   Net Income under Diesel-Engine Restrictions,
            Nominal Scenario/Infinite Supply Elasticity   222

8-17   Net Income under Diesel-Engine Restrictions,
            Oil-Shock Scenario/Post-1985 Retooling   222

A-1   Structure of the Model over Time   240

Tables

2–1	U.S. New-Car Vehicle Sales	17
2–2	U.S. Automotive-Market Segmentation	18
2–3	U.S. Car-Market Share, by Firm	20
2–4	After-Tax Return on Stockholders' Equity and Profit Margin for the U.S. Automobile Industry and All Manufacturing, 1965–1976	22
2–5	Annual Capital Investments of the Big Three U.S. Auto Makers, 1968–1977	24
2–6	Projected Capital Requirements of U.S. Auto Makers	25
2–7	Manufacturing-Cost Changes with Volume	25
2–8	1978 Manufacturing Capacity Utilization by Segment and Manufacturer	28
2–9	Vehicle Sales per Dealership, 1980	33
2–10	Worldwide Passenger-Car Market Shares, 1980	35
2–11	Car and Truck Market Shares outside the United States and Canada, 1976 and 1980	35
2–12	Percentage of Total Unit Sales: Cars and Trucks Sold in United States for Each Manufacturer	36
2–13	1980 Factory Unit Sales outside Home Country for Selected Firms: Cars and Trucks	37
2–14	Profitability of International versus Domestic Operations: Chrysler	39
2–15	Percentage Units Sold outside United States and Canada: Chrysler	39
2–16	Profitability of International versus Domestic Operations: General Motors	40
2–17	Percentage Units Sold outside United States and Canada: General Motors (Cars and Trucks)	41
2–18	Distribution of Net Assets: International versus North American: General Motors	41

2-19	Division of Assets and Capital Expenditures: International versus North America: Ford	42
2-20	Profitability of International versus Domestic Operations: Ford	42
2-21	Cash Flow for Domestic Producers over Time	55
2-22	Debt/Equity Ratios of Domestic Producers over Time	55
2-23	Actual and Projected Investment as Percentage Cash Flow	56
2-24	Projection of Chrysler Corporation Capital Flows under Normal Circumstances	58
2-25	Projection of General Motors Capital Flows under Normal Circumstances	59
2-26	Projection of Ford Motor Company Capital Flows under Normal Circumstances	60
3-1	Summary of Low and High World-Demand Projections, 1980-1990	67
3-2	New Passenger Automobiles: Japanese Production, Exports, Imports, 1956-1979	71
3-3	Motor-Vehicle Sales in Japan	71
3-4	Japanese Car Production by Engine Size	72
3-5	Japanese Export Shares by Region	73
3-6	Japan, U.S. and European Community Tariff Rates on Passenger Cars, 1967-1978	74
3-7	Japanese Market Share by Firm	75
3-8	Financial Status: Japanese Producers	75
3-9	Exports as Percentage of Total Production: Japanese Producers	76
3-10	Relative Growth of Production and Exports: Japanese Producers	77
3-11	Quality Comparisons of Foreign and Domestic Automobiles, 1979	81
3-12	Prices in Japan Compared with the United States for Selected Models	81

3–13   Average April Rates of Yen/Dollar Exchange,
        1964–1980   83

3–14   Dependence of Japanese Producers on U.S. Sales,
        1979   84

3–15   Japanese Automobile-Production Capacity   85

4–1   1979 Manufacturer Baseline Fleet, Market Share
        by Class   102

4–2   1979 Sales by Manufacturer   103

4–3   Manufacturer Measures to Improve Fuel Economy   104

4–4   1979 Base Auto Market   107

4–5   Demand Elasticities   110

4–6   Supply Elasticities   112

4–7   U.S. Consumer Repurchase Loyalty, 1979   113

4–8   Total Variable Production Costs   114

4–9   Financial Data: U.S. Passenger-Car Operations   117

4–10   Balance Sheet: U.S. Passenger-Car Operations, 31
        December 1979   117

4–11   General Motors: Income Statement for Year 1981   119

5–1   Nominal Economic Conditions   130

5–2   Pessimistic Economic Conditions   131

5–3   Optimistic Economic Conditions   132

5–4   Schedule for Downsizing, Front-Wheel-Drive
        Conversion, and Material Substitution   133

5–5   Schedule for Efficiency Improvements   134

5–6   Price Shifts under Different U.S. Supply Elasticities,
        Nominal Scenario   138

5–7   Market-Mix Shifts: Base Case   138

6–1   Annualized Percentage Change in Selling Prices under
        Different Levels of Japanese Future-Market Capture,
        1980–1990   153

6–2   Japanese Mix: Percent Small Luxury Cars   159

6–3	Japanese Vehicle Prices: Small Luxury Cars	159
6–4	Japanese Vehicle Prices: Small Basic Cars	160
6–5	Net Present Value of Japanese Profit: 1980–1995; Nominal Scenario, Japanese Profit Maximization	160
6–6	Net Present Value of Japanese Profit: 1980–1995; Nominal Scenario, Japanese Expansion	168
6–7	Japanese Mix: Percent Small Luxury Cars	168
7–1	Manufacturer-Specific Schedules for Post–1985 Fuel-Economy Improvements	180
7–2	Schedule for Post–1985 Efficiency Improvements	181
7–3	Oil-Shock Economic Conditions	183
7–4	Oil-Price-Reduction Economic Conditions	184
7–5	Net Present Value of Japanese Profits: 1985, 1990, 1995; Nominal, Oil-Shock, Oil-Price-Reduction Scenarios	190
7–6	Price Changes due to Post–1985 Retooling	191
7–7	Price Changes due to Trade Policy	199
7–8	Net Present Value of Japanese Profits: 1985, 1990, 1995; Oil-Shock Scenario and Trade Policy	200
7–9	Energy-Policy Scenario	203
7–10	U.S. Vehicle Price Changes under Energy-Policy Scenario	203
A–1	Labor Share of Total Variable Production Cost	254
A–2	Piecewise Linear Approximation to Production Scale Economies	255
A–3	Pro-Forma Income-Statement Relationships	259

Foreword

These are unusually complicated times for the U.S. auto industry, and there is a compelling need for unusually creative analytical approaches to the industry's problems. Jeffrey Hunker has responded to this need by undertaking a rigorous, computer-based analysis of the U.S. auto industry using principles of corporate strategic planning. The notion of corporate strategy has been the basis of professional management education and the object of corporate-planning staffs in individual companies for decades. But it has only recently matured as an acceptable intellectual discipline for analyzing industrywide phenomena. Hunker makes full use of its techniques.

Hunker has avoided the temptation to second-guess corporate strategists and public policymakers responsible for the industry's current condition. While his analysis is based on historical behavior and performance, its focus is on the future. Hunker blames no one for the industry's present condition and makes no comments on what should have been done. This alone is a refreshing perspective at a time when laying blame seems preferred to solving the industry's problems.

Because the analysis is prospective and in the planning mode, some will view it as nonscientific in that various behavioral hypotheses about structural change in the years ahead are not empirically testable. While this may bother some academic purists, it will certainly not bother those in the industry who constantly must make decisions based on today's limited information. Hunker attempts to minimize the limitations inherent in a prospective analysis through the discipline of the computer, insistence on a strong base of historical statistics, and a long list of alternative future scenarios.

Perhaps the most innovative aspect of Hunker's analysis is its recognition that the auto industry's future is the simultaneous product of both private and public decisions. Thus Hunker explicitly treats issues of industrial policy and their likely impact on the auto industry. By showing the relationship between regulatory policies, in particular, and corporate strategies in this industry, Hunker brings together managerial and public-policy approaches that tend to be isolated one from another. His effort is clearly ambitious—perhaps overly ambitious—but there can be no doubt of the need to join the intellectual perspectives of industrial policymakers and corporate strategists in studying this industry.

As our appreciation of the forces reshaping the U.S. auto industry improves, others will improve upon Hunker's analysis. The usefulness of his analysis is not its forecasts for the year 1995. His concern is not the accuracy of forecasts, but the systematic and rigorous evaluation of alternative private and public strategies for successful adaptation to change in this industry.

I suspect that Hunker's attempt to rigorously describe and scrutinize individual corporate strategies in the context of an industrywide analysis is only the first of many attempts. The success of his approach will be measured by the willingness of decision makers to subject their own judgments about sound strategy to the rigors of a similar analysis and by the willingness of analysts to acknowledge the relevance and susceptibility to analysis of strategic concepts.

The automobile industry is unquestionably a major force in the U.S. economy, as economic statistics readily show. But the importance of the automobile to the U.S. economy today goes well beyond measures of economic statistics. Changes facing U.S. auto manufacturers, in particular, are not merely challenges to existing jobs and entrenched economic interests; they are fundamental challenges to an American economic ego that finds it virtually impossible to think of the U.S. economy without thinking of the automobile industry. Whether as consumers, laborers, or stockholders, we all have a stake in Hunker's analysis.

Robert A. Leone
John F. Kennedy School of Government
Harvard University

Acknowledgments

This book is the result of work that I did while at the Harvard Business School. During that time, I had the privilege of working under Professors Stephen Bradley, William Abernathy, and Robert Leone. I benefited greatly from their many comments, and I am grateful for the guidance they provided.

My work was supported by a grant from the Division of Research of the Harvard Business School.

On a more personal note, my parents were a source of great comfort and support throughout this project. I am also grateful to Farnell Cowan for her encouragement, assistance, and good cheer; it is more than appropriate that to her this book is dedicated.

The views in this book are my own, and not those of either the Harvard Business School or the Boston Consulting Group.

1

Introduction

The automobile industry is only one of several domestic industries—including textiles, consumer electronics, and steel—whose competitive luster has tarnished under increasing foreign competition, changing markets, and new technology. Many industry observers argue that the auto industry's difficulties are largely temporary. Others, meanwhile, regard the current problems as representative of a more fundamental challenge to the industry and to important national capabilities in automobile production.

Contained within this debate is a set of broader issues concerning the consequences of changing industrial structure and the appropriate role corporate strategy and government policy should play in responding effectively to its perceived problems. The automobile industry is, of course, not unique as an industry facing structural change. However, a growing recognition of the broader social and economic consequences of structural change within this sector, coming on the heels of a decade of trade deficits and generally lackluster economic performance, has focused interest on developing a more effective response to the challenges of structural evolution.

This book examines the future of the U.S. automobile industry, and the effect some possible developments in corporate strategy, government policy, and other social and economic factors may have on its future viability and competitiveness. The broader objective is to address the critical interactions between corporate strategic decisions and industrial policy, as a guide to better understanding of and more effective response to the problems of industry structural change.

Structural Change as a Generic Problem

Structural change has always been a recognized aspect of economic growth. Only relatively recently, however, has structural change as a generic problem attracted the attention of managers, policymakers, and analysts. There appear to be several reasons for this increased interest.

One reason is that the past decade has witnessed what may be a permanent acceleration in the pace of economic change.[1] Sharply increased energy prices, the increasing internationalization of markets, and rapid technological change each in itself is a major force for economic adjustment. Together they have served to magnify and accelerate the pressures for readjustment in some sectors, disrupting not only the competitive performance of firms and long-standing patterns of industrial organization but also causing problems of regional and demographic adjustment.

The interest in structural change also undoubtedly reflects a concern over the perception of economic decline in this country. On a macro-economic level, the generally sluggish performance of the economy, low rates of productivity improvement, and high and persistent trade deficits have ceased to be regarded merely as transitory. On a more disaggregate level, the loss of worldwide competitive advantage in some sectors, such as automobiles, and the virtual disappearance of other U.S. industries, such as consumer electronics, have posed troubling questions both as to the competitiveness of the U.S. economy and the appropriate responses of policy-makers and managers.

A third reason is the growing awareness that government involvement in many sectors of the economy carries with it substantial and oftentimes unanticipated consequences for the performance and structure of industries. Regardless of their normative or social goals, these policies have changed, frequently in subtle fashion, the structure of competitive advantage in industries and the range of options facing managers. As it is unlikely the social goals that originally prompted such interventions will be abandoned, the expanding scope of government intervention challenges policy-makers to develop new tools for achieving these goals, while accounting for the unintended impacts on economic activity.[2]

Trends in some basic and mature industrial sectors highlight the concern over these issues of economic adjustment and illustrate their complexity. In the steel industry, a variety of circumstances have contributed to the loss of competitive advantage by major integrated producers: changes in both the location and composition of demand, lagging response to technological change, capital drains from mandated pollution control, and the rise of vigorous foreign competition. In the automobile industry, the sudden rise in gasoline prices and changing demand have altered the sources of competitive advantage in the market. The shift in competition from styling to technology and quality has challenged the existing competitive strengths of domestic producers and forced high levels of capital expenditure at the same time that foreign competitors have increased their presence markedly.[3]

In the past, of course other mature industries have undergone structural readjustments. Textile manufacturers, for example, migrated from obsolete Northeastern locations to low-cost areas in the Southeast and concentrated in high value-added or specialty products. In these and other cases a complex set of circumstances has altered the competitive value of established strategic positions, and opened up new ways of competing successfully.

Unfortunately, the current pressures for structural adjustment are coming at a time when slow economic growth may have reduced the capacity of the economy to absorb the shocks of major structural adjustment.[4] Furthermore, sectors like automobiles are important both as large employers and also as key links in the industrial base of a modern economy. Any permanent loss of competitiveness in these sectors may have profound consequences far beyond the immediate effects of individual sectors.

The automobile industry represents a sector in which the increasing concern about structural adjustment in the economy has taken the form of a tangible debate.[5] The importance of the auto industry as a base for a modern industrial economy and its role in providing employment have challenged both policymakers and managers to develop more effective ways of dealing with the concerns raised by a complex set of circumstances. The complexity of these problems and the importance of this sector suggest that merely fine tuning of past actions may not be the appropriate reponse if important national capabilities in auto manufacturing are to be maintained.

The situation in the automobile industry is in many ways typical of those in several other sectors: mature industries that have lost their international competitiveness and are facing structural change driven by increasing foreign competition, shifts in markets, new technologies, or regulatory initiatives. While the specifics of an analysis of structural change in autos may be applicable only to that sector, the more general conclusions—and the methodology that produced them—may contribute to guiding policy and strategy in other sectors.

Responses to Structural Change

These circumstances have led to increased interest on the part of both managers and policymakers in developing more effective ways to cope with and direct structural change.

For managers, a variety of increasingly sophisticated tools for strategic planning and industry analysis have been developed over the past two decades. Paralleling the increasing sophistication of managers, the past several years have witnessed numerous proposals for a revised industrial policy. Such a policy, generally speaking, would attempt to guide the broad collection of governmental activities affecting individual industries and sectors to promote economic growth. While the exact form of such proposals varies with the proponent, the interest in a revised industrial policy reflects a recognition of the substantial influence government policies exert on individual sectors of the economy.[6]

As a practical matter, however, formulating effective responses to the problems of structural change has been frustrated by a lack of understanding both in theory and in practice as to what role decision makers in government and firms can actually play. This limited understanding is particularly acute in the following areas:

1. *Implications of government policy on competitive performance:* By its very nature industrial policy concerns itself with the coordination of numerous policy tools to influence performance in the so-called unregulated industries. However, the understanding of the competitive implications of policy interventions is yet limited. Bradley and Leone[7] have expanded upon the different competitive impacts of regulatory changes. A few regulatory impact studies have also shown a sophisticated appreciation of policy impacts and their competitive effects. Hartman and his colleagues[8] simulated the impacts on the U.S. copper industry of pollution-abatement regulations promulgated by the U.S. Environmental Protection Agency. Joskow and Baughman used a simulation model of the U.S. electric-utility industry to examine the demand for nuclear reactors under several different scenarios, including different regulatory conditions.[9]

2. *Dynamics of structural change:* Only a few studies have addressed the dynamics of structural evolution directly. Porter and Spence[10] studied the capacity-expansion process in the corn wet-milling industry. They employed a rational-expectations framework to describe the dynamic-equilibrium evolution of capacity addition in this oligopolistic industry. In a theoretical paper in the same spirit, Spence[11] studied the optimal level of preemptive investment in a growing industry and the implications for the long-run structure of the market. Leone,[12] in analyzing the impact of effluent-control regulations of the pulp industry, also used a model of rational expectations of plant closure and investment to describe industry evolution under the new regulatory regime. Abernathy,[13] in a different approach, outlined the dynamic consequences of technological change on productive units of the automobile-manufacturing system and assessed the broader implications for industry structure and performance.

3. *Risk:* There is little understanding of how the choice of corporate strategy and industrial policy affects the degree of risk facing firms or how issues of risk influence the pattern of structural change. In one of the few studies dealing with this topic, Bradley and Karnani[14] studied the effects of fuel-economy regulations on the degree of risk facing U.S. automobile manufacturers.

The complexity of issues relating to structural change has meant that much of the work done is descriptive rather than prescriptive. Most analytical work has largely taken as fixed the conditions under which the industry operates, analyzing only a limited number of issues. Yet, in fact, effective response to pressures for structural change requires understanding the interactions and consequences of a conceivably wide range of possible developments. No past studies have attempted to address this reality analytically as a means of clarifying the critical issues—and their implications for both managers and policymakers. Yet if the challenges of structural change are to be met effectively, it is precisely this knowledge that is required.

Framework for Addressing Structural-Change Issues

The interest in better coping with structural change poses several challenges to analysts and decision makers. First, it is necessary to define what is meant by structural change so as to be able to focus the areas of interest in this research. Second, it is necessary to better understand the strategic implications of government policies on the competitive performance of firms. These effects are both substantial and poorly understood.[15] Yet it is precisely an understanding of these impacts that is required if policies aimed at responding to structural-change issues are not to exacerbate the problems they are intended to correct. Third, effective analysis requires a better understanding of the consequences of the increasing internationalization of many industries. The markets for many products have expanded across national borders. The rise of substantial foreign competition in these sectors has altered the pattern of competitive interaction and challenged the notion that the domestic market is the appropriate frame of analysis.

The dynamics of structural evolution are a final subtle, but very important, aspect that must be addressed. Almost by definition there exist numerous interdependencies between public and private actions, although the manner and mechanism by which the decisions of firms and the choices of policymakers condition each other remain unclear. With the internationalization of markets, these dynamics extend to foreign as well as domestic spheres.

A framework for addressing these issues is developed in the following sections.

The Concept of Strategy

Fundamental to the process of structural change are the long-term strategic decisions of firms. Ultimately, it is these decisions that lie at the heart of industry evolution. It is important, therefore, to understand this concept better as a means of clarifying the linkages between strategy, public policy, and external events.

Strategy is defined here as an organization's marshalling and organizing of resources to achieve objectives over its planning horizon. The choice of strategy establishes the manner in which a firm competes in the market, organizes and allocates its resources, and responds to competitive and other challenges. It is the overwhelming factor in defining the firm's ability to respond to change and the vulnerability and exposure of the firm to risk and change. The elements of strategy define the numerous and frequently subtle means by which public policy affects firm performance.

The concept of strategy provides a means of defining what is meant by structural change. Structural change is the process whereby firms redefine how they participate in the market. These changes can be understood through an analysis of corporate strategy.

While the specifics of strategy are unique to individual firms and their industrial context, strategic position may be described along three dimensions. The first is the firm's scope of participation in various markets: the breadth of its product line, vertical integration, participation in related markets, and consumer franchise, among others. For example, in the automobile industry, General Motors competes with a broad product line and high level of vertical integration, while American Motors has a much more limited product line and lower levels of integration.

Competitive emphasis—those characteristics along which the firm especially chooses to compete—is a second dimension of strategy. A sports-car or specialty-vehicle producer may choose to emphasize performance or advanced technology, while a full-line producer may be more likely to emphasize uniform quality and low cost. Competitive emphasis can differ within the same producer, of course. The competitive emphasis a full-line producer places on its luxury vehicles may differ from that of its mass-production lines.

The third element of strategy concerns the locus of change within the corporate organization—that is, the sorts of fundamental structural change to which the organization is best prepared to respond. U.S. automobile manufacturers for many years followed policies of *trickle-down innovation,* in which new developments were first introduced at the top of the line and gradually were introduced into their lower-priced, high-volume lines later. These incremental changes in technology were allied with annual or biennial model changes. In contrast, foreign producers often followed strategies of long production runs of a virtually unchanged model, followed by a radical redesign of the entire vehicle. In another area, U.S. producers were geared toward the production of large vehicles with a major styling input, while most foreign producers built smaller cars in which styling was not intrinsically as important.

Policy Impacts

While the manner in which government policies influence the strategic decisions and performance of firms is a complex issue, it is important to recognize the effect of these sometimes subtle interactions.

For example, the Corporate Average Fuel Economy (CAFE) regulations require auto makers to meet fuel-economy standards averaged over all cars they sell each year. Since vehicles vary drastically in their respective fuel economies, the CAFE requirements may encourage or discourage manufacturers from selling certain types of cars; for example, a manufacturer specializing in large, fuel-inefficient cars may be encouraged to sell more small, fuel-efficient vehicles so as to improve the average fleet mileage. CAFE regulations, therefore, may influence the manufacturer's scope of market participation. Import quotas, by constraining a high-volume, low-profit margin strategy, may encourage auto importers to shift their competitive emphasis toward more profitable, but lower volume, cars. When the 1970 Clean Air Act mandated reductions in emissions, the probable effect was to give a competitive advantage to foreign producers, both because smaller cars were inherently easier to clean up and also because the sorts of across-the-board massive redesign required by regulation fit the sorts of change that foreign producers were accustomed to. U.S. producers, on the other hand, were forced to respond in an unfamiliar manner.

Generalizing, the choice of policy impacts corporate performance in at least the following dimensions:

1. *Cost:* Government regulations induce both changes in the level and structure of costs. While changes in the level of costs may have competitive implications, more importance may center on changing cost structures and their consequences not only for the short-term profitability but also for longer-term profitability. For example, regulatory requirements in safety, emissions, and fuel economy have vastly increased vehicle-design requirements. Because of very high-scale economies of design, these regulations have had the probable effect of increasing the relative cost advantages of the largest producers.

2. *Demand:* Government policies affect the level and structure of demand in at least two fashions. One is by affecting extensive demand—that is, the total size of the market. For example, in Japan safety and other regulations that substantially increase the cost of owning a vehicle after the fourth year may increase vehicle turnover and thus the size of the market.[16]

Intensive demand describes the share of the total consumer dollar spent on a good that is captured by a particular sector. In the case of automobiles, consumer spending breaks down between vehicle purchase, accruing to auto makers, and vehicle operation, primarily fuel costs. Regulations that mandate improved fuel efficiency, for instance, reduce the fuel-related costs of driving. As a hypothetical example, if technology permits, a manufacturer can improve fuel economy, sell higher-priced cars (a greater share of the consumer dollar accruing to him), and possibly still keep the total cost of driving constant. The net effect is that even if extensive demand remains relatively unchanged, intensive demand of auto manufacturers can increase or decrease.

3. *Risk:* Government policy influences the level and composition of risk facing firms in several ways. Policy can create strategic dimensions where none existed before, thus exposing firms to new risks (as in the case of emissions and pollution regulations). Incoherent sets of policies can impose a multiplicity of conflicting strategic signals. For example, the imposition of CAFE regulations mandating improved fleet fuel economy, together with low and regulated gasoline prices, sent conflicting signals to firms and consumers. On one hand firms were required to improve fuel economy, while on the other hand consumers were denied at least one impetus (higher gasoline prices) to buy more fuel-efficient cars.

Since firms differ in their strategies, these policy impacts will affect even firms within the same industry differently. The net result is to create "winners" and "losers" among the affected firms, as some firms are strategically positioned to benefit more from the consequences of changing policy so others are strategically better positioned to benefit from changes in markets or technology.

Exposure to Risk

Through the choice of strategy, firms condition the manner in which they can best respond to changes in markets, competition, and government policy. For example, U.S. automobile producers, accustomed to operating in a market where low gasoline prices and excellent roads prompted the demand for large vehicles, were less well prepared for the sudden shift in demand resulting from higher oil prices than foreign producers, accustomed to operating in markets with a substantial small-car demand.

By virtue of the investments made in physical and human capital, the explicit or implicit recognition of goals throughout the organization, and the institutional relationships that develop, a coherent strategy develops a momentum about it. This momentum discourages short-run deviations, but it also implies that there is a cost associated with major strategic changes. These costs can be physical, as in the need for new plants and equipment, or they can be human and organizational. New personal and institutional relationships have to be created, new organizational structures developed, and new skills learned if there is significant change.

Because strategy cannot prepare a firm equally well for all contingencies, the choice of strategy defines the firm's exposure to effects of future changes for which it is unprepared. For example, high levels of vertical integration may result in cost advantages but may also reduce the flexibility and speed of retooling if technological or market changes make the manufacturing structure obsolete. Frequent model changes in automobiles may promote replacement demand but sacrifice scale and experience effects and expose the producer to lower-cost competition. Exposure to risk is merely a recognition that an organization cannot do all things equally well, nor can it respond equally well to all sorts of change.

These issues of exposure are particularly important when the firm's environment is changing rapidly or in unexpected fashions. New goverment regulations may quite unintendedly expose firms to significant risks—as do also unstable economic and competitive conditions. Facing such an environment, firms may hedge their actions to reduce their exposure to unwanted risk.

Issues to Address in the Analysis of Structural Change

The definition of strategy and the discussion of public policy have suggested some of the ways in which the critical strategic choices of firms and policy changes of government officials interact. These dynamic and interactive effects are an important element to understanding the evolution of industries.

While it is clear that government policy affects the choice of firm strategy—and in fact is one of the legitimate purposes of policy—the choice of firm strategy may also influence the development of public policy. Just as government policy creates winners and losers among the affected firms, and so creates pressures for strategic change, so too the strategies of firms condition the success and cost of government actions. Through the choice of technology, capital, and human investment, firms can alter the efficacy and relative economic and social costs of different regulatory policies. Firms may invest in human or physical capital that regulators are reluctant to destroy through policy initiatives, or otherwise choose strategies that increase the "cost" of achieving selected goals. The choice of firm position may make it impossible to "get from here to there" in a policy framework within an acceptable cost. There is a range of interactions between public policy and firm strategy. These links are as of yet poorly understood, but given the importance of public policy in shaping competitive outcomes, this interaction represents a critical reality of structural change.

The analysis of public-policy impacts must further distinguish between normative questions, which properly concern themselves with the broader ideological and social merits of policy, and positive questions about the direct and indirect consequences of such interventions. Independent of the broader social goals, the choice of public policy may alter cost levels and structure, determine the form of new organizational and managerial relationships, and require that firms utilize new skills and resources to meet the challenge. These effects are often unintended, and their nature and magnitude are intimately tied to the specific character of the regulation as much as to the overall policy goals.

A final point is that issues of structural change are not confined exclusively to the domestic market or industry but are multinational in scope. Many of the sectors that have undergone or are now undergoing structural change are characterized by growing internationalization of markets. Textiles, steel, and automobiles, and increasingly semiconductors, computers, and other high-technology industries have or will likely undergo this maturation and internationalization.[17]

For analysts studying issues of structural change, and for managers and policymakers attempting to deal with it, this internationalization of many sectors has several consequences. First, it heightens the interdependence between the industrial policies of different nations. Though the form of intervention varies, many countries have sought to improve the international competitiveness of selected sectors through explicit government policy.

Internationalization also brings increased interdependence between competitive and market developments throughout the world. As a consequence, the choice of firm strategies in one market may be driven by developments elsewhere. In particular, the strategies of importers or firms with a substantial multinational breadth may be very different from those of firms operating strictly in the domestic market—not only in the manner in which they compete but in the manner in which they will respond to change. The strategies of such firms may be driven by developments in markets elsewhere, and the manner in which such firms respond to regulatory and competitive developments here will depend upon more than just their posture in this single market.

The point is that, whether domestically or internationally, choices of strategy and policy are conditioned by each other. This interaction is an important and dynamic element of structural change. Effective analysis and understanding of industry evolution must deal not only with the consequences of an uncertain environment but also with the critical reality of these interactions.

Choice of Methodology

There are several approaches one could take to studying these issues. One approach would be the construction of a purely theoretical industry to study structural change. Too little is understood of the problem now to make such an approach very effective in addressing issues of interest. In particular, the decision structure of the problem outlined is complex and poorly understood.

A second approach would be a historical study of several industries that have undergone structural change. While effective in addressing many of the subtleties of the issues of interest, such an approach is inherently limited in the insight it provides. In a historic context it is often difficult to isolate the effects of one single policy or strategic instrument. Furthermore, without substantial second-guessing of the industry's evolution, the framework for analysis is limited to what actually went on.

Instead, this research models structural change in a single sector—the U.S. automobile industry—using both historical and analytical techniques. Issues of structural change are complex and sometimes subtle. A focused approach is necessary to identify the important aspects to a problem that is ill-defined at the onset. Furthermore, issues of structural change are critically linked to the particulars of corporate strategy and competitve dynamics. A detailed knowledge of the industry is required to understand them.

To address these issues effectively, the analysis needs to be firm specific. Firms position themselves differently on the relevant competitive dimensions of their industry depending on their history, resources, and perception of the environment. While the overall industry response to policy interventions of external change may be of interest, it is important to realize that industry response is merely the aggregation of individual firm responses, and an analysis of the consequences of change must begin at the component level of firms. It is important to look at the manner in which these differences among firms translate into differences in competitive viability in the face of changes in government policy, competition, and the environment.

Because the issues are complex, the first step is to understand more about the structure and functioning of the industry and the forces that shape it. Although the concern is with the domestic industry, the importance of the international developments here means that both the domestic industry and international dimensions should be studied. The second step is to study the impacts of alternative strategies, public policies, and external developments on the future development in the U.S. industry. A mathematical model of the industry is used, which incorporates the likely patterns of action by the different participants and their consequences for the evolution of the industry. A final step is a critique of these results and an evaluation of their contribution toward a more advanced understanding of industrial policy and structural change.

The Audience Addressed by This Research

The interface of industrial policy and structural adjustment is fraught with implications for the performance of individual firms and the achievement of broader social and policy goals. This fact suggests that for both managers and public policymakers there is a great value in better understanding the underlying process, the conditions that drive it, and the impli-

cations for decision makers. For managers, there is a need to better understand the determinants of firm performance and the manners in which the
choice of firm strategy influences industry evolution. For public policymakers, there is a growing recognition that many industries will face
pressures for restructuring. The development of effective and coordinated
policies requires an understanding of the industry's condition now and its
pattern of future development.

Such analysis must also recognize that, as well as being viewed in the
broader context of social goals, regulation also can be analyzed in terms of
its specific competitive impacts. Strategic use of the regulatory process, in
other words, can be a means of obtaining competitive advantage for firms.

While political issues are certainly an important dimension of the questions examined here, it is crucial to note that this analysis does not stress the
institutional dimensions of political behavior. There is an important distinction between understanding a process and influencing it. The issues just
presented are not only areas of action for specific decision makers but also
problems that demand new analytical methods and greater understanding.
There is a need for analytical methods to accommodate political factors in a
rigorous framework of competitive behavior. It is this latter concern that
this research shall address.

Outline of the Research

Chapter 1 has developed a framework for analyzing the critical industrial-
policy issues relating to structural change. The rest of this research is a study
of structural change in the U.S. automobile industry.

Chapters 2 and 3 comprise a strategic analysis of the automobile industry. Chapter 2 examines the structural change experienced by the U.S. automobile industry over the past fifteen years and discusses both past and
possible future evolutions in firm strategies. Chapter 3 focuses on the industry outside of the United States. It is principally concerned with the
Japanese auto industry and possible paths for its future evolution as they
may affect the U.S. market.

The second part of this book is an examination of possible future structural change in the U.S. auto industry over the 1980–1995 period. Chapter 4
develops the simulation methodology used to analyze these issues. Following that, chapters 5 through 8 examine some of the principal sources of risk
and forces for future structural change as they affect the industry.

The first critical issue addressed is to identify the pressures for structural change in the U.S. auto industry. To do so, a base case is developed to
determine whether the current industry stucture and firm strategies will
remain viable in the future. The base case presents a view of the industry

future without major structural change and evaluates individual firm performance under it.

The following chapters (chs. 6, 7, 8) then study some of the potential major forces for structural change facing the U.S. industry. Chapter 6 looks at the impact of non-U.S.-chartered auto makers on the U.S. market and industry. The analysis is tied to developments in the international industry as well as to the effects of possible trade policies. Chapter 7 studies the effect of future changes in petroleum prices and the consequences of further fleet fuel-economy improvements after 1985 on the viability and risk exposure of individual firms. Chapter 8 then looks at a variety of other public policy initiatives. These initiatives include restrictions on diesel engines, subsidies to the domestic industry, extreme changes in antitrust policy, and extreme changes in industry cost structure.

While the issues examined here are not an exhaustive list of the factors influencing the U.S. industry, they are intended to cover the principal forces for structural change facing the industry and address those dimensions that have attracted the most concern by analysts, policymakers, and managers.

The final chapter outlines the principal conclusions reached here and their relevance to both an extended understanding of structural change and the choice of public policy and corporate strategy in other sectors.

Notes

1. Stephen Bradley and Robert Leone, "Toward an Effective Industrial Policy," *Harvard Business Review,* (forthcoming).

2. U.S., President, Council of Economic Advisers, *Economic Report of the President* (Washington, D.C.: U.S. Government Printing Office, 1981), pp. 99–107.

3. Ibid., p. 127–128.

4. Ibid., p. 90.

5. Douglas H. Ginsburg and William J. Abernathy, eds.: *Government, Technology, and the Future of the Automobile* (New York: McGraw-Hill Book Co., 1980).

6. Bradley and Leone; Jeffrey Hunker, "National Industrial Policy: A Background Note" (Boston: Harvard Business School, forthcoming).

7. See, for example, Robert Leone, "Competition and the Regulatory Boom," in *Government Regulation of Business: Its Growth, Impact, and Future,* ed. Dorothy M. Tella (Washington, D.C.: Chamber of Commerce of the United States, 1979); idem, "The Real Costs of Regulation," *Harvard Business Review,* (November–December 1977); idem, ed., *Environmental Controls: The Impact on Industry* (Lexington, Mass.: Lexington Books, D.C. Heath and Co., 1976).

8. Raymond S. Hartman, K. Bozdogan, and R.M. Nadkarni, "The Economic Impacts of Environmental Regulations on the U.S. Copper Industry," *The Bell Journal of Economics* (Autumn 1979), pp. 589-618.

9. P.L. Joskow and M.L. Baughman, "The Future of the U.S. Nuclear Energy Industry." *The Bell Journal of Economics* (Spring 1976), pp. 3-32.

10. Michael Porter and A. Michael Spence, *The Capacity Expansion Process in a Growing Oligopoly: The Case of Corn Wet Milling* (Cambridge, Mass: Harvard University, 1980). (Mimeographed.)

11. A. Michael Spence, "Investment Strategy and Growth in a New Market," *The Bell Journal of Economics* (Spring 1979), pp. 1-19.

12. Leone, *Environmental Controls.*

13. William J. Abernathy, *The Productivity Dilemma: Roadblock to Innovation in the Automobile Industry* (Baltimore: Johns Hopkins University Press, 1978).

14. Stephen P. Bradley and Annel G. Karnani, *Automotive Manufacturer Risk Analysis: Meeting the Automotive Fuel Economy Standards,* Report prepared for the Department of Transportation, Transportation Systems Center (Bedford, Mass.: HH Aerospace Design Co., 1978).

15. Bradley and Leone; Hunker.

16. Mark Fuller, "Government Intervention in the Auto Industry: Japan" (Boston: Harvard Business School, 1980), p. 23.

17. U.S. Council of Economic Advisers, pp. 127-130.

2

The U.S. Automobile Industry, 1965–1980

Concern over the future of the domestic auto industry has its preface in the developments of the 1970s. This chapter will review the changes that have occurred in the U.S. auto industry over the period 1965 to 1980. From a premier symbol of U.S. industrial prowess at the beginning of this period, by its end the very survival of the industry was in doubt—with the combined losses of Ford and Chrysler amounting to $4.2 billion. This chapter will discuss the major forces that led to this change, the strategies of the individual participants, and how these strategies have adapted to changing competitive conditions.

Forces for Change in the U.S. Industry

To appreciate the magnitude of change that the auto industry has undergone, it is useful to review briefly the position of the industry in the mid-1960s. At that point, the industry could be described as a four-firm oligopoly composed of General Motors, Ford, Chrysler, and the American Motors Corporation (AMC). Foreign autos of any sort represented only a very small and specialized fraction of the market. Demand was principally for large or standard sized cars, and the level of demand was growing predictably as a function of the growth of the economy. The pace of technological innovation was at best slow; the basic automobile design was increasingly a V–8 front-engine, rear-wheel drive with automatic transmission. Sheet metal and styling were the principal loci of change. Government regulation of the automobile as a product was minimal.[1]

Since the mid-1960s changes in markets, regulations, and competition have altered the pattern of competition and requirements for success in the U.S. automobile industry. An understanding of these forces for change is necessary to understand why and how firms have performed in the fashion they have.

Demand

Over most of the postwar period, long-term auto demand has increased steadily. Between 1965 and 1977 automobile sales in the United States grew from 9.3 million units to 11.1 million units, an annual growth rate of about 1.5 percent. Since the mid-1970s, however, auto demand has been less easy to characterize. The market has shifted back and forth between large and small cars, while the characteristics valued by buyers have changed to include new attributes like fuel economy. The prolonged sales decline since 1979 has further called into question whether the size of the market will follow historic growth rates.

Factors Affecting Demand. The U.S. auto market is a mature market; in 1975, for example, 72 percent of North American demand was for replacement. While owning an automobile may be a necessity, potential purchasers also have the option of either buying a used car or of retaining their old car a while longer. Thus, new-car purchases, in particular, are deferable and discretionary. Moreover, new cars are bought by a relatively small segment of the total car-owning population each year; new-car buyers are a special group not representative of all people who own cars. Among other traits, new-car buyers tend to buy their new cars frequently.[2]

In the long run, demand historically has been largely a function of the growth and composition of the driving-age population and changes in aggregate income levels. Over the past thirty years, between 12 and 13 percent of personal-consumption expenditures consistently has gone toward automobile purchase and operation, while aggregate new-car prices in real terms have remained almost constant.[3] Consequently, auto sales have closely tracked overall economic growth.

In the short run, demand is sensitive to changes in individual income.[4] As a consequence, industry sales are highly cyclical. For example, averaging over the recessions of 1954, 1956, 1961, 1970, and 1974–1975, total real gross national product (GNP) and civilian employment declined only 0.4 percent from the previous year's level, while car and truck sales dropped 14.4 percent, and auto employment dropped 16.4 percent.[5] Increasing fuel prices and other changes in the components of ownership cost also have an impact on both the level and composition of sales. As fuel prices have risen both in absolute terms and as a fraction of total vehicle-operations costs, demand, at least in the short run, has shifted to smaller and more fuel-efficient cars. The level of demand also declined after the 1973–1974 and 1979 oil-price increases. However, whether high fuel costs will change the structure of long-term demand is unclear.

The market for automobiles is highly segmented, both in terms of size (mini or subcompact through standard) and by degree of luxury (basic, or stripped-down versions versus more luxurious versions). A definite hierarchy exists within each segment. For individual models, price and styling-design considerations are among the most important determinants of demand for individual models, although a wide variety of considerations seems to play in determining why some models become very popular.

Table 2–1
U.S. New-Car Vehicle Sales
(thousands)

Year	United States	Import	Total
1965	8,763	569	9,332
1966	8,377	658	9,035
1967	7,567	779	8,346
1968	8,624	985	9,609
1969	8,464	1,061	9,525
1970	7,115	1,231	8,346
1971	8,676	1,487	10,163
1972	9,321	1,529	10,850
1973	9,669	1,719	11,388
1974	7,448	1,369	8,817
1975	7,050	1,501	8,551
1976	8,606	1,446	10,052
1977	9,104	1,973	11,077
1978	9,308	1,950	11,258
1979	8,328	2,329	10,657
1980	6,578	2,469	9,047

Source: Adapted from *1981 Ward's Automotive Yearbook* (Detroit: Ward's Communications, 1981).

Level and Structure of Demand. Annual vehicle sales are shown in table 2–1. Although demand has grown steadily over time, cyclicality, related to business cycles and changes in consumer income, dominates the year-to-year changes in demand.

A major change in demand has been the shift toward smaller cars (table 2–2) and the consequent reduction in demand for standard-sized cars. This shift has been due to several factors. Declining family size, the growth of multiple-car households (in which the second car is generally smaller), and a young population are all factors favoring the purchase of small cars.

Increased oil prices are another principal reason for this shift. One part of this effect, of course, is due to the absolute increase in gasoline prices since the 1973 embargo, which has made fuel costs a much larger proportion of total auto-ownership costs. As fuel prices have risen, consumers have reacted by buying smaller cars, or driving less. Equally important, however, is the pattern of the price increase. Following a sharp increase in 1974, gasoline prices actually declined in real terms between 1975 and 1979. In 1974 demand shifted to smaller cars, but in the intervening 1975–1979 period the market again preferred larger vehicles. In 1979 a second sharp price increase shifted the market again in the space of just a few months toward small cars. The consequences of this zig-zag demand is a recurring theme throughout an analysis of structural change in the 1970s.

From the vantage point of the early 1980s, a critical question is whether

Table 2–2
U.S. Automotive-Market Segmentation
(in percentage)

Year	Subcompact	Compact	Intermediate	Standard	Luxury
1980	42.0	20.2	20.6	12.5	4.7
1979	34.0	20.0	24.2	15.3	5.5
1978	26.4	21.6	26.8	18.4	5.5
1977	27.1	21.2	26.9	29.4	4.6
1976	26.1	12.3	27.3	19.4	3.7
1975	32.4	20.3	24.1	17.9	4.0
1974	28.4	20	24.2	22.6	3.7
1973	24.9	17.7	23	30	3.6
1972	22.7	15.4	21.7	36.1	3.4
1971	22.7	15.8	20.3	37.1	3.4
1970	16.7	19.6	23.8	37.2	2.8
1969	11.2	16	25.1	43.9	3.4
1968	10.5	14.5	26.2	45.5	3.0
1967	9.3	15.7	23.6	47.9	3.1

Source: Adapted by author's calculations from 1967–1981 *Ward's Automotive Yearbook* (Detroit: Ward's Communications).

the developments of the past decade signal a fundamentally new pattern of demand or merely shorter-term disruptions. This uncertainty extends to both the volume of demand and its composition. Demographic shifts, especially the slowing growth rate of both households and overall population, suggest that the rate of growth of the U.S. auto market may slow in the future. Other factors that may impel changes in the structure of demand include the increasing maturity of the U.S. market and future petroleum prices.

The evidence regarding any fundamental change in the structure of demand is mixed. On one hand, over the 1971–1981 period average vehicle age has increased by over a year; this trend is particularly evident at the end of the decade. The chronically low sales of the 1979–1982 period may be another sign of changing demand. On the other hand, Ford, for example, is anticipating a return to a more normal sales level of about twelve million auto sales before 1985.[6]

Government Regulation

Starting in the mid-1960s, the automobile industry became the subject of substantial regulatory intervention in the areas of safety, emissions, and fuel economy.

Safety. Safety regulation is based on the 1966 National Traffic and Motor Vehicle Act. This act granted regulatory power, now exercised by the National Highway Traffic Safety Administration (NHTSA), to publish safety standards yearly. The emphasis of these regulations has been on vehicle hardware; for example, safety belts, improved bumpers, and such, rather than trying to alter patterns of vehicle use.

Emissions. The Clean Air Act Amendments of 1970 established strict control standards for three automotive emissions: hydrocarbons (HC), carbon monoxide (CO), and nitrous oxides (NO_x). The standards required a 90 percent reduction in allowable HC and CO emissions between 1970 and 1975; allowable NO_x emissions were to be reduced by 90 percent between 1971 and 1976. Failure to meet these standards carried a very stiff penalty ($10,000 per vehicle). Concern about the effectiveness of the 1970 act led to further amendments in 1977. These amendments gave greater administrative flexibility in establishing and enforcing standards and provided some direct incentives for innovation; in particular, NO_x standards could be relaxed to permit the use of diesel-engine technology.

Fuel Economy. The 1975 Energy Policy and Conservation Act provided mandatory fuel-economy standards for the average mileage attained by each auto maker's model-year fleet. The Corporate Average Fuel Economy standards (CAFE) set were 18 miles per gallon (mpg) for 1978, 19 mpg for 1979, 20 mpg for 1980, and 27.5 mpg for 1985, with the interim standards to be established by NHTSA. These interim standards were subsequently set at 22 mpg for 1981, 24 mpg for 1982, 26 mpg for 1983, and 27 mpg for 1984.

Internationalization and Changing Competitive Position

Perhaps one of the most significant changes has been the increasing internationalization of the U.S. auto industry. Whereas in the 1960s the U.S. industry and market were largely isolated from the motor industries of the rest of the world, issues of multinational competition are now important factors in deriving structural change.

Table 2–3 lists the U.S. market shares for nine of the major manufacturers operating in this country since 1965. In 1965, GM, Chrysler, and Ford had combined market shares in excess of 85 percent. AMC, imports, and specialty vehicles took up the rest. At that time, the U.S. market was effectively isolated from other markets, with the largest three domestic producers manufacturing domestically for home demand only. Volkswagen (VW), at that time near its peak U.S. market share, was filling a specialty demand for small, utilitarian vehicles. A few other imports, including the Japanese producers, were operating on the fringes of the market.

Table 2-3
U.S. Car-Market Share, by Firm
(in percentage)

Firm	1980	1979	1978	1977	1976	1975	1974	1973	1972	1971	1970	1969	1968	1967	1966	1965
General Motors	46.0	46.6	48.3	46.7	48.0	43.9	41.9	44.5	44.4	45.2	39.7	48.6	46.7	49.5	48.1	50.1
Ford	17.3	20.7	23.6	23.4	22.6	23.6	25.0	23.5	24.4	23.5	26.4	24.3	23.7	22.2	26.1	25.5
Chrysler	8.8	10.0	10.7	11.7	13.3	11.8	13.6	13.3	13.8	13.7	16.1	15.1	16.2	16.0	15.4	14.7
American Motors Corporation	2.0	1.6	1.5	1.7	2.5	3.7	3.8	3.4	2.8	2.5	3.0	2.5	2.8	2.8	3.0	3.5
Volkswagen	3.6	3.3	2.7	2.9	2.0	3.0	3.8	4.1	4.7	5.4	6.3	6.0	6.2	5.4	4.7	4.1
Volvo	.7	.5	.4	.4	.4	.7	.6	.5	.6	.5	.5	.4	.4	.4	.3	.2
Toyota	6.3	4.7	3.8	4.5	3.4	3.1	2.7	2.4	3.0	3.1	2.5	1.4	.8	.5	.2	—
Nissan	5.7	4.4	3.0	3.6	2.7	3.0	2.1	2.0	2.6	2.6	1.8	.9	.5	.5	.3	.1
Honda	4.1	3.3	2.4	2.0	1.5	1.2	.5	.3	.2	.1	—	—	—	—	—	—

Source: Adapted from *Ward's Automotive Yearbook* (Detroit: Ward's Communications); and corporate annual reports, 1965–1981.

Since 1968, a major change in the market has been the increase in import share and the change in its composition. Whereas in the 1960s VW was the principal importer, accounting for over half of the total imports into this country, by 1971 the total Japanese market share of imports had exceeded VW's, and by 1975 Toyota and Nissan each exceeded VW's share. This shift was due both to the growth of Japanese imports and the simultaneous decline in VW's share between 1970 and 1976. As the market has shifted toward Japanese imports, the total share of imports has grown from 10 percent in 1968 to 27 percent in 1980. In 1980, Japanese vehicles accounted for 82 percent of all imports.

Accompanying this increasing internationalization has been a shift in the relative size of competitors. Between 1968 and 1979 the share of the market accounted for by the three largest domestic producers dropped from 85 percent to 75 percent. This decline masks an even greater change in relative positions of the U.S. producers. In 1968 the ratio of market shares was General Motors (GM) 3, Ford 1.5, and Chrysler 1. In 1979 the ratio had changed to GM 9, Ford 2.5, and Chrysler 1. While GM has consistently retained between 45 percent and 50 percent of the total market, both Ford and Chrysler have lost market shares.

These figures tell a consistent story of the progressive deconcentration of the U.S. market. Whereas in 1968 there were five producers with market shares greater than 1 percent—GM, Ford, Chrysler, AMC, and VW—there are now at least nine, with the addition of Toyota, Nissan, Honda, and Mitsubishi. This change has come about because foreign entrants have captured most of the growth in the domestic market. Sales of U.S.-produced cars have increased little since 1965; between 1965 and 1977 imports captured about 85 percent of the U.S. auto market.[7]

Financial Pressures

The ongoing changes in markets, competition, and regulation all have their impacts on financial performance. Financial pressures therefore become the common denominator in the analysis of competitive performance and structural change.

Historically the U.S. automobile industry has had higher profitability than that for all manufacturing (table 2–4a). However, cyclicality in earnings is an important factor in putting industry earnings in proper perspective. Both industry sales and earnings are far from smooth; between 1960 and 1977 aggregate industry earnings varied by as much as 52 percent above and 63 percent below the average. This cyclicality and consequently increased risk are important justification for higher-than-average industry returns.

Table 2-4
After-Tax Return on Stockholders' Equity and Profit Margin for the U.S. Automobile Industry and All Manufacturing, 1965-1976

Table 2-4A. After-Tax Return of Stockholders' Equity

Year	U.S. Automobile Industry	All Manufacturing
1965	21.0	13.0
1966	16.8	13.4
1967	11.6	11.7
1968	15.7	12.1
1969	13.2	11.5
1970	6.0	9.3
1971	14.2	9.7
1972	16.1	10.6
1973	16.4	12.8
1974	5.9	14.9
1975	5.8	11.5
1976[a]	22.2	14.4

Table 2-4B. Profit Margin: Net Income after Tax as a Percent of Net Sales

Year	U.S. Automobile Industry	All Manufacturing
1965	8.0	5.6
1966	6.7	5.6
1967	4.9	5.0
1968	5.9	5.1
1969	5.0	4.8
1970	2.5	4.0
1971	5.0	4.1
1972	5.3	4.3
1973	5.0	4.7
1974	1.9	5.5
1975	1.8	4.5
1976[b]	5.6	5.5

Source: Council on Wage and Price Stability, Ann R. Horowitz (Senior Staff Economist COWPS), *1977 Automobile Prices,* no date, table 9, p. 14.
[a]First six months of 1976 annualized, but not seasonally adjusted.
[b]First six months of 1976.

Since the mid-1960s the industry has been undergoing a long-term decline in profitability (table 2-4b). Industry average return on sales has declined from over 7 percent in the early 1960s to under 4 percent by the late 1970s. This decline is the result of a combination of factors—regulatory requirements, foreign competition, a shift to smaller and less profitable cars, and changes in manufacturing cost structure.

Industry aggregates also conceal considerable differences in the relative profitability of the domestic producers. While return on sales for both GM and Ford was about halved between 1960 and 1977, they have both been consistently more profitable than the smaller two producers and have shown less cyclicality in earnings.

One consequence of the shifts in market demand and regulatory initiatives has been a vast increase in capital requirements. Table 2–5 lists historical capital investments of the domestic producers, and table 2–6 gives projections through 1985. Between 1976 and 1978 capital expenditures by Ford, Chrysler, and GM doubled—and will remain at high levels at least through 1985. These increased capital expenditures are coming about mostly because of the need to retool to meet government mandates and produce smaller cars. Regulatory initiatives—especially the CAFE standards—significantly have changed both the scope and character of the capital requirements facing domestic producers. Meeting these regulatory standards has increased nondiscretionary capital-spending requirements greatly. Most foreign producers are not facing the same rapid and required escalation in capital expenditures since most do not have to radically and rapidly redesign their product lines.

Strategies of Automotive Companies

The changes in markets, competition, and regulation that have occurred over the past fifteen years have forced major shifts in the structure of the automobile industry and the patterns of competition. This section describes the functional areas of strategy in the automobile industry, the pressures and objectives that different firms have faced in these dimensions, and what policies they have actually followed. An understanding of these corporate strategies and competitive positions is critical to understanding the effects of market, regulatory, and competitive developments, and the manner in which firms can respond in the future.

Manufacturing Policy

Salient characteristics of automobile manufacturing include high economies of scale, flexibility in assembly operations, a long product-development cycle, and high costs in designing and tooling a new model. As a result, the industry is both capital intensive and has volume-sensitive unit costs. Reportedly, GM's profit changes at a rate two and a half times greater than volume, while corresponding figures for Ford and Chrysler are three and four times.[8]

Table 2-5
Annual Capital Investments of the Big Three U.S. Auto Makers, 1968-1977
(millions of dollars)

Firm	1968	1969	1970	1971	1972	1973	1974	1975	1976	1977	1978	Total
General Motors												
Property, plant, and equipment	860	1,044	1,134	1,013	940	1,163	1,459	1,201	999	1,871	2,738	11,684
Special tools	866	863	1,149	613	899	941	1,096	1,036	1,308	1,776	1,827	10,565
Total	1,726	1,907	2,283	1,644	1,839	2,104	2,555	2,237	2,307	3,647	4,565	22,249
Ford												
Property, plant, and equipment	462	534	564	609	691	892	833	614	551	1,090	1,572	6,840
Special tools	417	424	484	430	463	594	619	342	504	673	970	4,950
Total	879	958	1,048	1,039	1,154	1,486	1,452	956	1,055	1,763	2,542	11,790
Chrysler												
Property, plant, and equipment	217	375	174	114	169	331	226	164	227	386	338	2,383
Special tools	205	272	242	136	166	298	242	220	197	337	333	2,315
Total	422	647	416	250	335	629	468	384	424	723	671	4,698

Source: Adapted from annual reports of General Motors, Ford, and Chrysler, 1969-1978.

Table 2–6
Projected Capital Requirements of U.S. Auto Makers
(billions of 1979 dollars)

Year	General Motors	Ford	Chrysler
1979 (actual)	5.4	3.4	.7
1980–1985	6.7	4	.8
Total 1979–1985	45.6	27.4	5.5

Source: Transportation Systems Center, U.S. Department of Transportation, April 1980.

Scale economies dominate automobile production. Small cars require a greater volume to achieve efficient scale than do larger models. While 250,000 units exhaust most of the scale economies for standard and luxury models, small cars require a volume closer to 400,000 units to achieve minimum efficient scale. The per-unit-cost penalties for producing below efficient scale are also greater for smaller than for larger cars. As table 2–7 shows, the percentage-cost penalties for producing 300,000 or fewer units per year is much greater for small-car production than for larger cars.

Communality in components and parts between models allows greater manufacturing scale economies to be achieved. There are limits, however, to the extent of sharing between lines. Small cars, in particular, require a subtly different manufacturing base than larger models.

In addition to scale economies in production, the economies of scale in design and development are increasingly important. Engineering, design, and launch costs—primarily incurred prior to volume production—have increased as vehicle designs have had to meet fuel-economy and emissions

Table 2–7
Manufacturing-Cost Changes with Volume
(production cost as percent of minimum cost)

Number of Units	Subcompact	Compact	Standard
400,000	100.00	100.00	100.00
300,000	104.83	100.98	100.04
200,000	114.68	108.89	101.02
100,000	144.70	133.37	116.50
50,000	204.78	182.31	147.43

Source: Adapted from Eric J. Toder, *Trade Policy and the U.S. Automobile Industry* (New York: Praeger Special Studies, 1978), p. 133.

requirements. These costs subsequently have to be spread over the total model production. Scale economies in design are thus almost infinite and are now an important factor in the ongoing worldwide consolidation of the auto industry.

There are also substantial economies from corporate size. Larger corporations are able to support a range of models to cover most segments of the market. They have a larger investment capability, so they may more frequently retool to change models. High volume and large size allow fixed costs—including those resulting from government-mandated changes—to be spread over more vehicles at a consequently lower per-unit charge.

The requirements for a different manufacturing base and the associated greater scale economies help to explain why domestic small-car production has generally been less profitable than large-car production. From a manufacturing point of view, small cars are not just scaled-down versions of big cars but require a different manufacturing base—different enough to negate the large-car volume advantages enjoyed by U.S. producers. The especially high scale economies of small-car production work to the disadvantage of U.S. producers. In 1977 no U.S. producer made even 200,000 units of any subcompact configuration while Toyota produced 450,000 to 500,000 Corollas and Nissan produced 300,000 to 400,000 B210s. Because the U.S. small-car market is fragmented and domestic production is not exported, the domestic producers have difficulty achieving the necessary scale to become competitive in small-car production. Japanese firms achieve scale efficiencies by concentrating production for the world market in Japan. Counterbalancing this domestic fragmentation to some extent is the ability by domestic producers to gain scale economies on components shared between large and small cars.

International cost differences are a second element forcing change in manufacturing policy. International comparative advantage can change with exchange rates, relative domestic price levels, relative labor costs, and relative productivity levels. A combination of these factors has given Japanese producers a substantial cost advantage over U.S. auto producers, reportedly on the order of $1,250 to $2,000 per vehicle.[9] While lower Japanese wage rates are a major part of this production-costs advantage, at least half is reputedly due to other factors, such as improved management and more efficient production systems.

For European-based firms, on the other hand, U.S. value added may be an attractive option due to the relative cost disadvantage of European production. Since 1976 Volkswagen has been steadily increasing its U.S. manufacturing presence—the intent was to reduce manufacturing costs 5 to 15 percent and become more price competitive in the U.S. market.[10] In addition to its Westmoreland, Pennsylvania, facility, with a 1980 capacity of 200,000 units, Volkswagen of America (VWA) has two U.S. component facilities and is constructing a second assembly facility. These facilities produce only the VW Rabbit. Local content in 1980 was 60 percent, anticipated to rise to 75 percent in 1981.[11]

Renault will begin U.S. manufacturing through the aegis of AMC, of which it owns 46 percent. AMC will domestically produce Renault-designed vehicles while phasing out its own passenger-car line.

These generalizations about international comparative advantage do not entirely dominate the choice of production location. Honda, for example, is constructing a U.S. manufacturing facility. Honda's high dependence on the U.S. market, the threat of trade barriers, and capacity constraints on its Japanese manufacturing facilities are all factors contributing to this choice.

Domestic manufacturing policies have had to respond to two fundamental pressures. One is the increasing need for improved manufacturing efficiency and quality. Domestic producers have faced a cost squeeze due to an inability to increase prices as rapidly as costs. Domestic producers have been unable to achieve additional manufacturing economies through volume increases because most domestic-market growth over the past ten years has gone to imports. Nor have the domestic producers been able to obtain volume increases and scale economies through export production, as do Japanese producers.

The second pressure manufacturing policy has had to deal with has been the shift in demand toward smaller cars, requiring a restructuring of manufacturing capacity. Efforts to roll over the capital stock have been hampered by a worldwide shortage in the machine-tool industry. Furthermore, while domestic producers face the challenge of retooling a large part of their capacity, on a worldwide basis there may be a developing excess capacity in small cars.

As the market has shifted downward, U.S. producers at times have had redundant capacity in large cars while capacity constrained in domestic small-car production. A rough indication of this situation is given by table 2–8, which estimates domestic capacity utilization by size class in 1978. It suggests that for both Ford and GM there were substantial capacity misallocations.

In efforts by domestic producers to reduce costs, basic components have been standardized between models, lighter-weight, lower-cost materials are substituted and the number of models have been reduced. For GM, part of this rationalization began in 1965 with the merger of the Buick-Oldsmobile-Pontiac assembly division with the Chevrolet assembly division to form the GM assembly division. With this has come a greater centralization of engineering design and production decision making. Other efforts to reduce production costs include reducing the number of parts required per car and building them faster—Lordstown was to have been the first one-hundred-car-per-hour assembly line.

Ford's manufacturing policies have had to live with the fairly steady

Table 2-8
1978 Manufacturing Capacity Utilization by Segment and Manufacturer

	Subcompact	Compact	Intermediate	Standard	Luxury
				Excess Capacity Here	
General Motors					
Capacity[b]	681,768	1,188,408	2,076,948	1,880,724	470,160
Production[c]	574,826	980,877	1,798,558	1,463,251	350,761
Capacity utilization	84%	83%	87%	78%	75%
Percent of total capacity	11%	19%	33%	30%	7%
Ford					
Capacity[b]	688,464	872,460[a]	923,256[a]	686,532	372,720
Production[c]	500,997[d]	710,681	679,509	431,098	189,523
Capacity utilization	78%[e]	81%	74%	63%	51%
Percent of total capacity	19%	25%	26%	19%	11%
Chrysler					
Capacity[b]	338,400	486,924	289,776[d]	145,396	—
Production[c]	288,236	384,408	231,156	101,049	—
Capacity utilization	85%	79%	80%	69%	—
Percent of total capacity	27%	39%	23%	12%	—
American Motors					
Capacity[b]	72,432	167,664	—	—	—
Production[c]	35,749	123,799	—	—	—
Capacity utilization	49%	74%	—	—	—
Percent of total capacity	30%	70%	—	—	—

Source: Author's calculations.
[a]March production figures times twelve.
[b]By calendar year, twelve times October production.
[c]By calendar year.
[d]Excludes discountinued models.
[e]Mustang capacity utilization: September–December: 106658/123092 = 87%; January–August: 133504/246184 = 64%—suggests a slow model start without Mustang capacity utilization 82%.

relative advantage GM has in scale and vertical integration versus Ford's stronger international positioning. In response to increasing cost pressures, as well as tightening capital allocation and improving manufacturing efficiency, Ford began to produce more luxurious cars or vehicles targeted for specialty niches with higher margins and greater opportunity for optional equipment.[12] Ford has also begun to source more components outside of the United States. This multinational sourcing compliments Ford's developing network of international manufacturing facilities and outside suppliers, allowing Ford to take advantage of lowest-cost production situations and to conserve capital.

While Ford moved toward a more international production strategy Chrysler suffered from manufacturing inefficiencies throughout the 1970s. In the 1960s the international expansion designed to put Chrysler on an equal basis with Ford and GM was done at the expense of financial stability and manufacturing efficiency. Neglect of manufacturing improvements reportedly resulted in manufacturing costs 10 percent higher than those of GM.[13] Chrysler also has a much lower level of vertical integration than either Ford or GM.

While pressures for more efficient domestic manufacturing are long-standing, events since the mid-1970s have increased the imperatives for a fundamental restructuring of manufacturing. Pressures for restructuring basically fall into two areas.

First are efforts to reduce production costs and related manufacturing break-even levels. The intense competition from lower-cost, Japanese-based manufacturing is one reason for greater efforts in this area. Another is the chronically low sales of the 1979–1982 period that, coming during a period of exceptionally high capital requirements, has made previous break-even levels unacceptable.

A second area of manufacturing restructuring is quality improvements. While quality is hard to define, there exists a widespread perception that U.S.-made autos are of inferior quality to many foreign, and particularly Japanese, vehicles.

Increasing manufacturing flexibility is a third area. The substantial uncertainty about the future level and composition of demand has placed a premium on a product line and manufacturing base capable of accommodating a wide variety of consumer preferences.

These pressures have led to what may be a fundamental change in labor relations. The labor-cost reductions and increased labor flexibility accompanying the renegotiated United Auto Workers contract may reflect part of such a shift—although from the viewpoint of late 1982 it is yet too early to tell. In any event, U.S. producers are independently taking measures to reduce labor costs. GM has for several years been pursuing its so-called Southern strategy of placing new plants in nonunion areas. Unionization efforts at these facilities have not always been successful. Both Ford and Chrysler have been increasing foreign value through non-U.S. components. The manual transaxle for the Ford Escort-Lynx, for example, is produced by Toyo Kyogo.

Increased factory automation through robotics is another way of reducing labor costs. It is difficult to make comparisons on robot usage between producers of national groups, since the definition of *robot* is unclear; what is clear is that robotics will mean permanently lower levels of auto-manufacturing employment in the future. General Motors and the major Japanese producers appear to be the most aggressive in using robots.

Efforts to improve manufacturing efficiency have also increased interest in copying some Japanese practices, especially in light of evidence that only a portion of the Japanese cost advantage is due to lower labor costs. For example, Japanese auto manufacturing is based on very tight inventory control, a practice that is now being adopted by U.S. manufacturers. Similarly, quality circles and other redefinitions of the traditional labor-management relation are being copied from the Japanese by U.S. firms.

In other areas, the degree of restructuring has appeared to be largely a function of the overall competitive strength—or weakness—of the firm. AMC, for example, has completely abrogated any design responsibility for its forthcoming passenger-car line, choosing instead to produce Renault designs. This move reflects a recognition that AMC could not finance new product development for both its passenger-car and Jeep lines.

Chrysler has completely restructured its manufacturing operations since 1979. Break-even in 1979–1980 was 2,426,000 vehicles. In 1982 it is estimated to be 1,244,000 units.[14] At the same time it has converted 90 percent of its production capacity to front-wheel-drive vehicles. It has also eliminated most of its international operations, becoming an almost entirely North American company.

Ford and General Motors have been less radical in their restructuring. Ford, for example, is anticipating a substantial sales increase from the 1981–1982 levels and thus is not reducing manufacturing capacity to maximize profitability of 1981 sales levels. This is not to say that it has not reduced its cost and break-even levels. In 1981 Ford cut its salaried staff by 25 percent, reduced overhead costs by $2.5 billion, and consequently reduced its North American break-even level by one million units.[15] It anticipates another $1 billion reduction in overhead costs by 1982.[16] Ford has also integrated its design function—with small cars the responsibility of one group and large and luxury cars under a separate group.[17] This move will presumably allow for greater commonality and integration between different models.

General Motors has made similar moves. In 1981 it integrated its worldwide truck and bus operations. It has also integrated its advanced-product and advanced-manufacturing groups to improve manufacturing efficiency and quality. G.M. has also redesigned its manufacturing facilities for increased flexibility. For example, the Oldsmobile division has production lines capable of producing either diesel or gasoline V–6 engines.

Vertical Integration and the Automobile-Supplier Industry

The choice of sourcing for parts and components is a critical part of manufacturing policy. The make-or-buy decision depends not only upon the strict production economies but also relates to choices of risk spreading, capital allocation, innovation emphasis, and competitive positioning.

Supplying the automobile industry in the United States is in itself a huge business despite the high degree of vertical integration among producers; in 1978 the automotive-components industry had at least $40 billion in sales.[18] At the same time, the inhouse capabilities of the U.S. producers were awesome; Ford, for example, is a major steel producer.

The domestic producers have followed different supply strategies. For standard components GM has historically bought 10 percent to 15 percent outside and produced the rest inhouse. Ford sourced 40 percent to 50 percent outside and Chrysler's proportion varied, sometimes producing 100 percent inhouse, sometimes depending entirely on outside suppliers.[19] AMC has had a very low level of vertical integration.

These differences in purchasing patterns presumably reflect both capital requirements and economies of scale in component production. GM has used its volume to achieve the low-cost-position inhouse, depending upon suppliers to second source and take up the slack and variance in production. Any additional volume supplied GM from the outside merely might reduce GM's internal advantage and pass scale economies on to the suppliers. Ford, with a similar volume, does not enjoy the same relative cost advantages that GM does. For a small producer like AMC, dependence upon suppliers reduces capital requirements. Futhermore, AMC has insufficient volume to justify inhouse production of many components. Chrysler internally produces all of the components for which it can obtain scale economies through its volume, depending upon outside suppliers for the rest.

The changes in manufacturing policy by the domestic auto makers have disrupted the preexisting structure of the supplier sector. For example, the V–8 engine will virtually disappear from the U.S. industry by the mid-1980s, eliminating what was once a major component market. Accompanying these transitions is the need for increased productivity and the possibility that the auto market in the future—at least for domestically produced cars—will be permanently smaller. This trend suggests that employment, and possibly overall size, of the supplier sector will decline.

It is also anticipated that the domestic industry will increase its usage of foreign components for reasons of both lower price and higher quality. One estimate is that non-U.S. suppliers will provide 26 percent of auto components for U.S. automobiles in 1985, and 36 percent by 1990.[20] Thus, it seems probable that there will be fundamental changes in the supplier sector.

Marketing

The marketing function operates under a number of constraints in the automobile industry. The product cannot be changed quickly in response to consumer reactions. Sales are largely a function of factors, such as macroeconomic conditions, which marketing efforts cannot change.[21] The tools available for marketing in the short run are limited: advertising, price, and dealer promotions. Increased marketing efforts with these tools can overcome only some consumer resistance, and at the cost of reduced profit. In the long run, what really counts in marketing is the effectiveness of the product strategy and the strength of the dealer and service network.

Although the percentages of sales spent on advertising by U.S. producers are relatively modest, the absolute sums spent are substantial. In 1978, for manufacturer advertising alone, GM spent $266.3 million, Ford $210 million, Chrysler $188.9 million, and AMC $43.4 million. While the relative domestic unit sales of these companies is roughly in the ratio of 25:10:5:1, their spending on advertising is in the ratio of 6:5:4:1 suggesting that there are substantial scale economies in some aspects of marketing.

The strength of the dealer network is an important element of marketing success and one of the most valuable assets of the company. The system of independently franchised dealers purchasing vehicles from the manufacturer is a risk-spreading device allowing manufacturers to pass on to dealers at least some of the risks of the industry.[22] During a slump, dealers may be forced to take more inventory than they want. The limited number of dealerships is a way of achieving efficiencies and economies of scale in retailing.[23] Developing a dealer network to provide sales and service is both expensive and time consuming and serves as a major barrier to entry into a market. The success of VW during the 1960s and the failure of the other importers that entered at the same time is due partially to VW's careful insistence on a strong service network.

Since dealers are independent businessmen, manufacturers have had to develop various tools for influencing the behavior of their sales channels. For example, dealer discounts traditionally have been greater for larger than for smaller cars, encouraging dealers to sell more larger—and more profitable to the manufacturer—cars. Recently, however, reflecting the market shift toward smaller cars, this premium on larger-car sales has been removed, so that dealer profit margins are basically uniform across all size classes.

Vehicle sales per dealership, shown in table 2–9, indicate roughly the strength of a dealer network. High sales per dealership mean that the best potential or actual dealers will find such a franchise attractive. Weaker lines with lower sales per dealer find their strongest dealers leaving them for more attractive opportunities and have difficulty attracting highly qualified new dealers. The position of the Japanese producers suggests the strength of

Table 2-9
Vehicle Sales per Dealership, 1980

Firm	Unit Sales/Dealership
Toyota	538
Honda	507
Datsun	473
Chevrolet	308
Oldsmobile	252
Buick	241
Ford	208
Pontiac	197

Source: Author's calculations based on data in 1981 *Ward's Automotive Yearbook* (Detroit: Ward's Communications).

their dealer networks; it may also suggest, however, a policy of locating dealers only in high-volume areas.

While the absence of a dealer network is a substantial barrier to entry, there are possible substitute channels to the market. Sears, for example, handled Kaiser-Frazer cars for a few years in the early 1950s. Furthermore, the use of dual dealerships means that an entrant need not set up a completely de novo dealer network. Dual dealerships are those situations in which a dealer carries two or more manufacturers' lines, as for example a Ford-Honda dealership.

Another mechanism for bypassing this entry barrier is through a cooperative arrangement with an existing marketer. Renault's controlling interest in AMC gives it access to AMC's distribution network. Without the difficulty of trying to build up a separate sales network Renault has entered the U.S. market. If Chrysler's financial difficulties continue it is likely that pressure will grow for it to share its distribution network with a foreign producer seeking entry into the U.S. market.

While all dealers provide service, a special emphasis upon service and warranty provisions has been used successfully by both VW and then later by AMC. VW's initial growth was both slowed and strengthened by a *service-first strategy* that assured buyers that a dense service network was already in place when the car was bought. While good service is important to all companies, a service-based marketing emphasis allows a small firm a market niche protected somewhat from its larger competitors.

International Positioning

Through the end of the 1960s the U.S. auto industry could be viewed in isolation from developments overseas. The U.S. market was largely insulated from the rest of the world through the demand for uniquely large cars, annual model changes, and other mechanisms that differentiated the U.S. market from the rest of the world. By the end of the 1970s, of course, these differences were disappearing.

In part this trend reflects changes unique to the U.S. market. During the 1970s, fundamental shifts in government regulation, fuel prices, and consumer preferences helped to destroy the distinctions between U.S. and foreign demand. The sorts of cars demanded in the U.S. market today are increasingly similar to those demanded in the European and Japanese markets.

In part this shift also reflects a broader internationalization of the industry. Strictly national markets and producers are giving way to multi-national positioning. There are two aspects to this trend. One is the increase in the number of effective world-scale producers. Using the reciprocal of the Herfindahl index to calculate the "equivalent number of firms" in the world auto industry, in 1950 it was less than five (GM, Ford, Chrysler, and essentially one other), but by 1980 it had increased to around twelve, suggesting a progressive deconcentration of the world industry.[24] As was noted earlier, this trend toward deconcentration is also mirrored in the domestic market.

The other aspect is the decline of isolated national markets. The current U.S. experience with rising imports is not unique. With the exception of Japan, most major advanced countries have seen import share rise.

A primary force behind this increasingly global scale of the industry is the high scale economies in both design and production. These scale economies have placed a premium on attaining as long a production run as possible, both at the vehicle and component level. The pervasiveness of these scale economies is such that many analysts anticipate a future auto industry consisting of no more than half a dozen major firms worldwide.

The international scope of the auto industry can be examined in several ways. World market share is one measure. Table 2–10 and 2–11 list world market share outside North America for major producers. Excluding North America, for example, GM has a comparatively weak position, second to Ford, in fact. The extent that U.S. firms depend upon the U.S. market, versus the dependence of foreign producers on the same market, is given by table 2–12.

With the exception of some Japanese firms, non-U.S. auto producers exhibit far less dependence upon the U.S. market. These differences in dependence suggest that changes in the U.S. market will much more severely affect domestic and some Japanese producers than they will other firms.

Table 2–13 list the percentage of sales outside the home country (as opposed to the U.S. market) for different firms. Again U.S. firms are unique in their dependence upon their home market. The dependence upon

Table 2–10
Worldwide Passenger-Car Market Shares, 1980

Firm	Share
General Motors	19.7%
Ford	12.3
Chrysler	3.4
Volkswagen	7.9
Fiat	4.8
Renault	5.7
Toyota	7.2
Nissan	5.9
Honda	2.4

Source: Author's calculations from data supplied by annual reports; Motor Vehicle Manufacturer's Association, *World Motor Vehicle Data, 1981; 1981 Ward's Automotive Yearbook.*

Table 2–11
Car and Truck Market Shares outside the United States and Canada, 1976 and 1980

Firm	1980	1976	Percent of Change
Toyota	10.9	10.1	7.9
Nissan	9.4	8.9	5.6
Volkswagen	9.3	9.5	−0.6
Ford	9.0	9.2	−0.2
Peugeot-Citroen[a]	8.7	11.1	−21.6
Renault	8.5	7.6	11.8
Fiat	7.6	8.3	−8.4
General Motors	7.5	8.4	−10.7

Source: Adapted from Ford Motor Company, *1980 10-K,* p. 10, and author's calculations.
[a]Adjusted to include retail sales of Talbot.

the U.S. market would be even more striking if sales to Canada were not considered foreign purchases. Thus, world-market-share figures for GM and Chrysler are misleading: in fact, these firms remain dependent upon a single market, unlike the greater international positioning of their foreign competitors.

Table 2–12
Percentage of Total Unit Sales: Cars and Trucks Sold in United States for Each Manufacturer

Year	Ford	General Motors	Chrysler	American Motors Corporation	Datsun	Toyota	Honda	Volkswagen[a]	Volvo
1978	63	—	78	—	18	18	37	10	20
1977	62	—	60	92	21	21	34	12	21
1976	61	73	60	91	15	16	27	9	15
1975	58	71	53	—	16	14	25	13	21
1974	63	70	55	—	14	13	10	—	23
1973	64	75	58	—	16	12	11	—	24
1972	64	—	60	—	14	13	6	—	25
1971	63	—	61	—	16	13	3	—	22

Source: Author's calculations based upon Corporate Annual Reports; *Ward's Automotive Yearbooks, 1972–1979.*
[a]Includes U.S. and foreign-assembled cars. Total production statistics based on Volkswagen Group.

Table 2–13
1980 Factory Unit Sales outside Home Country for Selected Firms: Cars and Trucks

Firm	Percentage
General Motors[a]	22.0
Ford[a]	44.5
Chrysler[a]	10.3
Toyota[b]	55.4
Nissan[b]	58.2
Honda[b]	69.2
Mitsubishi[b]	58.6
Volkswagen	69.7
Renault[c,d]	57.6
Peugeot-Citroen[c]	57.7

Source: Author's calculations based on data from annual reports; Motor Vehicle Manufacturers Association, *1981 World Motor Vehicle Data.*
[a]Outside United States and Canada.
[b]Includes knock-down vehicles.
[c]Passenger cars only.
[d]Excludes American Motors Corporation.

A second measure of internationalization is the developing network of link ups and coproduction agreements between firms. Chrysler, for example, has noncontrolling equity interests in both P.S.A. Peugeot Citroen and Mitsubishi Motor Corporation. Renault has a 46 percent interest in AMC, which could rise to absolute majority ownership. Ford and Toyota have had negotiations about vehicle coproduction, while Toyo Kogyo produces components for some Ford vehicles. These and other relationships are shaping not only the international competitiveness of U.S. firms but also competition in the domestic market.

The degree of manufacturing integration across markets is a final measure of international presence. At one extreme, Toyota has preferred to centralize all production in Japan except where trade barriers require local value added; on the other extreme Ford has been a leader in the transnational integration of manufacturing.

The key point is that multinational positioning will reflect increasingly on much of what happens in the U.S. market—in the determination of who are the significant competitors and in the choice of manufacturing and product strategy. Let us look now at the strategies of individual producers.

Strategies of the Individual Producers

AMC. By itself AMC has limited participation in the international market. International operations consist primarily of the export of knocked-down units for assembly and sale abroad. In 1980 non-North American sales were 57,245 units or 11 percent of total dollar sales.

The principal component of AMC's international posture is its close link with Renault. According to company statements, in 1977 AMC recognized that it did not have the internal resources to develop both fuel-efficient front-wheel-drive passenger cars and upgrade its four-wheel-drive specialty-vehicle line simultaneously. Its subsequent strategy has been to base AMC's further participation in passenger cars on an affiliation with a foreign producer, devoting internal resources to four-wheel-drive vehicles.

As of mid-1982 Renault had a controlling interest in AMC with 46 percent ownership. Since 1979 AMC has been the exclusive North American distributor for some Renault cars, while Renault has distributed Jeep vehicles internationally. Starting in the 1983 model year, AMC will produce Renault-designed passenger vehicles domestically, meanwhile phasing out its own line of now-outdated passenger cars.

Chrysler. Throughout the 1960s Chrysler expanded internationally in a move to match the international presence of Ford and GM. This expansion was done largely through the purchase of existing auto companies. In Europe, for example, it bought the Rootes Group in Great Britain, Simca in France, and Barreiros in Spain. In Japan it acquired a 15 percent equity interest in Mitsubishi Motor Corporation.

Chrysler also became the exclusive marketing agent for Mitsubishi in North America. The result was a rapid expansion of non-North American sales, from 15 percent of total sales in 1965 to 37 percent in 1975. However, Chrysler was unsuccessful in integrating these operations, and they proved to be consistently less profitable than domestic operations.

In the late 1970s Chrysler spun off its international operations as part of its restructuring. In 1978 it sold its European subsidiaries to Peugeot-Citroen for $230 million in cash and $200 million in stock, giving Chrysler a substantial equity position in P.S.A. Peugeot-Citroen. In 1979 and 1980 it sold its South American operations to GM and VW. As a result of this restructuring, Chrysler's operations are concentrated in the United States, Canada, and Mexico.

Chrysler still has equity interests in both Mitsubishi and Peugeot. At the time of purchase, both blocks of stock amounted to a 15 percent interest. Mitsubishi has recently renegotiated its marketing agreement with Chrysler to allow Mitsubishi to establish its own dealer network in North America while still providing Chrysler with certain models through 1990. Chrysler's interest in Peugeot has not led to any joint marketing efforts.

Table 2-14
Profitability of International versus Domestic Operations: Chrysler

	Outside North America		North America		Return on Sales	
Year	Sales	Net Earnings[a]	Sales	Net Income	Outside North America	North America
1978	4808.8[b]	53.5	15492.9	(258.1)	1.1	(1.7)
1977	4760	(49.2)	1567.8	174.0	(1.0)	1.1
1976	4391.3	91.3	1146.5	331.3	2.1	3.0
1975	4020.0	(46.7)	7578.4	(212.8)	(1.2)	2.8
1974	3410.3	(6.6)	7561.1	(45.5)	(0.2)	(0.6)
1973	3467.1	120.9	8307.2	134.5	3.5	1.6
1972	2478.9	29.6	7280.2	190.8	1.2	2.6
1971	1936.2	5.1	6063.1	78.6	0.3	1.3

Source: Author's calculations based on data from Chrysler Corporation Annual Reports, 1971–1978.
[a]Including extraordinary tax credits.
[b]Includes discontinued operations.

Table 2-15
Percentage Units Sold outside United States and Canada: Chrysler

Year	Percent outside United States and Canada
1978	12.0
1977	31.0
1976	31.0
1975	37.0
1974	36.0
1973	35.0
1972	35.0
1971	33.0[a]
1970	33.0
1969	30.0
1968	25.0
1967	23.0
1966	17.0
1965	15.0

Source: Author's calculations based on data from Chrysler Corporation Annual Reports, 1965–1978.
[a]15 percent interest in Mitsubishi acquired.

Peugeot and Chrysler have had discussions about joint production in the United States of a small car in the mid-1980s; in 1981 a letter of intent on small-car cooperation was signed.[25] More recently Chrysler has held discussions with Mitsubishi about a similar project.

General Motors. Despite its size, General Motors (see tables 2–16, 2–17, and 2–18) lacks any substantial diversity in the types of businesses and markets that generate its substantial revenues. In 1980 only 21 percent of GM's cars were sold outside of North America. GM has increasingly come to recognize the auto industry as a world industry and is attempting to cash in on growing automobile markets abroad—in spite of a rather dismal track record that has GM's international percentage of unit sales hanging around 20 percent. In 1978 GM Overseas Operations was reorganized along a product-line basis and brought closer to U.S. operations.

Like other U.S. auto makers, GM's involvement in foreign markets has depended on direct foreign investment. As a measure of GM's participation in overseas markets, GM's investment in plants outside the United States has grown from 12 percent of total gross plant in 1960 to 24 percent of total gross plant in 1974, while the number of vehicles manufactured abroad roughly doubled. GM still ranks second to Ford in overseas market share, however, with about 8.5 percent in 1977. Despite efforts to participate in international markets, GM's strength still lies in the North American market.

Table 2–16
Profitability of International versus Domestic Operations: General Motors

Year	Return on Sales		Percent of Total Net Income Attributable to International Operations
	Outside North America	North America	
1979	2.9	4.0	12.6
1978	2.6	5.4	8.4
1977	3.0	5.8	7.5
1976	n.a.	n.a.	12.0
1975	1.0	4.1	5.7
1974	0.0	3.7	0.0
1973	3.7	7.3	9.0
1972	3.6	7.8	7.8
1971	2.5	7.6	5.0
1970	3.2	3.3	19.0

Source: General Motors Annual Reports, 1970–1979.
n.a. = Not available.

Table 2-17
Percentage Units Sold outside United States and Canada: General Motors (Cars and Trucks)

Year	Overseas Market Share	Percent International Sales
1979	8.8	20
1978	8.5	19
1977	8.8	20
1976	8.1	22
1975	7.7	20
1974	8.1	19
1973	n.a.	21

Source: Adapted from General Motors Annual Reports, 1973–1979.
n.a. = Not available.

Table 2-18
Distribution of Net Assets: International versus North American: General Motors

	Outside North America	North America	Percent Outside North America
	Net Assets	Net Assets	Assets
1979	2030.1	17227.3	12
1978	1683.6	16522.8	10
1977	1482.5	14321.5	10
1976	1688.8	12696.4[a]	13
1975	1522.2	11560.2[a]	13
1974	1250.0	11280.6[a]	11
1973	1265.0	11301.0	11
1972	1060.0	10623.0	11

Source: Author's calculations based on General Motors Annual Reports, 1972–1979.
[a]Author's calculations.

In addition to its other foreign operations GM owns 34.2 percent of Isuzu Motors of Japan. Isuzu manufactures certain models for GM, including for a while a light pickup truck (Chevrolet LUV) for the U.S. market.

Ford: Ford has been the leading U.S.-chartered auto maker in non-U.S. markets for the past three decades. Since the early 1970s non-U.S. operations have become increasingly important both in terms of volume and profitability (tables 2–19 and 2–20). U.S. operations have, over a long-term trend, become decreasingly profitable, so that a larger percentage of net

Table 2–19
Division of Assets and Capital Expenditures: International versus North America: Ford

	Outside North America	North America	Percent Outside North America	
Year	Capital Expenditures	Capital Expenditures	Assets	Capital Expenditures
1978	366	1206	39.0	23.0
1977	220	870	40.0	20.0
1976	200	3̌51	41.0	36.0
1975	402	212	n.a.	65.0
1974	250	582	n.a.	30.0
1973	334	557	n.a.	37.0

Source: Author's calculations based on Ford Annual Reports, 1973–1978.
n.a. = Not available.

Table 2–20
Profitability of International versus Domestic Operations: Ford
(in percentage)

	Return on Sales		Percent of Total Net Income Attributable to International Operations
Year	Outside North America	North America	
1979	5.2	(.01)	100.0
1978	5.4	2.9	48.0
1977	5.7	3.5	42.0
1976	4.9	2.7	44.0
1975	2.0	0.4	70.0
1974	1.1	1.7	20.0
1973	3.7	4.0	24.0
1972	2.9	4.8	17.0
1971[a]	0.6	5.1	4.0
1970	3.2	3.5	24.0[a]

Source: Author's calculations based on Ford Annual Reports, 1970–1979.
[a]Strike in United Kingdom.

income has come from abroad. This dependence on foreign operations is in contrast to GM, which is far more domestically oriented.

Ford has aggressively positioned itself for expansion in the European market while giving less emphasis to other overseas markets.[26] Ford of Europe has been the leader in pan-European manufacturing integration. In 1978 Ford had 12.5 percent of the European market, second only to Renault with 13.5 percent. This figure is a great increase over Ford's 1974 position with 8.9 percent market share. Unlike in the United States, in Europe Ford is often the price leader, allowing it more leeway in its pricing policies.[27]

The increased domestic capital demands resulting from CAFE and downsizing may be hurting Ford's investment program abroad. Table 2–19 lists the percentage of total capital expenditures going abroad. Until 1976 it averaged somewhere around 30 percent to 40 percent each year. In 1977 and 1978, years in which the regulatory-inspired capital requirements began to increase, the percentage of investment going abroad dropped to around 20 percent.

In 1979 Ford acquired a 25 percent interest in Toyo Kogyo. Ford has moved to integrate Toyo Kogyo into Ford's operations in several ways. Ford's Asia-Pacific product range includes two models based on Toyo Kogyo vehicles. Toyo Kogyo also supplies some components, such as the Lynx-Escort manual transaxle, to Ford. The two companies have also discussed the prospect of Toyo Kogyo producing captive-import minicars for Ford.

Major Foreign Producers. As is discussed in greater detail in the next chapter, international positioning of the Japanese producers is intimately tied to the vicissitudes of the Japanese auto market. Unlike U.S. producers, foreign participation by Japanese firms has been through export from Japan rather than investment abroad. In general Japanese producers have followed strategies of attaining cost reductions through economies of scale in high-volume production.[28] High export sales to the U.S. market are a function of two factors. One is the desire or need by Japanese firms to continue high rates of expansion after the initial explosive growth of the Japanese market slowed. Smaller firms in the fragmented and highly competitive Japanese industry find the scale and cost motivations for continued high growth especially pressing. The second factor is that the Japanese happened to be well positioned to provide the U.S. market with high-quality fuel-efficient cars during the period in 1979–1980 when the U.S. market shifted in that direction. From 1978 to 1980 the Japanese share of the U.S. car market went from 10.8 percent to 19.7 percent, while the share of non-Japanese imports went from 5.1 percent to 6.2 percent.

Current Japanese strategies may change under a variety of pressures. Dependence on the U.S. market leaves export sales at the mercy of fluctuating exchange rates. Higher raw material and labor costs may make the Japanese product more expensive while the growing home-market saturation lessens the potential for increased efficiencies through expanded domestic volume. The Japanese also may face a potential weakening of their position as U.S. producers become more competitive in the small-car segment. Finally, there is the threat of increased protectionist sentiments in countries such as the U.S. where Japanese imports are a substantial share of the market.

European firms, in contrast, face a different set of imperatives. Japanese penetration in the European market is regarded as a serious threat. Meanwhile, European auto exports have declined relatively over the past decade due to increasing European production costs, international trade barriers, and greater competition from Japanese and (possibly) U.S. producers.

As noted earlier, these pressures have led European producers toward U.S. production. Both VW and Renault have followed this strategy. In the future there may also be domestic cooperation between Chrysler and Peugot.

Product Strategy

Product strategy concerns the choice and design of automobiles the firm intends to market. As the nature of competition has altered over the past decade, product strategies have been the focus of substantial change both for domestic and foreign competitors.

Underlying product strategy is the new product-development cycle; the time from project commitment to first-volume production. Up until the early 1970s the product cycle was about three years.[29] The cycle was so short in the past because much of the newness of product changes was in styling or discretionary introductions of new technology.

Accustomed to operating in the stable market of the 1960s and early 1970s, U.S. producers chose strategies emphasizing styling, model changes, and model proliferation.[30] These strategies were well suited to the stable, mature U.S. market; emphasis upon styling and brand loyalty is a relatively risk-free way of encouraging frequent replacement and thus expanding sales.

Vehicle mix and the choice of optional equipment, pricing, and brand loyalty are among the important elements of such product strategies. As noted earlier, vehicle mix can be viewed in two dimensions: size (subcompact through luxury) and grade (basic versus luxury versions in each size class). Traditionally, the basic car in any size class has been attractively priced to bring new buyers into the so-called manufacturer's family, hopefully encouraging future sales and contributing additional volume to bring production levels above break-even. Profitability, however, resided in the larger cars, especially large luxury cars, due to a domestic pricing structure based on an essentially constant price per pound per car.[31] For domestic manufacturers smaller cars have been nearly as costly to produce as larger cars, but small cars historically not only sold for less but also tended to be equipped with much less profit-generating optional equipment than their larger counterparts.[32] Furthermore, foreign producers were price leaders in the small-car segment. It was only in response to increasing import competition that U.S. producers initially entered the compact and subcompact markets.

Brand loyalty is an important element of product strategy in a replacement market. Ideally from the producer's standpoint, a consumer is loyal to a particular manufacturer, moving only from model to model within the fleet. Brand loyalty makes for a much more stable and orderly market than if consumers were to switch producers randomly at every purchase. Industry-wide loyalty rates have declined over the past decade in part because of the tendency for small-car purchasers to be less loyal than large-car buyers.[33] Chrysler, for example, reports loyalty rates for full-sized car buyers of 65 percent, intermediates 60 percent, but only 45 percent and 40 percent for compact and subcompact buyers, respectively.[34]

These broad product-line, replacement-oriented strategies were pursued primarily by the larger auto producers. Smaller firms, like Volvo, found a market niche that stresses safety and engineering. AMC found a niche first in smaller cars and then in specialty vehicles. Importers initially shared little of the same mix—related product strategies that characterized U.S. manufacturers. Except at the luxury end, foreign manufacturers offered a limited number of small models designed initially to serve a growing home market.

Over the 1974–1980 period, and especially during the latter 1970s, several trends have made the product strategies pursued by domestic producers obsolete. The need for higher fuel economies due both to market demand and CAFE regulations has focused increased attention on smaller cars. Subcompacts have ceased to be a minor market segment, creating the imperative that small cars can no longer be unprofitable cars. Responding both to changes in U.S. and home-market demand, foreign producers have begun to offer luxury small cars, so that luxury cars are no longer equivalent to large cars. Profitability no longer necessarily resides with large cars.

Another change has been the lengthening of product-development time. Fuel-economy, emissions, and safety requirements have shifted much of the design effort from styling and minor body modifications to basic redesign of the frame and engine. As a result, product-development cycles are now on the order of seven years.[35]

Figures 2-1, 2-2, and 2-3 help indicate how domestic and imported product strategies have changed over the past fifteen years. These graphs position cars (the smallest in each model line or a representative sampling from each manufacturer if there are no model lines) on the basis of cubic-inch displacement (a proxy for the power and size of the engine) versus curb weight (representing the size of the car). In 1966 (figure 2-1) the market was well segmented; at the upper end there were the luxury cars with displacements of 400 cubic inches and curb weights of 4,500 pounds, in the center were the standard and intermediate-sized cars. Below 150 cubic inches and 3,000 pounds weight there are no domestic cars, only the VW with 5 percent of the market at that time.

By 1975 there was still the distinct market segmentation of large, medium, and small cars, although by that time a number of imports had entered that "strategic window" at the low end of the market. Of the imports shown, only Volvo, which had defined a specialty niche based on safety, was competing in the middle range of the market. By this time, of course, domestic producers had established a presence in the small-car market, although it is interesting to note that the domestically produced small cars (Pinto, Vega, and Pontiac Astre) are all close to the upper ends of that segment, while captive imports (Opel and Colt) are positioned further down in the low-end segment.

By 1978 the market had become very muddled as the distinct group segmentation disappeared. Domestically produced cars had moved down in size (for example, Chevette) while imports had invaded what used to be the middle end of the market. What started out in 1965 as a very clear demarcation between imports at the small end and domestics in the rest of the market, had disappeared. Foreign producers had also begun to develop a product mix, albeit still concentrated in the low and middle ranges of the market. Datsun offerings in 1978 ranged from the F-10, at under 2,000 pounds and 75 cubic inches, to the 280 Z 2 + 2 around 3,000 pounds and 170 cubic inches. VW group offerings similarly ranged from the Rabbit to the Audi 5000.

Thus, the market has changed substantially over the past fifteen years. What used to be a well-segmented market dominated by a few, large domestic producers, has seen two major changes. First is a shift downward in the size of the products offered. As cars have been getting smaller, the market has shifted into those segments in which imports have always been strong. Second, major importers concurrently have been developing product mixes that include larger as well as smaller cars. As the market moves down, the importers are also moving up.

This shift downward by the domestic producers will continue until at least 1985, because the domestic producers must downsize their cars to meet CAFE standards and consumer demands for more fuel-efficient vehicles.

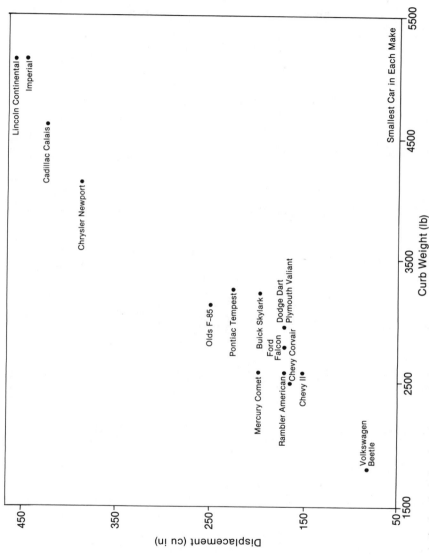

Figure 2-1. Relative Positioning of Car Models, 1966

Source: Author's calculations based upon information found in *1966 Ward's Automotive Yearbook* (Detroit: Ward's Communications).

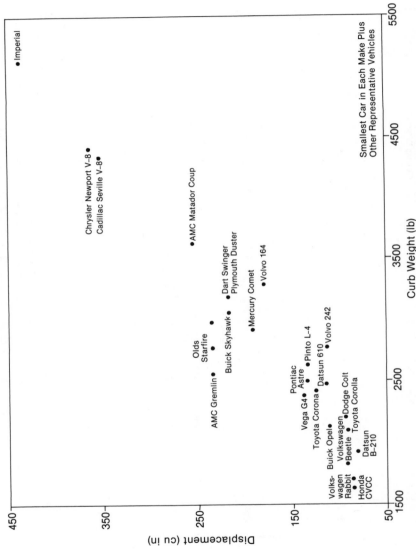

Figure 2-2. Relative Positioning of Car Models, 1975

Source: Author's calculations based upon information found in *1975 Ward's Automotive Yearbook* (Detroit: Ward's Communications).

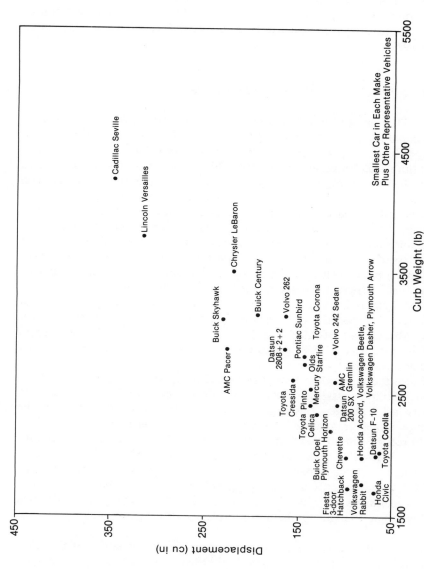

Figure 2–3. Relative Positioning of Car Models, 1978

Source: Author's calculations based upon information found in *1978 Ward's Automotive Yearbook* (Detroit: Ward's Communications).

An increasingly large segment of the market will continue to be pushed into those segments where imports—especially the Japanese—are strong and have a cost advantage. Between 1977 and 1985 it is expected that the average weight of a domestic vehicle will drop from 4,200 pounds to 3,000 pounds; in other words, the average car in 1985 will weigh less than the average small car in 1977.[36]

Present Strategies of Individual Manufacturers

AMC. Throughout the 1970s AMC almost could be viewed as three different companies. It was a leading producer of utility vehicles (Jeep), a contract producer of government postal and military vehicles, and a generally unprofitable passenger-car producer. This organization reflected a search for product niches neglected by the big three. In the passenger-car business, its so-called philosophy of difference made it first a specialist in the compact and subcompact segments. As other domestic producers entered this segment, AMC tried to differentiate its model line in other ways.[37] The Pacer was such a move, designed to be a new concept combining the interior roominess of a traditional U.S. produced car with the outside dimensions of the import, priced below luxury small cars but above the new subcompacts. It was fuel-inefficient, however, and was discontinued in 1979.

AMC entered the specialty-vehicle market with the 1970 purchase of Jeep. Jeep has become an increasingly important part of AMC's operations. Almost half of AMC's dollar sales were accounted for by Jeep in 1978, as compared with 11 percent in 1971. Jeep sales also have been quite profitable apparently.[38]

Since the mid-1970s AMC has lacked adequate financial resources to redesign both its passenger-car and Jeep lines. The 1975 Pacer introduction was its last truly new passenger-car model. The Concord and Spirit, its other passenger cars, are derivations of an even older design.

In recognition of this fact, AMC has formed an alliance with Renault. Over the 1980–1982 period Renault will have invested $350 million in AMC, acquiring a 46 percent share. AMC will phase out its own passenger-car line by 1984, producing Renault-designed vehicles instead. The first of these front-wheel-drive vehicles will appear in the 1983 model year. AMC will also use some Renault financing to introduce new Jeep models.

Chrysler. For several decades Chrysler has been the smallest of the three major full-line domestic producers. In the past Chrysler has depended upon a reputation for engineering excellence to sell cars.[39] Quoting former chairman Lynn Townsend, "We have traditionally sold our automobiles at prices above those of our competitors in each area of the market, because we maintain that our cars are worth more. They perform better; they've got better engineering." [40] By the mid 1970s, however, repeat purchases of Chrysler products were at a level consistently lower than those for Ford or GM, due at least partly to a deteriorating reputation for reliability. [41]

Throughout the 1970s Chrysler product policy hinged upon a strong belief that it had to produce a full line of cars to remain competitive, [42] despite its relative lack of resources in comparison to its competitors. Not having the resources to cover each market segment with a separate product line, Chrysler resorted to several stratagems. It dropped out of certain product segments; for example, withdrawing from luxury cars and heavy-duty trucks in 1975. It tried to broaden the appeal of its models to include several segments at once. [43] Through its relationship with Mitsubishi Motor Corporation, of which it owns 15 percent, Chrysler filled out parts of its product line with captive imports.

During this period, Chrysler's product mix was heavily dependent on compacts and vans. It was not until calendar 1978, for example, that Chrysler's domestically produced subcompact, the front-wheel-drive, L-body Omni-Horizon, achieved significant sales. Chrysler's subcompact sales were limited by engine availability, so that it could not take advantage of its positioning as the only domestic front-wheel-drive subcompact when the market shifted to small cars after 1978. This weak product positioning, together with high-cost manufacturing, is largely responsible for Chrysler's near bankruptcy.

Chrysler's product strategy for the 1980s is based on a limited range of front-wheel-drive designs—the K-body compact and intermediate range and the L-body subcompact range. By 1984 Chrysler anticipates that all of its production will be front-wheel drive; as of mid-1982, 90 percent of production capacity is front-wheel drive.

Chrysler's very weak financial position has sharply limited its product-development capabilities. With the introduction of the K-car, several years will elapse before any completely new design is expected. In response, Chrysler has taken two tacks. First, it has renegotiated its marketing agreement with Mitsubishi Motor Corporation to sell some Mitsubishi cars through 1990, meanwhile allowing Mitsubishi to develop its own dealer network. Second, it has been negotiating both with Mitsubishi and Peugeot about the possibility of joint production of a new small car in the United States in the mid-1980s, presumably as a successor to the L-body. [44]

General Motors. GM's product strategy emphasizes "a car for every purse and purpose," providing a wide variety of choices to the consumer while focusing on family-sized cars and the luxury market. GM has always led the intermediate and standard-sized markets, especially in the higher-priced, higher-profit ranges. [45] In the intermediate and standard-sized segments GM is the leader in pricing, styling, and innovation. They have been more successful than any other producer in selling luxury options such as automatic transmissions, air conditioners, and power steering.[46]

GM's downsizing program, announced in 1974, is central to its product policy. Faced with the need to provide a more fuel-efficient product line, GM chose to downsize from the top to protect the diversity and stratification of its product mix; it was felt that it would be easier to redefine the market's idea of a family-sized car and keep customers in them than to try to switch them to a new small car.[47] Downsizing from the top maintained product-line continuity, avoiding opening a gap in the line and possibly confusing consumers. Such a move marked a departure from the traditional competitive interaction. GM downsized its cars while Ford did not; 1977 was thus the first recent year in which Ford and GM did not have competitive models line for line.

Underlying General Motors' product strategy is the apparent commitment to remain the dominant full-line producer, with the financial resources to back up the commitment. Over the 1978–1985 period GM anticipates $40 billion in capital expenditures worldwide.

Ford. Ford, the number two producer, has long viewed itself as having to compete directly with GM.[48] Ford has been a follower in styling but until recently a leader in seeking out new product niches. Its strategy has been to occupy product niches that it could exploit profitably before its competitors could move in,[49] creating a product mix filled with speciality cars while still maintaining a full line. Ford also concentrated on producing high-volume products. In the late 1970s small cars accounted for about 50 percent of Ford Division sales versus 40 percent for Chevrolet. Ford was also very strong in vans and pickup trucks.

Ford's weakness as a full-line producer in the United States relative to GM is a critical factor. While Ford had great strength in small cars (47.2 percent of domestic subcompacts in 1975) and in specialty-car niches (for example, Mustang I and II, Cougar, and Thunderbird), Ford suffers from an overall weak mix especially in relation to GM's middle-range (Buick-Oldsmobile-Pontiac) markets. This inability to develop a rich product mix and lessen dependence upon small cars weakens Ford's position. Despite strenuous efforts, the scale and integration advantages of GM over Ford have remained constant while Ford's return on equity (ROE) and return on sales (ROS) continue to be, at best, 20 percent-30 percent lower than GM's.

Ford began its downsizing in the low end of its product line, leaving the downsizing of its full-sized cars until the 1979 model year, two years after GM. This decision was an apparent attempt to protect its small-car share from imports while remaining in a position to occupy the position in larger cars that GM had just vacated through its downsizing. In 1977 the market still preferred big cars and this move by Ford was designed to exploit that preference.

After the 1979 oil shortages and the market shift toward smaller cars, General Motors was successful in convincing buyers that its downsized versions, with interior dimensions even somewhat larger, but with smaller exteriors, were every bit comparable to the old big cars. In contrast, Ford's product strategy has been somewhat muddled.

Major Foreign Producers. Until the mid-1970s VW's product strategy was based on a narrow product line supported by a service-first strategy. VWs were not sold until there was a dense service network backing them.[50] This careful build up of dealer and service organizations allowed VW to survive in the U.S. market while other imports that had entered in the late 1950s could not. As figure 2–1 shows, the "Bug" filled a market niche for a small economic vehicle that domestic producers were not filling.

By the late 1960s both the strategy and the car were outdated designs. The mid 1970's finally saw VW grapple with the development of an efficient product line, during which time the company suffered massive losses both in the United States and in Europe. VW's product strategy was to replace the Beetle model and image with a line of water-cooled, front-wheel-drive, front-engine cars with improved component interchangeability.[51] VW also needed to recapture its U.S. share by regaining a cost-competitive position. Production of the VW Beetle in Germany was discontinued in January 1978 and efforts were made to more closely integrate Audi with VW—Audi, to cover the middle-range end of the market and VW, the lower end, with some overlap. VW now has a range of cars covering the small and inexpensive through the middle bracket (Rabbit) to the upper-middle-class Audi 5000.

Toyota and Nissan both entered the U.S. market for the second time in 1965 after a disastrous initial penetration in the late 1950s. Toyota's Corona, a very successful initial import, was priced slightly higher than the VW Beetle, had one-third more horsepower and an automatic transmission. Toyota's mix has always heavily emphasized small fuel-efficient cars. Toyota now follows a policy of product upgrading and differentiation, providing a broader product line than before. Nissan and Toyota closely match each other in the variety and size of their product line.

Honda is a late entrant into the Japanese and U.S. auto markets, not exporting to the United States until 1970. Unlike Toyota and Nissan, smaller Honda effected a relatively low risk, low cost entry into both markets with a narrow, distinctive product line based upon novel engineering features.[52] Having established a presence, though, it too is beginning to upgrade its models.

As discussed in greater detail in the next chapter, Japanese producers have in effect shifted the basis of competition from price, the original attraction when they were making their entry, to performance. By stressing quality and good service, their product strategies emphasize the nonprice appeal of their products. Part of this strategy involves broadening the product line to more adequately satisfy diverse tastes while studying shifts in U.S. tastes and desires closely.

Financial Issues

Central to the changes that have occured in the U.S. auto industry are the financial pressures that have arisen due to new competitive positions and changing firm strategies. The ability of individual firms to fund the required programs to maintain competitiveness is perhaps the critical element in determining the pattern of future structural change. Such issues are particularly important to examine because the need to retool entire product lines has vastly increased the capital requirements of domestic firms while not so affecting most foreign competitors. Furthermore, within the domestic industry there are wide variations in the relative financial strengths of individual producers. Analysis of this issue, thus, is central to understanding the competitive fortunes of domestic producers.

The financial strategies of the domestic firms must be viewed in the context of the several pressures that affect them. First, U.S. auto makers, particularly GM, reportedly rely upon investment strategies and capital allocation procedures that are very dependent upon the financial results achieved.[53] This approach contrasts sharply with the practices of most foreign producers. For example, financial criteria at VW apparently are applied in a much more flexible fashion, with the technical functions having at least as strong an influence on the product planning decision as the comptroller. Some observers have suggested that technical proposals accepted at VW would yield GM inadequate financial returns.[54]

Second, the high capital requirements arising from regulatory mandates and retooling have to be viewed in light of a fifteen-year trend of steadily decreasing profitability. Initially, domestic producers responded by decreasing the relative level of new investment, from about 9 percent of revenues in 1968 to about 6.3 percent in 1977. Since then, competitive and regulatory mandates have required the substantial increase in capital spending.

Domestic firms have very different resources to meet these increased capital requirements. Tables 2–21 and 2–22 list the cash flow and the debt/equity ratios for GM, Ford, Chrysler, and AMC. GM in the past has been in an extremely strong financial position, generating almost three times as much cash as Ford and keeping a debt/equity ratio similarly

Table 2–21
Cash Flow for Domestic Producers over Time
(in millions of dollars)

Year	General Motors	Ford	Chrysler	American Motors Corporation	American Motors Corporation Cash Flow from Operations Only
1979	6246.9	n.a.	n.a.	142.3	126.5
1978	6669.8	2902.6	433.9	104.3	87.6
1977	5828.6	2789.2	517.8	125.8	64.2
1976	5231.8	2003.8	779.3	16.9	16.9
1975	3437.1	1246.6	76.3	27.0	27.0
1974	2722.1	1284.4	279.0	67.2	67.2
1973	4449.0	1854.7	640.7	120.5	79
1972	4006.6	1783.3	606.4	54.0	n.a.
1971	3783.8	1480.3	457.6	41.6	n.a.
1970	2140.8	1339.2	356.7	99.5	n.a.
1969	n.a.	1350.2	459.9	39.1	n.a.
Total 1970–1978	38269.6	16684.1	4147.7	656.8	—
Ratio	(59)	(25)	(6)	(1)	—

Source: Author's calculations based upon Corporate Annual Reports, 1969–1979.
n.a. = Not available.

Table 2–22
Debt/Equity Ratios of Domestic Producers over Time

Year	American Motors Corporation	Chrysler	Ford	General Motors
1978	.22	.41	.12	.06
1977	.27	.42	.16	.07
1976	.36	.37	.20	.07
1975	.36	.44	.24	.09
1974	.21	.37	.23	.07
1973	.19	.35	.15	.06
1972	.29	.32	.17	.07
1971	.17	.36	.14	.06

Source: Author's calculations based upon Corporate Annual Reports, 1971–1978.

strong. This financial strength allowed GM to pursue a financial strategy emphasizing internal financing of capital needs, a return on equity of 20 percent or more, and the maintenance or increase of the dividend.[55] It is also interesting to note how AMC's financial position—traditionally regarded as the shakiest—improved over the 1975–1979 period while Chrysler's continued to deteriorate. Since 1974 AMC has been following a cash-preservation policy. Expenditures for facilities and tooling have gone down—halved, in fact—while cash has been used to reduce debt. This policy is possible because of AMC's disinvestment from new-model design.

Table 2–23 summarizes the financial strengths of the different domestic firms between 1970 and 1978. The key figure is the percentage investment to cash flow. AMC's financial strength measured by this statistic is surprisingly comparable to Ford, but it masks a weakness in product strategy that results from delaying the introduction of new models. Chrysler's financial position is at best precarious.

The obvious question is whether domestic producers will be able to fund their product-repositioning programs internally, and if not, how much will they have to obtain from outside. This section will not consider the question of how that money actually might be obtained from external sources.

Table 2–23
Actual and Projected Investment as Percentage Cash Flow
(in millions of dollars)

	General Motors	*Ford*	*Chrysler*	*American Motors Corporation*
Total capital investment				
1970–1977	18616.0	9953.0	3629.0	450.3
1970–1978	23180.0	12495.0	4300.0	491.5
Total cash flow				
1970–1977	28599.8	13781.5	3713.8	531.0
1970–1978	38265.6	16684.1	4147.7	656.8
Percent investment to cash flow				
1970–1978	61%	75%	104%	75%
Projected[a] ratio of investment to cash flow				
1979–1985	1.04	.97	1.74	b

Source: Author's calculations based upon tables presented in chapter 2.
[a]See tables 2–24, 2–25, 2–26.
[b]AMC projections are not made because of AMC's links with Renault.

Tables 2–24 through 2–26 present estimates of the capital flows of GM, Ford, and Chrysler over the 1979–1985 period. AMC is not included because of its close ties with Renault. The capital needs projected are those actually forecast by the producers. Profits are assumed to increase at 10 percent per year and dividend payouts are "restrained" from historic levels. These projections represent what might be called a best-case scenario. Profits increase steadily, if unspectacularly, and more importantly, there is no economic or market downturn, or strike, which would cause profits to drop.

Ford and GM, with relatively modest outside funding, succeed in meeting their capital requirements. Chrysler, however, will have to continually seek outside funding of almost 50 percent of its capital needs each year—a tremendous strain for any company. GM and Ford can just about supply their capital requirements internally but Chrysler's ratio of cash flow to capital requirements rises from 1.04 percent to 1.73 percent.

Implications and Conclusion

The events of the 1970s can be summarized in terms of three overall themes. The first is a shift in the basis of competition. During the 1970s a fundamental change in competition occurred in the U.S market as a result of a number of factors—increasing oil prices and the consequent shift in demand toward smaller cars, regulatory initiatives, and the entrance of foreign competitors. U.S. producers, operating in what could be characterized as a four-firm oligopoly, were accustomed to supplying a replacement market for large cars that was largely immune to foreign competition. At the same time, these competitive changes complimented the strategies of some foreign producers, particularly the Japanese, who already had a low-cost production base for the sorts of small cars the U.S. market was beginning to demand.

A second fundamental change, and one in which the automobile industry was by no means alone, was an increase in the degree of uncertainty and risk facing the established domestic producers. Risk increased for several reasons. Capital requirements increased as the locus of design change shifted from styling and sheet metal to fundamental redesign of the entire car. With this change, product lead times expanded, so that fundamental design choices had to be made increasingly far removed from accurate knowledge of the markets.

Another fundamental factor increasing risk for domestic producers particularly was the lack of coordination between energy policy and the CAFE regulations. After the initial 1973–1974 oil-price increase, in real terms gasoline prices actually declined until 1979, when they again increased dramatically. Consumers, responding rationally to these price sig-

Table 2-24
Projection of Chrysler Corporation Capital Flows under Normal Circumstances

Year	Capital Need	Increase in Working Capital	Profit	Dividend	Net	Depreciation	Amortization	Total	Variance
1979	.7	—	—	—	—	.2	.2	.4	(.3)
1980	.8	.1	—	—	—	.2	.3	.5	(.4)
1981	.8	—	—	—	—	.2	.3	.5	(.3)
1982	.8	.1	—	—	—	.2	.3	.5	(.4)
1983	.8	.1	—	—	—	.2	.3	.5	(.4)
1984	.8	—	—	—	—	.2	.3	.5	(.3)
1985	.8	.1	—	—	—	.2	.3	.5	(.4)

Capital need   5.9   Cash flow   3.4

Source: Author's calculations based upon tables presented in John B. Schnapp et al., Harbridge House, *Corporate Strategies of the Automotive Manufacturers* (Lexington, Mass.: Lexington Books, D.C. Heath and Company, 1979). Revised by author.

Notes: Working capital assumed to increase 5 percent annually. Base is 1 b, average for 1976–1978.

Profit averaged, 0.1 b is base, profits increase at 10 percent.

No dividends are paid.

Split between Planning, Preproduction and Engineering and Tooling: 54 percent Planning, Preproduction and Engineering, 46 percent Tooling (1973–1977 average).

Depreciation: 45 percent of investment (1974–1978 average: 45.9 percent, 1969–1978 average: 51.7 percent).

Amortization: 70 percent of investment (1974–1978 average: 70 percent, 1969–1978 average: 70.5 percent).

Table 2-25
Projection of General Motors Capital Flows under Normal Circumstances

Year	Capital Need	Increase in Working Capital	Profit	Dividend	Net	Depreciation	Amortization	Total	Variance
1979 (actual)	5.4 b	(1.3)	2.5	1.5	1.4	1.2	2.0	4.6	.5
1980	6.7	.3	3.6	1.8	1.8	1.7	2.7	6.2	(.8)
1981	6.7	.4	4.0	2.0	2.0	1.7	2.7	6.4	(.7)
1982	6.7	.4	4.4	2.2	2.2	1.7	2.7	6.6	(.5)
1983	6.7	.4	4.8	2.4	2.4	1.7	2.7	6.8	(.3)
1984	6.7	.4	5.3	2.6	2.7	1.7	2.7	7.1	—
1985	6.7	.5	5.8	2.9	2.9	1.7	2.7	7.3	.1

Capital need 46.7   Cash flow 45.0

Source: Author's calculations based upon tables presented in John B. Schnapp et al., Harbridge House, *Corporate Strategies of the Automotive Manufacturers* (Lexington, Mass.: Lexington Books, D.C. Heath and Company, 1979). Revised by author.

Notes: 3.3b is average of profit in 1977, 1978, and 1979. Profits increase at 10 percent.
50 percent dividend payout.
50/50 split between Planning, Preproduction and Engineering and Tooling.
Depreciation 50 percent of annual investment (average 1975-1979: 51.4 percent).
Amortization 80 percent of annual investment (average 1975-1979: 96.9 percent).
5 percent increase in working capital assumed, base is 7.4b (average 1977-1979).

Table 2–26
Projection of Ford Motor Company Capital Flows under Normal Circumstances

Year	Capital Need	Increase in Working Capital	Profit	Dividend	Net	Depreciation	Amortization	Total	Variance
1979	3.4	.1	1.6	.4	1.2	1.2	1.0	3.4	(.1)
1980	4	.1	1.8	.4	1.4	1.4	1.2	4.0	(.1)
1981	4	.2	2.0	.5	1.5	1.4	1.2	4.1	.1
1982	4	.2	2.2	.5	1.7	1.4	1.2	4.3	.1
1983	4	.2	2.4	.6	1.8	1.4	1.2	4.4	.2
1984	4	.2	2.6	.6	2.0	1.4	1.2	4.6	.4
1985	4	.2	2.9	.6	2.2	1.4	1.2	4.8	.6

Capital need　28.6　　　　　　　　　　　　Cash flow　29.6

Source: Author's calculations based upon tables presented in John B. Schnapp et al., Harbridge House, *Corporate Strategies of the Automotive Manufacturers* (Lexington, Mass.: Lexington Books, D.C. Heath and Company, 1979). Revised by author.

Notes: Percent increase in working capital. Base is 2.8 b: average 1976–1978.

.5 b is average of profits 1976–1978, adjusting 1976 (strike year) by 350 m, Ford's estimate of lost profit.

Dividend rate is assumed 25 percent (1976–1978 rate is 26.4 percent).

Split between Planning, Preproduction and Engineering and Tooling: 58 percent Planning, Preproduction and Engineering, 42 percent Tooling.

Depreciation is 60 percent of annual investment (five-year average 1974–1978: 65.9 percent).

Amortization is 70 percent of annual investment (five-year average 1974–1978: 74.8 percent).

nals, shifted from large cars to small cars, back to large and finally to small cars again in the space of a decade. From the point of view of U.S. manufacturers facing CAFE requirements, the lack of a consistent energy pricing to encourage consumers to buy more fuel-efficient cars created great uncertainty.

More generally, it is important to note how regulatory efforts in fuel economy, emissions, and safety, coming from different political and administrative agendas, sent a series of contradictory strategic signals to firms. Emissions regulations, by promulgating a fleet standard, both tended to favor small cars (inherently easier to clean up) and also worked against the trickle-down pattern of innovation favored by U.S. auto makers. Safety standards implicitly favored larger and more crashworthy vehicles. CAFE regulations were at cross purposes with emissions standards, since reductions in emissions tend to reduce fuel efficiency too, although emissions standards did tend to favor small cars.

In several specific areas these changes have taken the form of specific pressures for structural change in the industry:

1. *Scale economies:* While always important, scale economies have increased in the automobile industry over the 1965–1980 period. The shift to smaller cars has increased volume requirements from those required for large cars. Equally important has been the need to increase volume to amortize very high vehicle-design costs that stem from the major engineering and design changes that have been required.

These increasing scale economies have put the smaller mass-market producers at a disadvantage. In response, AMC has moved to integrate itself more closely with Renault, while at the same time concentrating in specialty vehicles. Ford appears to be moving more toward international integration of its operations. How Chrysler will respond is yet unknown.

2. *Manufacturing cost differences:* The established basis of competition between U.S. companies has changed as Japanese firms with a significant cost advantage have entered the market. As the small-car market, in which imports are price leaders, becomes an increasingly large segment of the market, an imperative for U.S. producers is to reduce their production costs. Whether this reaction is feasible or even possible is unclear.

3. *Increased capital requirements:* For U.S. producers in particular, the need to retool the entire product line over the 1978–1985 period has sharply increased captial requirements at the same time that import competition has intensified.

Even if all domestic producers can satisfy these capital requirements, this capital crunch may have implications far beyond the mid-1980s. An important element of strategy is timing; for example, much of the success of Japanese imports in the United States depended upon their positioning with a strong distribution network when the market shifted to smaller cars. To the extent that the capital shortage facing domestic producers prevents them from taking advantage of strategic opportunities that open in the next few years—opportunities that firms with more cash might be able to take advantage of—domestic firms might find themselves disadvantaged in the future world market.

4. *Transition pressures:* A final issue is the importance of distinguishing between short- and long-term viability. A combination of developments, among them very low levels of demand and high-capital requirements, resulted in very poor 1980 financial results for the entire industry. It would indeed be an academic issue to examine the long-term viability of the industry without recognizing that short-term survival may be a principal driving force.

Notes

1. For a further discussion see, for example, Lawrence J. White, *The Automobile Industry since 1945* (Cambridge, Mass.: Harvard University Press, 1971).

2. Ibid., p. 96.

3. Office of the Assistant Secretary for Policy and International Affairs, U.S. Department of Transportation, *The U.S. Automobile Industry, 1980* (Washington, D.C.: U.S. Department of Transportation, January 1981), p. 4.

4. Harbridge House, Inc. *Corporate Strategies of the Automotive Manufacturers* (Lexington, Mass.: D.C. Heath and Co., 1979), p. 82.

5. Ford Motor Company, *State of the U.S. Automotive Industry* (Ford Motor Company, 13 June 1978), p. 2.

6. "U.S. Automakers Reshape for World Competition," *Business Week,* 21 June 1982, p. 85.

7. Ford Motor Company, *State of the Industry,* p. 16.

8. Harbridge House, *Corporate Strategies,* p. 83.

9. U.S. Department of Transportation, *Automobile Industry,* p. 40.

10. Harbridge House, Inc., *Corporate Strategies of the Automotive Manufacturers; Vol. I, Strategic Histories, prepared for the U.S. Department of Transportation, National Highway Traffic Safety Administration* (Boston: Harbridge House, Inc., June 1978), p. I–374.

11. *Ward's Automotive Yearbook, 1981* (Detroit: Ward's Communications, 1981), p. 217.

12. Harbridge House, *Corporate Strategies, Vol. I,* p. I–162.

13. Harbridge House, *Corporate Strategies* (Lexington, Mass.), pp. 18, 130.

14. "Chrysler Reduces Breakeven Point," *Ward's Automotive Reports,* 15 March 1982.

15. *Business Week,* "U.S. Automakers Reshape", p. 85.

16. Ibid.

17. Ibid.

18. Author's calculations.

19. Associate Professor Michael E. Porter, *Note on Supplying the Automobile Industry; Electronic Engine Controls* (Boston: Harvard Business School, 1978), p. 2.

20. *Business Week,* "U.S. Automakers Reshape", p. 92.

21. Harbridge House, *Corporate Strategies* (Lexington, Mass.), p. 111.

22. White, *Auto Industry since 1945,* p. 155.

23. Ibid., p. 138.

24. See, for example, Raymond Vernon, *Storm Over the Multinationals: The Real Issues* (Cambridge, Mass: Harvard University Press, 1977), p. 81.

25. Chrysler annual reports.

26. Harbridge House, *Corporate Strategies, Vol. I,* p. I-103.

27. Ibid., p. I-214.

28. Ibid., p. I-372.

29. Harbridge House, *Corporate Strategies* (Lexington, Mass.), p. 108.

30. White, *Auto Industry since 1945,* p. 208.

31. Harbridge House, *Corporate Strategies* (Lexington, Mass.), p. 93.

32. Ibid., p. 92.

33. *Automotive News,* 2 January 1978, p. 1.

34. Ibid.

35. Harbridge House, *Corporate Strategies* (Lexington, Mass.), pp. 108, 185, 141.

36. Ford Motor Company, *State of the Industry,* p. 20.

37. Harbridge House, *Corporate Strategies* (Lexington, Mass.), p. 126.

38. *U.S. Department of Transportation, Transportation Systems Center, Analysis of American Motor Corporation's Financial Status* (Cambridge, Mass: U.S. Department of Transportation–Transportation Systems Center, 21 February 1978), p. 4–9.

39. U.S. National Highway Traffic Safety Administration, Office of Automotive Fuel Economy, *Data and Analysis for 1981–1984 Passenger Automobile Fuel Economy Standards, Document 1* (Washington: U.S. Department of Transportation, 28 February 1977), p. 3–7.

40. Ibid.

41. Harbridge House, *Corporate Strategies, Vol. I,* p. I-31.

42. Ibid., p. I-67.

43. Ibid., p. I-65.

44. "GM-Toyota and Chrysler-Mitsubishi Play 'Let's Make a Deal,'" *Ward's Automotive Reports,* 15 March 1982, p. 34.

45. Harbridge House, *Corporate Strategies, Vol. I.,* p. I-147.

46. Ibid.

47. Ibid., p. I–163.
48. Harbridge House, *Corporate Strategies,* (Lexington, Mass.), p. 24.
49. White, *Auto Industry since 1945,* p. 188.
50. Harbridge House, *Corporate Strategies, Vol. I.,* p. I–340.
51. Ibid., p. I–353.
52. Ibid., p. I–294.
53. Harbridge House, *Corporate Strategies* (Lexington, Mass.), p. 34.
54. Ibid., p. 25.
55. Harbridge House, *Corporate Strategies, Vol. I,* p. I–151.

3

The Global Context of the Auto Industry

An understanding of the automotive industry outside of the United States is important to an analysis of structural change within the domestic industry for several reasons. First, in 1980 imported automobiles accounted for over 27 percent of the U.S. market, and many industry observers suggest that this share may grow in the future.[1] Whatever else high import share may connote, it is plain that the strategies of non-U.S. firms are a critical dimension of the domestic market. Furthermore, the strategies that foreign-based firms adopt in the U.S. market are only partially a function of developments here. Their strategies may be influenced by forces outside as well as within the domestic market. Similarly, the domestic passenger-car operations of U.S.-chartered multinationals are only one part of a larger operation.

The first two sections of chapter 3 outline the major forces conditioning developments in the evolving world auto industry. A major portion of the chapter is then devoted to an analysis of the Japanese industry and its likely patterns of future evolution as they affect the North American market.

Forces for Increasing Industry Internationalization

Over the past decades several developments have propelled the automobile industry into an evolving worldwide competitive system. First is the growing similarity in demand among major markets. The maturation of European and Japanese markets and the end of cheap gasoline in the United States have eliminated much of the basis for product differentiation between domestic and European or Japanese vehicles.[2]

Scale economies are a second impetus for increasing internationalization. Excluding organizational and administrative diseconomies, it appears that scale economies are never really exhausted in automotive manufacture. While the magnitude of scale economies is uncertain, production up to two million identical units a year probably confers some advantage, although most of the gains are made at lower levels.[3] Economies also differ between size classes: there are higher scale economies associated with small-car production. Table 2–7, chapter 2, is one estimate of production scale economies.

Increasingly significant are economies in development costs. Associated with the introduction of any model are substantial initial costs that must be spread over the total lifetime model output. The potential for scale economies in these engineering, research and development, and launch costs are substantial. Such concerns recently have become more important to auto makers because of the enormous design requirements for pollution controls and energy conservation.

The competitive pressures to achieve scale economies unavailable in any single national market have led to two evolving worldwide manufacturing strategies. In the decentralized or *world-car approach* followed by U.S. firms, production facilities are distributed among many countries to take advantage of scale and relative cost advantages while gaining access to markets that would otherwise be hidden behind trade barriers. The international integration of manufacturing offers the potential for significant economies for multinational producers. This so-called world-car strategy also provides a mechanism for competing in developing markets protected by substantial trade barriers. Through the location of component facilities in developing countries, a competitive presence in the market can be established within the framework of an integrated worldwide manufacturing system.[4]

A second response to the need for increased volume has been followed by the Japanese up to the present. Japanese producers have chosen to achieve volume and scale economies through integrated manufacturing in Japan, exporting production throughout the world.[5]

The increasing internationalization of the auto industry has profound implications for the competitive structure and performance of the industry in the future. On the one hand, mature markets may grow increasingly consolidated, as the industry responds to a slowdown or actual decline in market growth and increasing costs due to technological and market shifts. On the other, the development of new automotive capacity in developing markets such as South America or the Communist bloc may alter trading patterns and the position of the currently dominant producers and producing regions significantly.

Risks in Multinational Strategies

While the increasing homogeneity of the major world markets has created opportunities for economies of scale in production and design of the world car, it has also raised the stakes for successful competition in the auto industry. As the scale of the industry increases, the investments required to build increasingly complex manufacturing and marketing structures in multiple locations also increase. The massive commitment of resources and time magnifies the strategic and financial consequences of mistakes. These risks are heightened by the substantial uncertainty surrounding the evolving structure of the world automotive industry. While the sources of this uncertainty are numerous, three critical factors particularly bear on the strategies multinational firms will adopt in the future.

1. *Future demand in world markets:* Table 3–1 gives a summary of available projections of world demand by major area. The most notable characteristic of these projections is their variation, which reflects the uncertainty about future developments in three underlying determinants of automobile demand: oil prices, the rate of economic growth, and the policies that developing markets may choose to follow.[6] With no accepted consensus on future oil-price developments, and with the increased pessimism about the prospects for future real economic growth, especially in the non-OPEC less-developed countries (LDCs), it is unclear what are the prospects for substantial automobile-demand growth in the future. Furthermore, regardless of the underlying economic conditions, government policies may discourage vehicle demand for a variety of reasons—for example, to avoid increased petroleum imports or the need to invest in transportation infrastructure. A striking example is the Communist-bloc countries, where the relatively few private vehicles reflect the policy decisions of centralized economic planners.

While future demand in less-developed markets is highly uncertain, demand projections for the developed markets also show great variation. Projections for both Western Europe and the United States show the same range—on one hand, reduced demand at replacement-market levels, and on the other, a steadily increasing market.

Table 3–1
Summary of Low and High World-Demand Projections, 1980–1990
(millions of units)

Region	1980[a]	1985	1990
North America	9	9.9–12.0	8.0–14.4
Western Europe	10.1	10.0–12.0	9.0–14.6
Japan	3.1	2.5–03.5	2.0–05.8
Rest of world	5.8	5.8–16.0	5.8–27.0
Total	28.9	28.2–43.5	24.8–62.8

Source: Adapted from projections by Economic Models Ltd., Euro-Finance, *The Future of the World Motor Industry;* industry projections; and A. Gary Shilling and Co., as cited in U.S., Department of Transportation, Research and Special Programs Administration, "World New Car Demand Projections, 1980–1990." (Typewritten).
[a]Estimated actual sales.

Projections for the Japanese market reflect a degree of uncertainty exceeded only by projections for less-developed markets. The range of projections extends from a one-third reduction in demand over the next decade to a market growth of 6 percent, which would make Japan the greatest growth market outside of newly developing markets. This fact is important because, as will be discussed later, Japanese market growth is a critical element in determining the sorts of future strategies Japanese producers may adopt.

2. *Government policies of the expanding markets:* The automobile industry is viewed by many LDCs as an engine for economic progress and development. Policies to promote the local development of an auto industry often take the form of steep trade barriers or local-content requirements. In some countries that have already established local auto capacity, imports are strictly tied to exports.

The desire by some developing countries to have their own auto industries and the plethora of trade restrictions that many nations have imposed may condition future multinational strategies. First, it is unclear whether the types of vehicles demanded in the more mature U.S., European, and Japanese markets will be desirable in the developing markets. Furthermore, the goal of attaining world scale in production is complicated by various trade restrictions. As there are plans for major capacity expansions in a number of countries, there seems to be an implicit assumption that export markets will absorb much of the new capacity. Where and whether these export markets will absorb the proposed capacity is a question left begging.

3. *The next wave of major producers:* There are now three major emerging automotive markets in the world—the USSR and Eastern Europe, parts of South America, and parts of the Middle East. In the Communist bloc, demand has been constrained by central economic planners, while in the other countries rising economic status is producing an increased demand for automobiles. Each of these expanding markets is close to much larger markets, and each has already established the basis of a viable motor industry. There are also many differences, however. Middle East growth depends critically upon petrodollar revenues; Communist bloc growth is centrally planned; and South America is a large, fragmented, and diverse market with steady but less spectacular growth.[7]

The Communist bloc countries and South America are the most likely candidates to become the next major producers. With a total output in the late 1970s of over two million cars and one million commercial vehicles, the auto production in the Communist bloc had a twenty-percent growth rate. In South America, Argentina, Brazil, and Mexico—the most densely populated South American countries—have well-established motor industries. Brazilian production already exceeds one million vehicles annually. GM, Ford, and VW have taken aggressive positions in South America, which will probably lead to a coming three-way fight.[8]

It is unclear in many instances where existing multinationals fit into all of this. In some countries, as in Spain and Brazil, they have participated in the growth of the industry, while in others, such as South Korea, they have largely been excluded.

Again, scale economies will determine the success of these development efforts. Some countries can probably never develop a viable motor industry unless it is a part of a broader regional development. One advantage of less-developed countries is their low labor costs. Despite the efficiencies of assembly lines, for example, the labor content in assembling motor vehicles and motor components is still fairly high. Low-cost labor in less-developed countries is sometimes less expensive than automation.[9]

The Japanese Auto Industry

In 1980, over 80 percent of U.S. auto imports, or 23 percent of the market, came from Japan. That same year, Japanese motor-vehicle production exceeded that of the United States—the first time U.S. production had ever been exceeded by another national industry. These two statistics suggest the importance of the Japanese industry to developments in the United States. Although the increased penetration of Japanese imports has been ascribed to changes in factor costs that exposed U.S. producers to risks they were unprepared to meet, this reason does not explain why, for example, the Japanese have been enjoying similar import success in Europe, where small, fuel-efficient cars have always predominated. Clearly the competitive success of the Japanese involves more than merely the timely production of small cars. An analysis of the Japanese competitive advantage, and a better understanding of the forces shaping its future, may provide valuable insight into a critical force for structural change in the auto industry.

Continued references to "the Japanese" in auto-industry discussions tend to numb the mind to the fact that, just as with the U.S. industry, the Japanese industry is not a monolith. An understanding of the sorts of behavior that can be expected from the Japanese industry in the future must hinge upon a more sophisticated appreciation of competitive dynamics.

Development of the Japanese Industry

Though the origins of the postwar Japanese auto industry were outside of government sanctions, the industry's development is closely linked with national policies. Government policies first protected the initial industry development, then encouraged industry consolidation, and are now aimed at correcting social externalities of auto use and addressing international trade issues. Directly or indirectly, the Japanese government has extended substantial financial assistance to the auto sector as well as playing the role of international representative for the industry through the use of trade barriers and the promotion of exports.[10]

The Ministry of International Trade and Industry (MITI) has been the government agency most involved with the auto industry. During the 1950s, the ministry first succeeded in gathering together institutional support for a program of auto-industry development; during the next two decades, it encouraged its international competitiveness, and today it is concerned with reducing the trade friction resulting from high automobile exports.[11] Throughout, MITI has actively supported the industry's development,[12] playing the role of mediator vis-a-vis the auto industry.[13]

By the end of the 1950s, the Japanese industry had become sufficiently well established to supply almost the entire domestic market with domestically designed and produced vehicles. At that point the industry was poised for a period of dramatic expansion.

Between 1960 and 1973, domestic auto demand increased an average of 25.5 percent per year. The combination of high levels of trade protection and a very rapidly expanding market allowed Japanese producers to achieve sizeable cost reductions through volume and experience effects, while generating large profits for reinvestment.[14] This rapid growth, and the accompanying scale and volume effects, enhanced the international competitiveness of the industry. Auto exports increased from 7,013 in 1960 to 3,383,000 in 1979. The effects of rapid domestic growth and increasing export sales reinforced each other, allowing the industry to attain a size and level of economies that the domestic market alone would never have supported.

Throughout the 1960s, MITI policy was directed toward limiting competition to allow the surviving firms an efficient scale of production. Such efforts at consolidation were in general unsuccessful. The rapid growth of the Japanese market and the increasing strength of the firms both financially and technologically made it difficult for MITI to restructure the industry by fiat. The number of competitors grew from four in 1951 to six in 1960 to eleven in 1966.[15]

During the 1970s, Japanese firms had to adapt to changes both in the domestic market and in government policy. The spectacular market growth of the previous fifteen years ended as the economy became more mature. As shown in table 3-3, domestic automobile sales began to grow more slowly.[16]

This slowdown in growth sparked increased competition and strategic shifts.[17] The product lines of the larger producers shifted upwards and offered greater variety. In part, this shift was due to the greater sophistication of consumers, but it also reflected a significant change in production economies. While during the 1960s the price of vehicles had declined both in real and current terms, this trend was reversed in the following decade. Thus, the market demand for bigger, more sophisticated, and more comfortable vehicles complimented the manufacturers' shifting cost structure.[18]

Table 3–2

New Passenger Automobiles: Japanese Production, Exports, Imports, 1956–1979

Year	Production	Exports (Percent of production)	Exports to United States (Percent of production)	Total Imports
1956	32,056	0.1	0.0	6,684
1957	47,121	0.8	0.0	6,179
1958	50,643	4.7	2.9	5,450
1959	78,958	6.2	3.4	5,994
1960	165,094	4.2	0.5	3,540
1961	249,508	4.6	0.3	4,310
1962	268,784	6.0	1.0	5,648
1963	407,830	7.7	0.7	9,339
1964	579,660	11.6	2.0	12,185
1965	696,176	14.5	3.2	12,881
1966	887,656	17.4	5.8	15,244
1967	1,375,755	16.2	4.8	14,352
1968	2,055,821	19.8	7.4	15,000
1969	2,611,499	21.5	8.4	15,748
1970	3,178,708	22.8	7.3	19,080
1971	3,717,858	34.9	17.6	18,551
1972	4,022,289	35.0	14.7	24,759
1973	4,470,550	32.5	13.1	36,922
1974	3,931,842	43.9	17.4	42,218
1975	4,567,854	40.0	15.6	45,480
1976	5,027,792	50.5	20.9	40,416
1977	5,431,045	54.5	24.7	41,395
1978	5,975,968	50.9	23.6	54,517
1979	6,175,771	54.8	25.0	64,808

Source: Adapted from *World Motor Vehicle Data,* 1979, Motor Vehicle Manufacturers Association, as cited in U.S. House of Representatives, *Auto Situation 1980,* p. 30., and author's calculations.

Table 3–3

Motor-Vehicle Sales in Japan

Year	Passenger Cars	Percent Change from Last Year	Total Vehicles	Percent Change from Last Year
1965	585,091	–	1,703,564	–
1966	741,124	26.4	2,079,070	22.0
1967	1,129,131	52.4	2,725,024	31.1
1968	1,561,559	38.3	3,307,665	21.4
1969	2,031,969	30.1	3,844,372	16.2
1970	2,374,123	16.8	4,106,528	6.8

Table 3–3 continued

Year	Passenger Cars	Percent Change from Last Year	Total Vehicles	Percent Change from Last Year
1971	2,394,520	8.6	4,024,036	– 2.0
1972	2,618,037	9.3	4,369,295	8.6
1973	2,941,389	12.4	4,954,039	13.4
1974	2,279,997	– 22.5	4,391,662	– 22.2
1975	2,730,609	19.8	4,953,427	11.9
1976	2,450,334	– 10.3	3,852,750	– 4.8
1977	2,500,632	2.1	4,311,359	2.2
1978	2,856,710	14.2	4,681,863	11.6
1979	3,036,872	6.3	5,153,750	10.1

Source: Adapted from Toyota Motor Sales Company, *The Motor Industry of Japan* (annual), and author's calculations.

Table 3–4
Japanese Car Production by Engine Size
(in percentage)

Year	0–1500 cc	1501 cc–2000 cc	Over 2000 cc
1957	100.0	–	–
1958	100.0	–	–
1959	98.7	1.3	–
1960	98.8	1.2	–
1961	79.8	19.2	–
1962	74.3	25.7	–
1963	67.6	31.6	0.8
1964	72.7	23.8	1.0
1965	82.0	17.5	0.4
1966	82.3	17.1	0.5
1967	84.6	14.5	0.9
1968	79.5	19.3	1.2
1969	76.4	22.6	1.0
1970	68.4	30.0	1.6
1971	61.1	37.0	1.9
1972	60.4	37.2	2.4
1973	58.5	39.2	2.3
1974	58.3	38.0	3.7
1975	57.3	38.1	4.6
1976	44.9	48.9	6.2
1977	40.7	51.2	8.1

Source: Data from Japan Automobile Manufacturers Association as cited in Krish Bhaskar, *The Future of the World Motor Industry,* (New York: Nichols Publishing Company, 1980) p. 214, and revised by author.

Table 3-5
Japanese Export Shares by Region

Year	North America	Europe	Latin America
1979	47.1	21.6	4.5
1978	44.1	16.2	5.1
1977	42.6	17.5	6.3
1976	40.4	19.1	5.0
1975	43.5	15.0	5.9
1974	43.4	14.9	5.9
1973	44.1	19.6	5.9
1972	51.2	18.7	6.1
1971	53.2	12.1	6.5
1970	45.6	11.6	7.3

Source: Author's calculations based on data from Toyota Motor Sales Company, *The Motor Industry of Japan* (annual).

A second consequence of slowing domestic growth was an increased dependence upon exports (as shown in table 3–9). In 1976, exports exceeded production for the domestic market for the first time. As table 3–5 suggests, much of this export effort was directed toward North America. More recently, such exports have generated considerable trade friction, and MITI has increasingly played a role in the "administrative guidance" of exports.

With Japan's membership in the General Agreement on Tariffs and Trade (GATT) (February 1963) and Organization for Economic Cooperation and Development (OECD) (April 1964), formal trade and investment barriers were no longer feasible. Table 3–6 describes the reductions in some of these measures. In the 1960s the focus of government regulation shifted toward safety and emissions.

For the industry as a whole, Japanese safety and emissions regulations have probably complemented and encouraged industry positioning on a multiplicity of dimensions. The biennial safety inspections may have increased the demand for quality—a currently important competitive dimension in export markets. It has almost certainly shifted consumption patterns: as the inspections have gotten stricter, Japanese car owners have exhibited an increasing tendency to trade in cars after four years, thus increasing manufacturer production volumes.[19] Japanese emissions standards allow Japanese exports to meet emissions regulations in foreign markets as well. Japanese regulations may also serve as nontariff barriers to trade.[20]

Table 3-6
Japan, U.S., and European Community Tariff Rates on Passenger Cars,
1967-1978
(in percentage)

Year	Japan		United States	European Community
	Small Cars	*Other Cars*		
1967	40.0	28.0	6.5	22.0
1968	36.0	28.0	6.5	11.0
1969	36.0	17.5	5.0	11.0
1970	20.0	17.5	4.5	11.0
1971	10.0	10.0	4.0	11.0
1972	6.4	6.4	3.0	11.0
1978	0.0	0.0	3.0	11.0

Source: U.S., Congress, House of Representatives, *World Auto Trade*, 96th Congress, 7, 18 March, 1980.

Structure of the Japanese Industry

There are currently eleven vehicle manufacturing firms in Japan: Toyota, Nissan, Honda, Mitsubishi, Suzuki, Toyo Kogyo, Isuzu, Hino, Daihatsu, Nissan Diesel, and Fuji Heavy Industry. As a result of link-ups made during the 1960s, these eleven firms effectively form seven competing groups, with Toyota, Hino, and Daihatsu defining the Toyota Group, and Nissan, Nissan Diesel, and Fuji Heavy Industry the Nissan Group.

Table 3-7 lists domestic Japanese market share for each of these firms for recent years. Nissan and Toyota dominate the industry, with a combined two-thirds share of the market. There are also numerous smaller competitors, some of which have entered comparatively recently. For example, late entrants of the 1960s, like Honda and Toyo Kogyo, were able to enter on the strength of innovative products.

The seven competitors can be grouped into three categories. The two majors are the Toyota and Nissan groups, which by every measure dominate the industry both domestically and internationally. Small, independent producers include Honda and Suzuki. Third, there are those firms affiliated with U.S. capital: Isuzu (with GM), Toyo Kogyo (with Ford), and Mitsubishi (with Chrysler). Each of these firms differs in terms of its size, the breadth of its vehicle product line, and its geographical and product-line diversification.

Toyota is the world's third largest auto maker (after G.M. and Ford), and the largest auto maker in the Japanese industry. While over the past

Table 3-7
Japanese Market Share by Firm

Firm	1971	1972	1973	1974	1975	1976	1977	1978	1979
Toyota group	37.4	38.7	38.9	40.0	39.9	38.2	37.3	39.0	37.9
Nissan group	28.4	30.2	29.6	28.3	30.6	30.6	29.6	28.2	27.8
Toyo Kogyo	7.7	7.7	8.0	7.4	7.4	7.1	7.2	7.3	7.8
Mitsubishi	9.6	8.6	9.0	8.0	8.1	9.1	10.2	10.6	10.6
Isuzu	2.9	2.9	3.0	3.1	3.1	3.6	3.9	3.9	3.9
Honda	7.3	6.3	6.0	7.3	5.8	6.1	5.9	5.4	5.1
Suzuki	6.4	5.1	4.8	4.8	3.9	4.3	4.5	4.5	5.7

Source: Toyota Motor Sales Company, *The Motor Industry of Japan* (annual).

Table 3-8
Financial Status: Japanese Producers
(1979 fiscal year)

Firm	Sales (Y billion)	After-Tax Profits (Y billion)	Output (1,000 units)	Capital (Y billion)	Japanese Employees (1,000)
Toyota group	3,430.2	116.6	3,516.5	110.0	61.3
Nissan group	2,754.9	72.1	2,711.0	90.5	74.4
Isuzu	635.4	12.6	418.0	38.0	14.8
Mitsubishi	874.5	15.6	972.0	35.1	22.0
Toyo Kogyo	834.0	7.3	1,001.0	25.7	26.8
Honda	922.2	16.0	801.0	29.6	29.0
Suzuki	271.5	3.4	267.0	12.0	8.5

Source: Adapted from *Far Eastern Economic Review,* 15 February 1980, p. 40.

decade, Toyota's growth has occurred principally in overseas markets (table 3-9), growth and dependence upon expert sales (particularly sales to the United States) have been lower than for other Japanese firms.

Toyota's principal competitor is Nissan, which continues to strive to replace Toyota as the leading auto maker.[21] While the two firms have very similar product lines, there are major differences between the firms. In contrast to Toyota's emphasis on pricing, marketing, and styling, Nissan has emphasized technology and engine development.[22] In the future Nissan's product strategy is likely to stress further product differentiation and up-

Table 3-9
Exports as Percentage of Total Production: Japanese Producers
(passenger cars plus commercial vehicles)

Firm	1971	1972	1973	1974	1975	1976	1977	1978	1979
Toyota group	34.8	30.6	27.4	30.6	34.1	45.2	48.3	44.3	43.1
Nissan group	36.8	36.5	33.3	46.0	41.3	47.9	52.7	50.6	48.6
Toyo Kyogo	34.0	44.8	46.5	52.5	54.4	60.8	65.6	63.0	59.8
Mitsubishi	17.8	18.2	16.3	35.9	29.9	43.2	42.9	46.9	39.7
Isuzu	15.6	34.2	27.5	42.7	46.1	54.5	49.0	54.6	49.9
Honda	11.1	11.4	20.8	28.0	46.2	54.9	67.0	66.7	68.2
Suzuki (Subaru)	1.0	1.9	1.7	6.4	10.3	19.8	17.7	16.7	14.2

Source: Author's calculations based on data from Toyota Motor Sales Company, *The Motor Industry of Japan.*

Table 3–10
Relative Growth of Production and Exports: Japanese Producers

	Annualized Percent Change in Production	Annualized Percent Change in Exports	Relative Size of Firm[a]	
	(1971–1979)	(1971–1979)	1971	1979
Toyota group	5.0	7.9	8.7	10.0
Nissan group	5.3	9.0	6.7	7.9
Toyo Kogyo	8.4	16.3	1.9	2.8
Mitsubishi	8.6	20.1	1.8	2.7
Isuzu	15.3	33.4	.5	1.2
Honda	12.7	41.4	1.2	2.3
Suzuki	3.2	44.5	1.0	1.0

Source: Author's calculations based on data from Toyota Motor Sales Company, *The Motor Industry of Japan* (annual).
[a]Based on total production.

grading in response to the shifting Japanese market. Nissan's product mix is also filled with specialized products such as its sports car and diesel car, and these products, too, will likely be emphasized.[23]

Nissan has pursued a more internationally expansionist strategy than Toyota. Nissan's growth in export sales over the last decade (table 3–10) and the percentage of total production that it exports (3–9) have both been consistently higher than for Toyota. Its major area of export growth has been the United States, although more recently it has been aggressively pursuing cooperative link ups with European firms. Nissan also appears to be following a more international production strategy than Toyota. While Toyota has resisted any move away from centralized Japanese manufacturing, Nissan's future small truck plant in the United States, and the consideration of small-car production in Britain and Italy plus the recent pattern of capacity expansion in Asia-Pacific, suggests a more international positioning.

Honda is a diversified producer of motorcycles, four-wheeled vehicles, and agriculture and forestry machines, the common element being engine technology. Honda entered the auto industry in the early 1960s, when MITI's consolidation efforts threatened to foreclose new entrants. Honda's success in auto manufacturing has resulted from producing a narrow, distinctive product line based upon novel engineering features.[24]

Honda produces only two basic models, the Civic and the Prelude/Accord. Although its sales in Japan are good, the majority of Honda's growth has come from expansion into North America; it exports about

40 percent of its production to the United States. Such high dependence upon one export market leaves Honda vulnerable to the risks inherent in exchange-rate fluctuations and possible trade barriers.

Honda has been the only Japanese firm to announce its intention to assemble autos in North America, beginning in 1983. This decision may have been motivated both by a concern about possible trade barriers to the U.S. market and also because Honda's Japanese production facilities were already working at capacity.[25] Honda and BL (formerly British Leyland) have also reached an agreement on a collaborative manufacturing venture.

Suzuki, the other independent Japanese manufacturer, is both a motor-cycle manufacturer and a minicar maker.

Three Japanese firms have U.S. capital participation: Mitsubishi (Colt) with Chrysler, Isuzu with GM, and Toyo Kogyo (Mazda) with Ford. These relationships have grown more complicated over time, since the Japanese firms are not subsidiaries of the U.S. firms and have their own competitive interests.

Mitsubishi Motor is 15-percent owned by Chrysler Corporation, and 85-percent owned by Mitsubishi. It is in competition with Toyo Kogyo for the third-highest rank in Japanese production. Mitsubishi has a narrow product line, emphasizing a small number of conservatively engineered but carefully styled models.[26]

Mitsubishi's international expansion has been conditioned by its relationship with Chrysler. While it has its own sales network in Europe and southeast Asia, in the Middle East, South Africa, and Africa, it has been expanding its sales in cooperation with Chrysler International, and in North America Chrysler has the exclusive distribution rights.[27] Unlike most Japanese firms, which have expanded primarily in North America, Mitsubishi has spread its marketing effort throughout the developing world as well as in the West.[28]

Mitsubishi's future international position depends upon the future strength of Chrysler. Mitsubishi now has plans to create its own marketing network in North America independent of Chrysler.[29] A longer-term need is to acquire the volume necessary to become an internationally competitive multinational. One hypothetical expansion path to achieve this volume would be for Mitsubishi to merge with Chrysler and a smaller European producer like Volvo, Saab, or BMW, resulting in a multinational company with a total production capacity of around four million vehicles.[30]

Toyo Kogyo already has its own distribution system in North America. It will supply transaxles for Ford's small world cars, while Ford will market Toyo Kogyo products in Asia, the Middle East, and Australia under the Ford label.

Isuzu is 34.2 percent owned by General Motors. With the smallest domestic market share in the Japanese market, and a limited product line,

Isuzu is attempting to secure its future growth through international expansion and by supplying components for GM's new small cars.[31] Isuzu already has its own sales network in a few European countries, and has increased exports through the use of the GM sales network.[32] Isuzu is also beginning to develop its own North American distribution network independent of GM.

Japanese Competitive Advantage

The worldwide penetration of Japanese exports leaves no question as to Japanese competitiveness. The sources of this competitive advantage are important to identify, however, because changes in them will affect the competitive posture and strategies that Japanese producers adopt in the future. While issues of competitive advantage are often linked to issues of individual firm strategy, to the extent that certain elements of competitive advantage are country-wide rather than firm specific, it is useful to generalize about the entire industry.

Principal components of Japanese competitive advantage include:

1. *Japanese positioning for world-scale production:* Japanese producers have historically pursued a strategy of centralized production and the export of finished products to other markets. Until recently, local sourcing and assembly in other markets appear to have almost always been the result of political factors.[33]

Through centralized production Japanese manufacturers have been able to achieve low-cost production through close coordination and integration.[34] High levels of growth have created opportunities for greater scale economies and high-capacity utilization. By growing faster than the domestic market, Toyota and Nissan have achieved economies of scale and production equivalent to those of Ford, Chrysler, and the European producers.[35] Only GM has a greater volume.

While centralized production has generated large scale economies, it has also exposed the Japanese industry to the risks of high-export dependence. Exports now account for about 50 percent of total production. In particular, the importance of a single country—the United States—as a market for Japanese exports indicates the substantial risk the Japanese industry faces along this dimension.

2. *Production cost advantage:* While estimates as to the magnitude of the Japanese cost advantage vary, analysis suggests that in general Japanese producers have a $1,000 to $1,500 cost advantage over the North American industry.[36] The magnitude of this cost differential is important not only in itself, but also because it may subsequently be translated into superiority in other competitive dimensions—for example, increased durability.[37] Part of

this cost advantage is due to differences in labor costs. While comparisons of labor costs between national industries are complex, Japanese labor costs are substantially less than U.S. costs.[38] A second-factor cost advantage stems from the strong Japanese parts industry. The North American supplier industry has neither the quality nor the scale advantages of the Japanese industry, and the European parts industry is even further disadvantaged.[39] In a similar fashion, Japanese auto production benefits from low-cost domestic steel.[40]

Superior productivity is another source of Japanese cost advantage. After compensating for differing levels of vertical integration, analysis suggests that Japanese manufacturers require fewer man-hours than U.S. producers to build a vehicle of equivalent size.[41]

Levels of automation are again difficult to measure, although general opinion (albeit with some dissent) acknowledges the Japanese industry as leading the world in automation, particularly in the use of robots.[42] One estimate is that as of 1980 Japanese manufacturers were using over six times as many robots per million vehicles produced as were U.S. manufacturers.[43]

3. *Quality:* Superior quality is a frequently cited attribute of Japanese competitive advantage. Unfortunately, there is no generally accepted definition of quality. A main area of Japanese quality advantage seems to be in overall workmanship and body finish; on the other hand, there is some evidence that U.S. cars may be more durable.[44]

The perceived quality advantage of Japanese vehicles also has an important competitive implication. The market's preference for higher-quality Japanese vehicles may mean that even when U.S. producers have the capacity to meet the U.S. demand for fuel-efficient cars, they might not be able to sell them.[45] (For a more detailed discussion of the competitive implications stemming from higher rates of consumer loyalty to Japanese vehicles, see chapter 6.)

4. *Nontariff barriers to trade:* Substantial nontariff barriers appear to exist in the form of internal tax policy, homologation costs, and distribution systems.[46] The two-tier commodity tax discriminates against the sale of larger cars, which are principally imports. A road tax, applied annually on the owner of a vehicle, has a sharp break (a 270 percent increase) between vehicles under and over 2000 cc displacement. These policies make the purchase and operation of a large car very expensive, consistent on one hand with domestic policies that regard car ownership, especially of large vehicles, as a luxury, but on the other hand also effectively discouraging the demand for most imported vehicles.[47] The extensive documentation, testing, and modification that imported vehicles must undergo to meet safety and environmental standards may also be a source of trade barriers.

Distribution costs, however, are by far the most important source of competitive disadvantage for imports. Due to a system of exclusive dealer-

Table 3–11
Quality Comparisons of Foreign and Domestic Automobiles, 1979

Automotive Class	Condition of Car at Delivery[a]		Owner Satisfaction[b]	
	Domestic Make Average	Imports Average	Domestic Make Average	Import Average
Subcompacts	6.55	7.94	76.6	91.0
Light weight	—	—	83.0	—
Heavier weight	—	—	71.0	—
Small specialties	6.33	7.80	77.6	92.5
Compacts	6.20	7.65	72.2[c]	91.4
	—	—	77.4[d]	—
Midsize	6.51	8.05	75.3	94.5
Standard	6.75	—	81.8	—
Luxury	7.12	8.47	86.6	94.6

Source: Rogers National Research, Buyer Profiles, 1979 (data aggregated from proprietary data), as cited in U.S. Department of Transportation, *The U.S. Automobile Industry, 1980,* p. 45.
[a]Scale of 1 to 10: 10 is excellent.
[b]Would buy again, in percentage.
[c]Low-price domestic compacts.
[d]High-price domestic compacts.

Table 3–12
Prices in Japan Compared with the United States for Selected Models
(in U.S. dollars)

	1979 Models		
	Subcompact	Small Sporty Car	Compact Size
U.S. effective retail	$4,810	$4,915	6,635
Additional Japanese costs:			
Ocean freight and insurance	235	175	210
Port handling and make-ready	105	125	125
Japanese commodity tax	700	850	1,200
Net homologation costs	110	435	535
Dealer incentives	0	500	500
Higher dealer margin	950	1,425	2,100
Other costs and profits (net)	205	180	760
Effective retail in Japan	7,105	8,605	12,065

Source: "United States-Japan Trade: Issues and Problems" (automobile section). Report by the Comptroller of the United States, 21 September 1979 as cited in U.S., *Auto Situation 1980,* p. 34.

ships, imported vehicles usually cannot piggyback on some already-existing distribution network. Very high dealer-incentive margins, with associated low import volume, place imported vehicles at a substantial price disadvantage relative to domestically produced vehicles in the Japanese market.[48]

Future Development of the Japanese Industry

Issues Facing the Japanese Auto Industry. The spectacular growth of the Japanese auto industry to become the preeminent world producer has been a function of several factors: the explosive growth in domestic demand, government policies encouraging local production and high exports, and an array of social and industry characteristics that have given the Japanese producers a substantial competitive advantage in world markets. While these factors have combined to make the industry extraordinarily successful, other developments already evident or likely to emerge in the future could challenge the current positioning of Japanese firms. These developments include:

1. *Saturation of the domestic market:* Up until the mid-1970s, high domestic sales growth provided Japanese producers with the momentum to expand and achieve international volumes. While the future market will likely reflect increased replacement demand and the heightened sophistication of consumers,[49] there remains substantial uncertainty about future growth in Japanese markets over the next decade. There is little doubt that saturation levels in Japan will be lower than in North America, but otherwise there is little consensus.[50]

Whatever the ultimate penetration of motor vehicles, the rapid growth of the 1960s is unlikely to return. Nineteen seventy-four was the first year since the automotive market began to develop that production actually declined, and since then registrations have begun to exhibit the cyclicality characteristic of more mature markets. In 1977, used-car sales reached 150 percent of new-passenger-car sales, leading some observers to speculate that the Japanese market is taking on the shape of the European auto market, in which used-car sales are between 160 and 200 percent of new-car sales.[51] Demographics are also working against future expansion: the end of the postwar baby boom has meant that in the future fewer new-car buyers will enter the market.[52]

With increased market maturity, business cycles may increasingly influence sales. With reduced growth, there is also the prospect of excess capacity and reduced profitability. Until now, the industry has been structured to operate near capacity. For example, Toyota's break-even level is around 60 percent of capacity, which is high in comparison with non-Japanese firms.[53] With cyclicality and the prospect of generic overcapacity in the domestic market, Japanese producers may need to increase export sales and restructure their operations to lower break-even levels. It is likely that domestic-market competition will grow still more intense if the market matures and demand growth slows.[54]

2. *Shifting industry competitive advantage:* The form and magnitude of Japanese competitive advantage in autos has resulted from both structural characteristics of the Japanese economy as a whole and the specific strategic positionings of auto firms. While elements of this competitive advantage are likely to be enjoyed for some time to come, Japan's position as a low-cost producer may change in the future.[55] Two factors in particular may reduce Japan's cost advantage in auto production: labor costs and exchange-rate fluctuations. Demographics do not favor the Japanese auto industry. The system of lifetime employment requires periodic raises based on seniority. Over the next decade, due to changing mortality and birth rates, the work force will begin to age appreciably. By 1985, workers over the age of forty-five, the group that receives the highest pay, will comprise 40 percent of the automotive work force.[56]

Exchange-rate fluctuations are a second threat to continued Japanese competitive advantage. All else equal, a rise in the value of the yen would

Table 3–13

Average April Rates of Yen/Dollar Exchange, 1964–1980
(in U.S. cents per unit of foreign currency)

Year	Japan (Yen)
1964	.28
1965	.28
1966	.28
1967	.28
1968	.28
1969	.28
1970	.28
1971	.28
1972	.33
1973	.38
1974	.36
1975	.33
1976	.33
1977	.35
1978	.42
1979	.46
1980	.39

Source: Compiled from data published monthly by the International Monetary Fund in *International Financial Statistics* as cited in *Auto Situation 1980*, p. 44.

make Japanese exports less attractive in other markets. The increase in labor costs, coupled with an appreciation of the yen, could reduce the international competitiveness of the Japanese industry.[57]

3. *Limitation of export opportunities:* As noted above, in response to slowing domestic growth, Japanese producers have increased their dependence upon export sales to maintain high rates of growth. Smaller producers especially have been forced into a heavy dependence upon export sales, because of the dominance of the domestic market by Nissan and Toyota. In the future, if domestic growth slows, the percentage of production devoted to exports may rise even further. There are several reasons that a planned dependence upon high exports may prove unviable.

One threat to continued high Japanese exports will come from the increased competition of U.S. and European producers, and possibly from new entrants into auto making from developing countries. As the Japanese domestic market shifts away from simple, basic vehicles toward greater differentiation and sophistication, Japanese producers face the risk that their increasingly sophisticated products will prove undesirable for the developing markets of the future, most of which will be located in LDCs. At the same time, further penetration of the European and U.S. markets increases the risk of stricter trade barriers.

This threat of trade barriers to Japanese exports is a second force for strategic repositioning in the future Japanese industry. The major developing markets of the 1980s will most likely have steep trade barriers.[58] The

Table 3-14
Dependence of Japanese Producers on U.S. Sales, 1979

Manufacturer	Total Production	U.S. Sales	Percent
Toyota	2,996,225[a]	637,891	21.3
Nissan	2,337,821	574,165	24.6
Honda	801,869	353,291	44.1
Subaru	334,290	127,871	38.3
Mazda	971,421	242,920	25.0
Volkswagen	1,396,916	125,670 (imports)	9.0
		132,822 (U.S. produced)	
Mitsubishi (Chrysler)	938,517	138,053	14.7
Fiat	1,325,000	59,254	4.5
Volvo	238,788	56,602	23.7
Renault	1,544,955	18,842	1.2

Source: Adapted from *1980 Ward's Automotive Yearbook* (Detroit: Ward's Communications) and author's calculations.
[a]Domestic production (excludes foreign assembly).

existence of these barriers works directly against the strategic positioning of the Japanese producers. A principal way to compete for a substantial share of these developing and protected markets is through local production facilities to satisfy local-content or export requirements. The need to compete in this manner can be more easily integrated into a worldwide manufacturing network than into the centralized Japanese production system. In particular, local-content laws nullify much of the Japanese cost advantage.[59]

These changes in the conditions facing the Japanese industry—the slowdown in domestic growth, possible restrictions in export opportunities, and an eroding cost advantage—are all taking place against the backdrop of potential overcapacity in the Japanese industry. Japanese producers have ambitious plans for capacity increases over the next several years. It is estimated that by 1983 the Japanese industry will have increased capacity by 20 percent over 1980 levels.[60]

Table 3–15
Japanese Automobile-Production Capacity

Firm	1979	1980	1981	1982	1983
Toyota	2782	2902	3040	3305	3430
(CKD)	(72)	(72)	(90)	(115)	(120)
Nissan	2665	2665	2690	2720	2900
(CKD)	(180)	(180)	(200)	(220)	(400)
Toyo Kogyo	885	910	960	1070	1250
(CKD)	(55)	(80)	(130)	(160)	(160)
Honda	770	880	1010	1110	1290
(CKD)			(40)	(140)	(320)
Mitsubishi	1000	1000	1000	1000	1000
Isuzu	320	340	400	520	600
Daihatsu	350	350	350	390	390
Fuji	280	300	320	320	320
Hino	65	66	6	66	66
Nissan diesel	30	35	35	48	50
Grand total	9147	9363	9871	10,529	11,276

Source: Analysis by the U.S. Department of Transportation based upon published reports and estimates, as cited in U.S., Department of Transportation, *The U.S. Automobile Industry,* 1980, p. 62.

Notes: Above figures include both cars and trucks. Heavy trucks have been excluded where possible. Midget cars are not included.

All figures are for *normal operation,* usually equivalent to operation by two eight-hour shifts, approximately 250 days per year. Use of overtime could raise actual production substantially above nominal capacity. Actual production has exceeded a twelve-million-unit annual rate in recent months.

CKD: Completely knocked down.

The addition of this capacity is significant for several reasons. First, it suggests that the Japanese industry has not begun a major shift toward the more multinational producers. In fact, the expansion of capacity in Japan has been used as an excuse for not adding plant capacity overseas.[61] For some observers, the addition of this capacity also signals the further penetration of the North American market. As one U.S. government official noted, "We might be justifiably puzzled as to why certain Japanese firms are gearing up new automotive manufacturing capacity in Japan, part of which no doubt would be used for the manufacturing of cars for export to the United States, while predicting that demand for Japanese cars in the United States will be reduced."[62]

Trade Policy. With the increasing prominence of Japanese auto exports, the Japanese government has sought to reduce the resulting trade frictions. One prong of this policy has been to reduce barriers to the Japanese market; thus, there are no automotive tariffs, and foreign vehicles are exempt from emissions standards. The government has also encouraged Japanese producers to invest in foreign markets and to source foreign components.[63]

A more direct response to trade pressures has been MITI's "monitoring" of Japanese exports to various nations. For example, MITI reportedly used so-called administrative guidance to oversee an informal voluntary restraint of Japanese exports to the United Kingdom. When this agreement broke down, apparently as a result of the intransigence of the Japanese firms, MITI responded by undertaking direct supervision. Reportedly, MITI has also exercised similar guidance over exports to France.[64]

The manner in which Japanese firms respond to MITI guidelines is at best ambiguous, because such guidelines are not legally binding, although the ministry could—under the appropriate circumstances—organize an export cartel that would be. Japanese auto makers have resisted MITI efforts to restrict exports, and have reportedly even refused to acknowledge the existence of Orderly Marketing Agreements (OMAs) in the United Kingdom and France. The relationship between MITI and the industry is perhaps best summarized by a MITI official when in February 1980 the ministry announced its intentions to promote "orderly exports" of autos to the United States: "We can't force them [the auto makers] to reduce their exports, but that's what we have been telling them."[65]

To understand the dynamics of this interaction between the Japanese government and auto producers requires some appreciation of the competitive impacts of trade restrictions. An Orderly Marketing Agreement (OMA), or a Voluntary Restraint Agreement (VRA), is an agreement negotiated between governments (OMA) or between industries with government backing (VRA), that restrains imports of specific goods from a specific industry.[66] An OMA has two advantages over the procedure for import relief outlined under GATT: it is faster, and can discriminate among the imports of different nations.[67]

Like any government regulation, an OMA creates winners and losers. The impact of the OMA will depend largely upon how market share among the importing firms is assigned. Typically, share assignments are based on historic market share of, say, the past three years. A rational strategy for a Japanese firm facing the prospect of an OMA in the future, therefore, is to push hard for additional market share, even if this hastens the political reaction that brings on the trade restrictions. The winners under an OMA are firms with high market shares, which position will subsequently generate monopoly rents. Late entrants and firms with low market shares lose out, hence the reaction of Toyota and other late entrants into the British market who refused to obey MITI voluntary guidance.[68]

MITI is also a winner, in an institutional sense. It is usually MITI's responsibility to coordinate the OMA and allocate market share, a role that enforces an institutional role as economic planner and mediator, as well as its power vis-a-vis the industry.[69]

Future Competitive Strategies. The sorts of competitive strategies that Japanese producers adopt in the future can only be understood in the context of broader social, market, and competitive realities facing the industry. Three key points will condition future responses of Japanese producers:

1. The social and economic contribution of the Japanese auto industry to Japan is too great to allow responsible policymakers and managers to permit the industry to shift offshore. The auto industry is the largest single industry in Japan, accounting for over 10 percent of all manufacturing. About 10 percent of the total national work force is directly or indirectly employed in the manufacture of automobiles. Other national development programs, such as the advancement of the computer industry, are tied to the auto industry.[70]

Labor policies also limit future responses. The Japanese system of lifetime employment and seniority imposes high fixed costs and an inflexible labor force on manufacturers. The concern over possible losses of domestic employment stemming from a more multinational manufacturing strategy reduces firms' flexibility in this issue, even if international political and economic trends dictate its necessity. The high and increasing fixed costs of such labor policies also make it difficult for manufacturers to handle cyclical markets; manufacturers have few alternatives but to keep boosting production.[71]

2. The growth opportunities for Japanese producers are increasingly limited. The domestic market may be nearing saturation. Simultaneously, political realities in current or potential export markets may restrict future opportunities for growth through exports. Successful competition in devel-

oping markets may depend more upon the ability to manage and integrate worldwide manufacturing systems, which include facilities in these new markets. Non-Japanese firms are much better positioned to take advantage of such opportunities. Finally, in European and U.S. markets, Japanese producers will face increasing competition from newly redesigned U.S. vehicles.[72]

3. Changes in exchange rates and structural attributes of the Japanese economy threaten to erode the Japanese cost advantage. An important element of superior Japanese competitiveness has been the translation of a low-cost position into superior quality and durability. Appreciation of the yen and the aging of the labor force threaten the basis of the Japanese competitive strength.

In response to these developing critical realities, the Japanese industry as a whole is likely to move in the two following directions:

1. *Increased sophistication of product:* There are several reasons to suggest that the Japanese industry will position itself for higher value added in product. In the Japanese domestic market, rising incomes and the increasing sophistication of replacement purchasers have resulted in an increasing demand for larger and more sophisticated vehicles. While for many years minicars dominated the domestic market, now 90 percent of sales are in the 1200–2000 cc classes. Increasingly, Japanese manufacturers are following a strategy of encouraging consumers to trade up within diversified product lines.[73]

A second impetus for increased product sophistication is the growing importance of technology as a competitive dimension, driven by demands for fuel economy and emissions reductions. The perceived locus of change may have shifted to the recognition that in the future the winners in world automotive markets will be those who have most successfully adopted technologies that meet market demands.[74] In particular, the use of sophisticated electronics in automobiles—the so-called smart-car—may become an important competitive dimension, one in which the Japanese currently have a significant competitive lead.[75] In this regard, the strong links Japanese government policy makes between the development of a domestic computer industry and the domestic automobile industry may presage future developments.[76]

2. *Increased dependence upon non-Japanese markets as outlets for expansion:* With the probable slowing of domestic demand, exports may be a locus of growth for the Japanese industry in the future.[77] Where these exports are directed, and the manner in which they appear, is less certain.

Recent evidence suggests that Europe may be the next area of Japanese expansion. The European industry is still fragmented, and only GM and Ford really represent pan-European producers who might most successfully compete with Japanese imports.[78] Japanese expansion into Europe may also reflect a more sophisticated response to the trend toward globalization. While exporting finished products, the more internationally sophisticated Japanese producers are also attempting to penetrate Europe through cooperative link ups with local manufacturers. Nissan has acquired a 36 percent capital share in the Spanish producer Motor Iberica, which it is expected to use as a base to produce and sell its vehicles in Europe under the Nissan trademark.[79] Nissan has negotiated with Peugeot-Citroen to supply the French firm with technical advice on meeting Japanese emissions standards. It is also negotiating with Alfa Romeo for Nissan to grant a license to allow the Italian state-run car maker to produce 1300–1600 cc engines at a plant in southern Italy. Honda, meanwhile, has a licensing agreement with BL, which grants distribution rights in the European Economic Community (EEC) to a joint-production vehicle.

The developing model for foreign expansion by both Nissan and Honda seems to encompass both limited foreign production (for example, U.S. assembly plants) and close cooperative links with foreign firms. In the future, these links could stress the trade-offs of advanced Japanese automotive technology in return for access to local markets. This arrangement may well provide a model for the rest of the Japanese industry in the future.[80]

While this discussion has examined likely developments in the Japanese industry within the context of developing trends, the impact of these uncertain future trends has illuminated some dimensions more clearly than others. Because of the paucity of evidence and the complexity of the issues, it has proved difficult to say anything definite about at least two important issues that will shape the sorts of strategic postures Japanese firms will adopt in the future.

First, it seems clear that over the long term the Japanese industry is overcrowded and will have to undergo additional restructuring. Already, despite increased production volumes, profitability in the Japanese industry has declined since the early 1970s.[81]

In the future, the increased competition between Japanese, European, and U.S. firms, and the growing role of technology as a competitive dimension will up the required levels of capital investment.[82] These developments and the increasingly intense competition entailed by slowing domestic growth may encourage industry consolidation, with consequences for the sorts of strategies pursued by the surviving Japanese producers.

The role of MITI in the industry's future is a second uncertainty. Some observers note that the Japanese auto industry may have escaped from the administrative power that created it. In the past, administrative guidance was successful because the industry was catching up, and there was a model to look at when reformulating policy; the concern now is that with Japanese competitive preeminence, this form of policy guidance is no longer useful.[83]

The failure by MITI to get significant Japanese investment in the United States suggests the weakness of MITI in influencing industry behavior. A question for the future is whether new diplopmatic or economic developments might shift this power balance again. The question is of particular relevance to future developments in the U.S. market, since diplomatic efforts to restrain Japanese imports may depend upon MITI intervention.

Conclusion

In attempting to relate developments in the world auto industry to the evolution of the domestic industry, it has proved difficult to develop any single view of the future. The complexity of the world industry makes possible a multiplicity of developments affecting the United States. Several points, however, emerge from this discussion:

1. An understanding of likely shifts in the strategies of foreign-based firms requires a sophisticated understanding of the complexities of multinational positioning. Japanese expansion into the United States and other export markets can only be understood in the context of broader competitive and economic developments affecting the Japanese industry. The industry's development has been characterized by high growth rates, which during the 1960s were driven by the expansion of the domestic market, and during the 1970s taken up increasingly by exports, a large percentage of which have been directed toward the U.S. market.

In the future, efforts by many countries to promote or maintain their automobile industries, and the great uncertainty regarding future levels of demand, make it difficult to predict the extent to which exports may be targeted toward the domestic makret. There are indications that by 1985—just within the U.S., Japanese, and European industries—substantial excess small-car capacity may exist if the most optimistic of demand forecasts do not obtain. A possible consequence of these trends might be efforts by foreign auto industries to direct surplus capacity toward exports to the U.S. market which, because of its size, will be the central market of the future. This possible future convergence of competition makes it difficult to develop reliable and accepted forecasts of import share and behavior in the domestic market.

2. Government policies and industry-government relations are an important aspect to the analysis. The role of the Japanese government in shaping the strategies of the individual firms is both subtle and complex. While the term *Japan, Inc.* has gained some notoriety in describing patterns of industry-government relationships, MITI has never monopolized the initiative in auto-industry development, nor has it always been successful in enforcing its wishes. Government initiatives in safety and emissions, as well as MITI's role as international representative, impose a multi-

plicity of diverse policy objectives upon the industry. Analysis of their cumulative effect requires a sensitivity to the dynamics of Japanese industry-government relationships.

These conclusions have important implications for the future role of Japanese imports into the U.S. market. Currently the United States is the final destination of almost 40 percent of all Japanese auto exports. It has been suggested that one reason for this heavy dependence upon the U.S. market is that Japanese producers may be unable to export its cars elsewhere because of trade restrictions.[84] While political considerations may suggest that further increases in Japanese exports to the United States are not wise, the U.S. remains the largest and the most open car market in the world. Limiting exports to the current level, combined with a possibly slowing rate of growth in Japanese domestic demand and no other obvious markets for expansion, might force a lower rate of growth onto the industry—in particular choking off the opportunities for expansion by some of the smaller firms.

The issue remains unclear, however. Future Japanese domestic growth may be high (for example, 6 percent over the next decade) or Japanese producers may succeed in further penetration of European and Third World markets from their Japanese production base. There are also diplomatic and political issues involved. While the Japanese government has repeatedly announced that it does not foresee any increase in export capacity aimed at the U.S. market[85], the competitive interests of individual Japanese firms are not necessarily identical to those of the Japanese government. The dynamics of government-industry decision making that would resolve such issues can only be briefly discussed here, but it is important to keep in mind that competition between Japanese producers may obstruct a politically astute export policy.[86]

Notes

1. Statement of William Abernathy, *Automotive News,* 12 May 1980.

2. U.S. Congress, House Committee on Ways and Means, Subcommittee on Trade, *Auto Situation 1980, Report prepared by the Staff of the Subcommittee on Trade,* 1980, p. 67.

3. Krish N. Bhaskar, *The Future of the World Motor Industry,* (New York: Nichols Publishing Co., 1980), p. 89.

4. U.S. Department of Transportation, Office of the Assistant Secretary for Policy and International Affairs, *The U.S. Automobile Industry, 1980: Report to the President from the Secretary of Transportation* (Washington, D.C.: January 1981), p. 58.

5. Ibid., p. 55.

6. U.S. Department of Transportation, Research and Special Programs Administration, "World New Car Demand Projections, 1980–1990" (Cambridge, Mass., 1981) pp 1–2. (Typewritten.)

7. Bhaskar, pp. 66–76, 364.

8. Ibid., pp. 374–439.

9. Ibid., p. 109.

10. Bhaskar, p. 348; Mark Fuller, "Government Intervention in the Auto Industry: Japan" (Boston: Harvard Business School, 1980) p. 15. (Typewritten.); Amelia Porges, *Car Wars: Automobile Regulation, Policy, and Strategy in Japan* (Cambridge, Mass.: Center for Policy Alternatives, Massachusetts Institute of Technology, [1980]), p. 12; Harbridge House, Inc., *Corporate Strategies of the Automotive Manufacturers, Vol. I: Strategic Histories* (Boston: Harbridge House, [1978]), p. I-176.

11. Fuller, p. 31.

12. U.S., *Auto Situation 1980,* p. 80.

13. Fuller, p. 31.

14. Ibid., p. 7.

15. Porges, p. 14.

16. Harbridge House, p. I-188.

17. Fuller, p. 3.

18. Harbridge House, p. I-208.

19. Fuller, p. 23.

20. Ibid., p. 22.

21. Harbridge House, p. I-219.

22. Modan Bijineso Risachi, *Toyota to Nissan: Raiboro Monagatari* (Yunion Shuppankai, 1975), pp. 79–87, cited by Porges, p. 52.

23. Harbridge House, p. I-278.

24. Ibid., p. I-294.

25. Tracey Dahlby, "A Headlong Drive for Exports in a Race Against the Clock," *Far Eastern Economic Review,* 15 February 1980, p. 41.

26. Ibid., p. 45.

27. Hiroyo Ueno and Muto Hiromichi, "The Automobile Industry of Japan," 3 *Japan Economic Studies* 1 (Fall 1974):24.

28. Dahlby, p. 45.

29. Ueno and Hiromichi, p. 24.

30. Bhaskar, p. 360.

31. Booz, Allen and Hamilton, Inc., *Outlook: Summer 1980* (New York: Booz, Allen and Hamilton [1980]), p. 33.

32. Ueno and Hiromichi, p. 28.

33. U.S. Department of Transportation, *The U.S. Automobile Industry, 1980.* p. 55.

34. Ibid., p. 58.

35. Bhaskar, p. 333.

36. U.S. Department of Transportation, *The U.S. Automobile Industry, 1980* p. 40; William J. Abernathy, James E. Harbour, and Jay M. Henn, *Productivity and Comparative Cost Advantage: Some Estimates for Major Automotive Producers,* Report to the Transportation Systems Center, Department of Transportation (Cambridge, Mass.: December 1980), passim.

37. Wiliam J. Abernathy, James E. Harbour, and Jay M. Henn, "The Competitive Status of the Domestic Automobile Industry: Productivity, Product Quality, and Labor Style" (Boston: Harvard Business School, 31 July 1980), p. 3.

38. U.S. Department of Transportation, *The U.S. Automobile Industry, 1980,* pp. 40–43.

39. Porges, p. 14; U.S. Congress, House Committee on Ways and Means, *Auto Situation 1980,* p. 43.

40. Harbridge House, p. I–210.

41. Abernathy, Harbour, and Henn, *Productivity and Comparative Cost Advantage;* U.S. Congress, House Committee on Ways and Means, *World Auto Trade: Current Trends and Structural Problems, Hearings before the Subcommittee on Trade,* 96th Congress, 7, 18 March 1980.

42. Abernathy, Harbour, and Henn, "The Competitive Status of the Domestic Automobile Industry," p. 13; U.S. Congress, *World Auto Trade,* p. 318.

43. U.S. Congress, House, *World Auto Trade,* p. 96.

44. Abernathy, Harbour, and Henn, *Productivity and Comparative Cost Advantage,* p. 55.

45. U.S. Congress, House, *Auto Situation 1980,* p. 57.

46. Ibid., p. 34.

47. William Duncan, *U.S.-Japan Automobile Diplomacy* (Cambridge, Mass.: Ballinger, 1974), p. 75; U.S. Congress, House, *Auto Situation 1980,* p. 35.

48. U.S. Congress, House, *Auto Situation 1980,* p. 36.

49. Harbridge House, p. I–227.

50. Bhaskar, p. 350.

51. Porges, p. 60.

52. Ibid.

53. Abernathy, Harbour, and Henn.

54. Harbridge House, p. I–219.

55. Abernathy, Harbour, and Henn, *Productivity and Comparative Cost Advantage,* p. 62; Bhaskar, p. 347.

56. Abernathy, Harbour, and Henn, *Productivity and Comparative Cost Advantage,* p. 13.

57. Abernathy, Harbour, and Henn, "The Competitive Status of the Domestic Automobile Industry," p. 13.

58. U.S. Department of Transportation, *The U.S. Automobile Industry 1980*, p. 53.

59. Abernathy, Harbour, and Henn, "The Competitive Status of the Domestic Automobile Industry," p. 22.

60. U.S. Department of Transportation, *The U.S. Automobile Industry 1980*, p. 61.

61. U.S. Congress, House, *Auto Situation 1980*, p. 46.

62. U.S. Congress, House, *World Auto Trade*, Statement of Ambassador Robert D. Hormats, Deputy U.S. Trade Representative, p. 189.

63. U.S. Congress, House, *Auto Situation 1980*, p. 37.

64. Fuller, "Government Intervention in the Auto Industry: Japan," p. 38.

65. Ibid.

66. Porges, p. 3 of notes to chapter 2.

67. Ibid.

68. Ibid., p. 16.

69. Ibid., p. 17; for a more complete and general discussion of these issues, see C. Fred Bergsten, "On the Non-Equivalence of Import Quotas and 'Voluntary' Export Restraints," in *Toward a New World Trade Policy: The Maidenhead Papers*, ed. C. Fred Bergsten (Lexington, Mass.: Lexington Books, D.C. Heath and Co., 1975), pp 239–271.

70. Booz, Allen and Hamilton, *Outlook: Summer 1980*, p. 32.

71. Dahlby, p. 44.

72. Harbridge House, p. 219.

73. Porges, pp. 59–66.

74. Booz, Allen and Hamilton, p. 22.

75. Dahlby, p. 41.

76. Porges, p. 66.

77. Ibid., p. 15.

78. Dahlby, p. 43.

79. Ibid.

80. Ibid., p. 40.

81. Bhaskar, p. 342; Harbridge House, p. I–270; Dahlby, p. 44.

82. Bhaskar, p. 357.

83. Porges, p. 15.

84. U.S. Congress, House, *World Auto Trade*, p. 158.

85. U.S. Department of Transportation, *The U.S. Automobile Industry, 1980*, p. 61.

86. Bhaskar, p. 354.

4

Methodology for Analyzing Future Structural Change

Critical to an understanding of the future evolution of the U.S. automobile industry is a recognition of the manner in which firm strategy, government policy, and environmental changes interact to influence structural change. As discussions in the past two chapters have shown, for both firm performance and the attainment of policy goals, the implications of these dynamic interactions may be quite subtle.

The choice of methodology is driven by the need to estimate the effects of these different strategic, policy, and external developments on the future performance and structure of the U.S. auto industry. To do so, a simulation model of the U.S. auto industry is developed. The model is designed to capture the critical underlying forces for structural change in the U.S. auto industry and relate them to the financial performance of industry participants. Future oil prices, economic conditions, public policy, and the strategies of foreign and domestic firms are all important inputs into the formulation.

The use of a simulation model to examine future structural change in the U.S. auto industry has several advantages. The dynamics of the choice of public policy and firm strategy may complicate the analysis of structural evolution. Each of the participants—government policymakers, domestic firms, importers, and potential entrants—has a wide range of possible actions that it can take. The objective functions of each of these groups are likely to be complex and perhaps poorly understood. A simulation model allows the decision structure of each participant to be exogenously supplied, and so a wide variety of different strategies and patterns of behavior can be examined. Furthermore, structural change in the automobile industry is characterized by a high degree of uncertainty about many underlying factors, such as oil prices. By using the computer to simulate the industry under alternative specifications, the model evaluates the different consequences for industry performance and the achievement of policy goals.

Structure of the Model

The model is formulated with sections separately representing each firm modeled, and the domestic market for automobiles. For each firm, investment, manufacturing cost, and profitability relationships are used to generate a set of financial statements for each of the years 1980 through 1995.

The model is designed to move forward through time, using last year's final results as this year's base values, and covering the period 1980–1995. Conditional on the choice of strategy and the environmental scenario that obtains, the supply and demand of autos are made equal through price adjustments. The choice of strategy and new levels of sales and prices are then translated into financial and market performance of the individual firms.

As depicted in figure 4–1, over time the model operates as follows:

The period is entered with a given strategic positioning and financial strength for each firm, plus policy and market structure as defined by the previous period.

Also conditional on the current state, a new policy and multinational context are revealed. This context is exogenously supplied to the model.

Vehicle prices and sales are determined, and, conditional on each firm's strategic position for the previous period, new financial and market positions for each of the firms are calculated.

Within each time period, the basic structure of the model consists of the following sections (figure 4–2):

Fuel economy: U.S. producers upgrade the fuel economy for each vehicle class through downsizing, material substitution, front-wheel drive, and increased use of efficiency-improving technologies.

Market: The model is concerned with the long-term trend in demand rather than trying to model short-term cyclicality. Demand for vehicles is a function of the price to consumers and the level of consumer spending on vehicle purchase and operation. Consumer price is the sum of the discounted vehicle operating costs and the original manufacturer selling price. Discounted vehicle operating costs are a function of vehicle fuel efficiency and the current gasoline price. The manner in which consumer price is determined is described in the market-module section.

Investment calculated for domestic producers: Capital investment calculated for domestic producers is the sum of new investment in fuel-economy improvement and *other,* nonfuel-economy-related investment to maintain the competitiveness of product lines.

Manufacturing costs: Manufacturing costs are based on historical experience, but change due to the incorporation of fuel-economy improvements, scale economies, and changes in productivity.

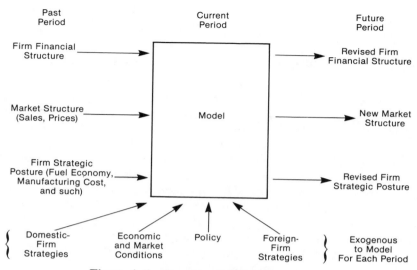

Figure 4-1. Structure of Model over Time

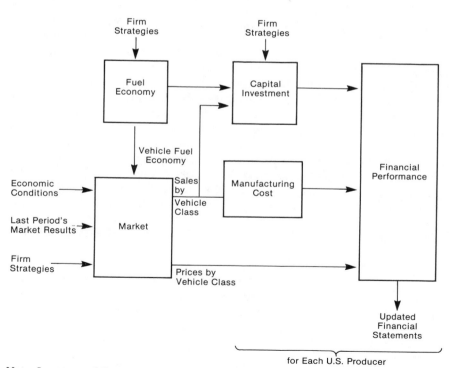

Note: Japanese and European producers are modeled in less detail.

Figure 4-2. Structure of Model within Each Time Period

Financial performance: Accounting relationships for depreciation, amortization, capital changes, taxes, and so forth are used to update financial statements for each U.S. producer for each period.

In the model formulation, five "firms" compete in the domestic passenger-car market: the U.S. passenger-car operations of General Motors, Ford, and Chrysler, plus two aggregated manufacturers representing as national groups the Japanese and the Europeans. Truck or nonautomotive operations are not considered. The Japanese and European manufacturers are aggregated to avoid having to explicitly model the intragroup dynamics in these sectors. Instead, alternative models of behavior for these national groups will be abstracted from earlier discussions as inputs into the model.

AMC and Volkswagen of America are included with the European group. VW of America is a wholly owned subsidiary of VW, and Renault has effective controlling interest in AMC. The dependence of both AMC and Volkswagen of America on European firms and strategies is the key reason for their grouping with the Europeans.

Another point regards the treatment of *captive imports,* vehicles produced abroad either by a foreign division of a U.S.-chartered multinational or through a joint-venture arrangement, and then sold through the marketing channels of the U.S. manufacturer. Since the concern is with the future evolution of U.S. manufacturing, captive imports are classed with the region of origin.

For the same reason, the three U.S. firms are modeled in greater detail than are the two foreign groups. Importer performance is considered only to the extent that it influences behavior in the domestic market.

Before describing in more detail the structure of the model, the philosophy of the model deserves comment. The model is normative. It projects results for the future based upon a series of relationships and submodels, each of which has attempted to capture a part of the future reality of the auto industry. The U.S. auto industry is in the process of change, and a modeling approach that was estimated using historical relationships would be inappropriate for studying a period when these relationships themselves are changing. The analysis that follows is designed to reflect that change.

A final point regards the model's limitations. Because a number of simplifying assumptions are made, the results generated are best suited for studying the relative impact on the manufacturers of various policy, strategic, and environmental developments. It is less likely that the absolute level of results generated will be entirely accurate because of the types of simplifying assumptions made.[1]

The remainder of this section will describe in greater detail the structure of the model employed.

Firm Strategy

This model does not attempt to optimize the strategies of domestic auto makers against competitive, policy, and exogenous developments. There are several reasons for this. It is difficult to adequately characterize the strategies of automobile manufacturers with a limited number of strategic decision variables. Automobile manufacturing involves several complex stages, at each of which there are commonalities among different product lines. An explicit modeling and optimization of manufacturer strategy would properly have to be cognizant of such intrafirm linkages. Furthermore, it is difficult to link some important strategic dimensions to identifiable investment streams or management decisions. Vehicle quality and productivity improvements are two such examples.

In the model, alternative firm strategies are defined exogenously for each domestic producer. These strategies vary along dimensions of technological implementation and vehicle fuel-economy improvement, manufacturing cost structure, quality, and pricing. The exogenous specification of these strategies avoids the problem of explicitly modeling the intrafirm details that underlie strategic choice. Instead, these considerations are implicit in the specifications of alternative strategies.

External Environment

The simulation model evaluates domestic-firm strategic choice conditional upon the firm environment which describes developments in government policy, the strategies of non-U.S.-chartered auto makers, and broad economic, social, and demographic changes. The very complexity of these exogenous developments is itself an issue for the modeler, since each environmental attribute can take on a wide range of values. The full range of possible government policies, non-U.S.-chartered-firm strategies, and exogenous environmental changes is not separately represented. Instead, the set of possible combinations is aggregated into a manageable number of reasonable alternatives. In this model this structuring of alternatives is done through the use of scenarios. A range of alternative scenarios can be used to approximate the full range of possible developments. This approach, while an approximation, is particularly useful in dealing with high levels of complexity created by a large number of possible outcomes. In particular, the use of scenarios to represent the environment separates the effects of environmental risk from other sources of risk.[2]

In the model, the environment remains fixed for one year. The unfolding of the environment over time is therefore described by a series of static environments succeeding one another, the entire sequence over the 1980-

1995 period defining a single scenario. Because of the complexity of possible future environmental developments, several alternative scenarios are used to capture the range of possible developments.

Each scenario is defined in terms of the following parameters:

1. *Government policy:* The representation of government policy may include the following:

    a. Trade policy: There are parameters for quotas or orderly marketing agreements and tariffs by vehicle class. Local-content requirements are handled through adjustments to non-U.S.-chartered-firm production costs.

    b. Tax and financial policy: These areas include the corporate income-tax rate, depreciation and amortization schedules, loan guarantees and subsidies, and tax credits.

    c. Fuel economy: Corporate average fuel-economy requirements are included.

2. *Foreign-firm strategies:* Non-U.S.-chartered-firm strategies are described in terms of the level of sales penetration, production costs, and the degree to which future sales are taken into account in the pricing policies.

3. *Exogenous environment:* The environment is defined in terms of four parameters: the inflation rate, the level of real personal-consumption expenditure, the fraction of real personal-consumption expenditure that goes toward user-operated vehicles, and automobile-fuel price per gallon.

Financial analysis must be done in current dollars because of inflation's effect upon depreciation, amortization, and the value of debt. While inflation has a neutral effect upon most income-statement items, the book values of assets and debt remain unaffected by changes in the price level. Since depreciation and amortization are calculated on the basis of book value, inflation implies a steadily eroding depreciation and amortization tax shield, which affects firm profitability. Conversely, inflation reduces the real value of a fixed dollar amount of debt.

Consumer spending on automobiles and automobile-fuel price are included as determinants of automobile demand. Historically the fraction of personal-consumption expenditures devoted to automobiles has remained fairly constant, between 11.3 and 13.4 percent.[3] In the future, social and demographic developments may shift this parameter. Automobile-fuel prices, of course, are highly uncertain, and, as the past decade has demonstrated, are an important determinant of automobile demand.

Structure of the Model within Each Time Period

Fuel-Economy Improvement

Improvements in fleet average fuel economy result both from mix shifts to more fuel-efficient vehicles and technological changes improving the fuel efficiency of individual models. This section of the model calculates the improvement in individual-vehicle fuel efficiency. Such changes are important both because of the consequences for capital and manufacturing costs and also because fuel-economy improvements alter vehicle operating-cost characteristics.

Analysis of future fuel-economy improvements requires three steps. First is the characterization of the *baseline* passenger-car fleet as a starting point for fuel-economy improvements. The calendar-year 1979 fleet is used. The second step is the identification and characterization of new technologies for fuel-economy improvement over the period of the model. With this information, the fuel-economy module calculates updated fuel-economy values for each U.S. manufacturer's vehicle class for each year, based upon the previous year's fuel-economy rating, the manufacturer's schedule for implementing the various fuel-economy-improvement measures, and the fuel-economy improvement resulting from the implementation of each technology.

For the calculation of vehicle fuel economy and for manufacturing cost analysis, each manufacturer's product line is segmented into six groups:

1. *Minicompacts:* This class includes the very smallest and most economical of vehicles in the U.S. market; these vehicles are not produced domestically.

2. *Subcompacts:* The smallest domestically produced cars, larger than minicompacts.

3. *Compact regulars:* This class includes cars like the Citation, Fairmont, and K-car.

4. *Compact specialty:* This group contains small cars that because of their degree of luxury or special purpose are differentiated in the market from the standard subcompact and compact vehicles. Sports cars and the so-called up-market compact cars are included here.

5. *Large regular cars:* Until recently these cars were the mainstay of the U.S. market, the standard-sized vehicle. Intermediates are also grouped here.

6. *Large specialty cars:* These cars are vehicles, such as the Cadillac, which provide both a high degree of luxury and large amounts of passenger and luggage space.

While the original classification of the 1979 baseline fleet (tables 4–1 and 4–2) into these segments was done primarily in terms of physical dimensions, future physical attributes of vehicles will likely change. This analysis

Table 4–1
1979 Manufacturer Baseline Fleet, Market Share by Class

Class	Weight	Fuel Economy	Market Share within Class
Minicompact			
Europeans	1768	32.0	.25
Japanese	1741	31.1	.75
Subcompact			
General Motors	2453	27.5	.21
Ford	2589	22.8	.21
Chrysler	2227	28.3	.08
Europeans	2074	29.0	.12
Japanese	2150	28.7	.39
Compact Regular			
General Motors	2773	22.8	.37
Ford	2760	20.7	.36
Chrysler	3281	19.9	.22
Europeans	3060	22.0	.04
Japanese	—	—	—
Compact Special			
General Motors	3451	17.2	.43
Ford	3210	18.8	.22
Chrysler	—	—	—
Europeans	2527	22.4	.13
Japanese	2668	23.5	.22
Large Regular			
General Motors	3400	19.4	.73
Ford	3831	17.1	.19
Chrysler	3641	16.7	.08
Europeans	—	—	—
Japanese	—	—	—
Large Specialty			
General Motors	4135	17.1	.61
Ford	4683	13.3	.24
Chrysler	3908	16.8	.05
Europeans	3362	18.8	.10
Japanese	—	—	—

Source: Author's calculations based on data supplied by Mellon Institute and found in *1980 Ward's Automotive Yearbook* (Detroit: Ward's Communications).

Table 4–2
1979 Sales by Manufacturer

Manufacturer	Mini-compact	Sub-compact	Compact Regular	Compact Specialty	Large Regular	Large Specialty
General Motors	—	643,774	554,392	392,584	3,184,250	412,281
Ford	—	627,285	438,154	197,084	707,756	131,271
Chrysler	—	271,118	284,868	—	382,219	40,000
Europeans	78,109	384,774	55,573	118,550	—	75,300
Japanese	235,161	1,260,905	—	199,481	—	—

Source: Author's calculations based upon figures found in *1980 Ward's Automotive Yearbook* (Detroit: Ward's Communications).

therefore treats these vehicle classes as expressions of marketing intent rather than strict definitions of vehicle size.

Technologies to improve fuel economy are divided into weight reduction and efficiency-improving technologies. The first set improves fuel economy by reducing the weight of the vehicles—all else constant, a lighter vehicle is more fuel-efficient. The second set of technologies primarily improves fuel economy through greater vehicle efficiency. The set of improvements used in this analysis is listed in table 4–3. This table is an aggregation of analyses performed separately by the National Highway Traffic Safety Administration (NHTSA)[4], and the Mellon Institute[5]; it represents on a somewhat aggregated level the measures available to manufacturers over the next fifteen years to improve fuel economy.[6]

Associated with each technology is a per-vehicle capital and variable cost, based upon NHTSA and Mellon Institute analysis. Cost figures are uniform across the industry. It would, of course, be more appropriate to show a range of capital and variable costs that reflected differing levels of vertical integration and unique technological or manufacturing expertise in each firm. However, to calculate such a range of costs would require proprietary data that was not available.

In some cases, it is assumed that the capital costs of a technology are borne by automotive suppliers, rather than by the manufacturers. Since the analysis is concerned with the financial performance of the auto makers, no consideration is made of the consequences for the supply industry.

The program of fuel-economy improvement for each U.S. manufacturer is defined in terms of the manufacturer's schedule for downsizing, material substitution, front-wheel-drive conversion, and the implementation of other technologies. The penetration of weight-reduction technologies (downsizing, material substitution, front-wheel drive) is manufacturer-vehicle-class specific, while efficiency-improving technologies are applied

Table 4-3
Manufacturer Measures to Improve Fuel Economy

Weight Reduction Technologies

Technology	Percent Weight Reduction	Capital Cost per Unit 1979 Dollars	Variable Cost per Unit 1979 Dollars
Downsizing (2 rounds)	13.5/6	2000/2000	250/250
Material Substitution (3 rounds)	1.5/3.5/8.0	0/0/200	15/60/120
Front-wheel-drive	8	200	30

Efficiency-Improving Technologies

Technology	Percent Fuel-Economy Improvement	Capital Cost per Unit	Variable Cost per Unit
Aerodynamic-drag reduction	4	0	18
Rolling-resistance reduction	2	12	12
Lubrication improvements	2	0	6
Accessories	5	90	15
Manual transmission	5	200	30
Automatic transmission	10	600	115
Engine-operating parameters	5	60	110
New gas engine	10	1080	100
Turbocharging	5	260	400
Diesel	25	1200	370
Brayton	20	2600	610
Stirling	30	3900	915

Sources: Author's calculations and interpolations based on Richard H. Shackson and H. James Leach, *Maintaining Automotive Mobility: Using Fuel Economy and Synthetic Fuels to Compete with OPEC Oil* (Arlington, Va.: Mellon Institute, [1980]); and U.S. Department of Transportation, NHTSA, *Rulemaking Support Paper Concerning the 1981-1984 Passenger Auto Fuel Economy Standards,* July 1977, p. 7-3.

Notes: Some of the technology options have been consolidated from the source material. Mellon Institute study presents values for *consumer cost/unit,* which the author has translated into variable cost per unit by assuming that the cost structure of these technologies is comparable to that of GM North American vehicle operations as a whole. A comparison shows the U.S. Department of Transportation and adjusted Mellon Institute figures to be close.

equally throughout the manufacturer's fleet. Weight-reduction technologies are part of a total vehicle-redesign program and hence are introduced only periodically, when that class of vehicles is redesigned. Efficiency-improving technologies depend more upon improved components, and their introduction usually does not require the total redesign of the vehicle.[7]

Calculating this period's fuel economy for each manufacturer vehicle class begins with last year's fuel economy and curb weight for that class. The model then updates these based on the manufacturer specific schedule for implementing fuel-economy-improvement measures.

The first step is to update vehicle weight and calculate fuel-economy gains only from weight reduction. If the manufacturer's strategy specifies that a round of downsizing, material substitution, or front-wheel-drive conversion will take place this period, vehicle weight is reduced by the corresponding percentage given in table 4-2. Implementation of more than one weight-reduction technology can take place during the same period; if so, weight reductions are cumulative. A new vehicle fuel economy reflecting only weight reductions is then calculated using a relationship based upon NHTSA studies.

Fuel-economy gains through weight reduction and improved efficiency are cumulative in the model. Fuel-economy improvement due to improved efficiency is calculated by multiplying vehicle fuel economy (which already reflects gains due to weight reduction) by the increased penetration of each technology in the manufacturer's fleet times the percentage fuel-economy improvement resulting from that technology. The result is the updated value of manufacturer-vehicle-class fuel economy for that period.

Detailed information about the future fuel-economy-improvement programs for European and Japanese manufacturers is not available. It is reasonable to assume, however, that their fuel economy for each vehicle class will remain at least on a par with that of domestic producers. Percentage improvements in European and Japanese fuel economy for each vehicle class are set equal to the equivalent General Motors change. Since no domestic firm manufactures a minicompact car, improvements in minicompact fuel economy are set proportional to subcompact fuel-economy improvements.

Market Clearing

Crucial to the effectiveness of this analysis is the accurate estimation of relationships between auto sales, price, fuel economy, and other determinants of demand. This section describes a simple comparative static model of auto market clearing that generates sales and price forecasts by vehicle class.[8] While simple, the market-clearing model is responsive to the sorts of behavioral and environmental shifts that this analysis will examine. A number of assumptions and design considerations underlie the structure of the market-clearing mechanism that this section will describe.

Description of the Market

In response to changes in the automobile market, the industry's historic price structure is changing. The price differential between small and large cars is disappearing.[9] With the trend towards smaller, lighter, and more fuel-efficient vehicles, size has ceased to be the critical discriminating dimension of market pricing, although a careful delineation of vehicle-size classes still is important in characterizing manufacturer product plans.

On the basis of these observations, the market is segmented into the following classes:

Small basic cars: These cars are small, fuel-efficient vehicles sold with few options. Until recently, they comprised nearly all imports and still constitute a majority in that group.

Small luxury cars: These cars comprise a broader and more diverse group. They are principally distinguished from small basic cars by their greater luxury and comfort.

Large basic cars: Once the mainstay of the U.S. market, these cars are large, relatively fuel-inefficient, six-passenger vehicles.

Large luxury cars: These cars comprise a small and relatively isolated section of the market for vehicles that provide both a high degree of luxury and a large amount of passenger space.

The relationship between these segments is complex in part because imports, which have significant penetration in the small segments, are perceived as distinct from domestically produced vehicles. Japanese cars in particular, which comprise over 80 percent of imports, are differentiated from domestic vehicles in perceived quality and the composition of their product mix. The analysis therefore treats Japanese cars as distinct from domestic vehicles. This separation of domestic and foreign vehicles into distinct classes has also been used in other auto-demand forecasting models.[10] Because European production is similar to that of domestic producers in mix and quality and also because European imports are only a small part of total imports, the analysis aggregates European imports with domestic production. Table 4–4 gives the 1979 breakdown of the market.

To use this market segmentation to forecast future sales, it is assumed that consumer perceptions and valuations of each class will remain unchanged. In fact, future vehicle performance and dimensions probably will differ from today's cars. However, if the perceived value to consumers of these vehicle attributes is not some absolute standard but relative to what else is offered, this assumption of unchanged consumer valuations is appropriate.[11]

Table 4-4
1979 Base Auto Market

Type	Japan	Europe	United States	Total
Small Basic	1.2	.3	1.6	3.1
Small Luxury	.5	.2	2.0	2.7
Large Basic	—	—	4.3	4.3
Large Luxury	—	.1	.5	.6
Total	1.7	.6	8.4	10.7

Source: Author's calculations.

Price and Market Share

Automobile price as a determinant of demand properly includes not only initial purchase price but also a measure of lifetime operating costs. The relevant comparison is not merely between the sales prices of different vehicles, but between the full costs of owning them.[12] To capture these effects, this formulation follows the pattern of other automobile-demand models that have defined price in terms of life-cycle costs.[13] Here market-clearing vehicle price is a function of manufacturer-specific selling price and the present value of future fuel costs of operation. Although fuel costs are only one part of the total vehicle operating costs, it is the component that will likely show the greatest volatility in the future.

The market-clearing price is calculated in the following manner. First, as the model enters a new period, new values for discounted vehicle operating costs are calculated to reflect changes in vehicle fuel economy and fuel cost. For Japanese vehicles, small-basic-car operating costs are calculated using Japanese subcompact-car fuel-economy ratings; small-luxury-car costs are calculated with compact-luxury fuel-economy ratings. For the aggregated market-clearing price for U.S. and European producers, corresponding General Motors fuel-economy ratings are used. Second, market-clearing price is adjusted to reflect competitive interactions. The manner in which price is calculated will be discussed shortly. Finally, revised values of manufacturer-specific selling prices are derived from the new set of market-clearing prices.

There are two complexities to calculating manufacturer-specific selling prices. First, market price is defined in terms of four vehicle categories, while, as discussed earlier, manufacturer product lines and prices are defined in greater detail with six. The conversion between market price and manufacturer selling price is handled by assuming fixed relationships between the two sets of prices. Second, the four U.S. and European firms have been aggregated, so that the market-clearing price for U.S.-European vehicles has to be broken down for each manufacturer.

The model solves this problem by working backwards. For each period, the market-clearing price is first updated to reflect competitive interactions and the new period environment. Then manufacturer-specific selling prices are calculated by subtracting from the market-clearing price the present-value cost of driving ten years at 10,000 miles yearly at current fuel prices and manufacturer-specific fuel economy. Thus, manufacturer selling prices vary according to fuel-economy levels. This approach accords with the intuition that, all else constant, more fuel-efficient vehicles should receive a market premium.

The definition of price to include both initial purchase and subsequent operating costs is designed to capture several effects that are important to understanding the dynamics of the market. Since smaller vehicles are generally more fuel-efficient than larger cars, the costs of owning and operating larger vehicles is more affected by fuel-price increases. Concomitantly, fuel-economy improvements reduce the combined operating and purchase cost differential between large and small cars, making larger vehicles relatively cheaper to operate. The net result of these two effects will depend upon the specifics of fuel-economy improvements and fuel prices.[14]

This pricing approach also makes explicit the critical distinction between extensive and intensive demand. Hypothetically, a manufacturer with a highly fuel-efficient vehicle could charge more for it than for an otherwise equivalent, less fuel-efficient vehicle and still keep the price to consumers constant. While the total vehicle cost—and hence extensive demand—will remain relatively unchanged, the share of the consumer dollar accruing to the manufacturer will have increased.

The market share of individual producers varies with the share of market taken by Japanese producers; otherwise the relative shares of General Motors, Ford, Chrysler, and the European producers among themselves within any market class are fixed (see table 4-2).[15]

Price Setting

In the model, the Japanese set price for their vehicles while the U.S. and European manufacturers respond according to their supply elasticities. The Japanese are assumed to act jointly to maximize profit subject to a sales target. This formulation reflects the developing realities of the automobile market, in particular the disappearance of the uniquely U.S. class of large car and the substantial Japanese competitive advantage in the evolving new market classes.

The assumption of Japanese profit maximization subject to a sales target does not, however, imply that Japanese producers act in a coordinated fashion as a monopolist. The Japanese sales target can be either a trade restraint or a short-run planning goal representing more complex underlying behavior.

Demand Elasticities

A detailed review of econometric estimates of demand elasticities reveals a lack of consistency—and none that followed the market separation used here.[16] More important, the significant structural change in the U.S. market over the last decade means that historical estimates of elasticities do not reflect the new reality of the auto market. Instead of using past estimates, the model uses a synthesized set of reasonable and internally consistent short-run demand elasticities for market clearing.[17]

In general, the estimates of elasticities produced by various studies are difficult to compare or evaluate because they are based on quite different data sets and variable definitions. The range of uncertainty associated with these estimates of elasticities is quite large. However, there are some generalizations that can be made:

Studies have generally estimated the price elasticities of demand for new cars as a whole to be in the neighborhood of -1.[18]

The own-price elasticity of demand for small cars taken as a whole (minicompacts, subcompacts, and compacts) is roughly -1.[19]

The cross-price elasticity of demand between imported and domestic vehicles is between -1.5 and 2.0.[20]

The cross elasticity of demand for large cars with respect to small-car prices is very low. One estimate is .02.[21]

On the basis of these relationships, a set of internally consistent elasticity estimates was developed; that is, all of the price and fuel-economy effects are of reasonable magnitude and in the proper direction.[22] It is assumed that the own-price elasticities are between 2.5 and 3.5 percent for each segment, with the basic cars showing a higher price responsiveness. The price elasticity of U.S. basic cars is set at -3.5 percent, based on an industry view that a 15 percent increase in the price of one product line would evoke a 50 percent decline in quantities sold.[23] The price elasticities for Japanese cars were set equal to those for the corresponding U.S. cars.

The cross-price elasticities were chosen to satisfy certain rules of con-

Table 4–5
Demand Elasticities

	Japanese Small Basic Cars	Japanese Small Luxury Cars	U.S.- European Small Basic Cars	U.S.- European Small Luxury Cars	U.S.- European Large Basic Cars	U.S.- European Large Luxury Cars
Japanese small basic cars	−3.5	0.10	2.00	0.50	2.90	0.03
Japanese small luxury cars	0.25	−2.50	0.40	3.40	2.50	0.30
U.S.-European small basic cars	0.80	0.10	−3.50	0.50	2.90	0.03
U.S.-European small luxury cars	0.25	0.20	0.40	−2.50	2.50	0.30
U.S.-European large basic cars	0.10	0.02	0.10	0.10	−4.00	0.10
U.S.-European large luxury cars	0.10	0.04	0.20	0.20	1.70	−2.50

Source: Author's calculations based upon existing demand-elasticity estimates (see text).

sumer behavior. With an increase in the price of one vehicle class, it is assumed that most consumers, dissuaded by the higher price of their preferred vehicle class, will seek out a vehicle in the most similar competing category. A few will go to other vehicle classes. For example, 50 percent of the expenditure deterred by rising prices from the Japanese basic-car segment is assumed to go to U.S. basic cars; 30 percent of that expenditure is assigned to luxury small cars in a manner that maintains the relative U.S.-European and Japanese market shares that prevailed in that category in 1980; 15 percent is assigned to large basic cars; and 5 percent to large luxury cars. Similar principles apply to other auto segments.

Income Elasticities

The model does not attempt to represent the short-term cyclicality of the market. Therefore, what is of interest is the long-run elasticity of demand with respect to income.

This figure was estimated over the 1959–1972 period using a constant elasticity specification:

$$\ln(SALES) = A + A \ln(Y)$$

where *SALES* were total U.S. passenger-car sales, and *Y* was real personal-consumptions expenditures in 1957–1959 dollars. The results are given in equation 4.1. Price is not included because of its constancy in real terms over this period.[24]

$$\ln(SALES) = 10.194 + .956\ln(Y) \qquad\qquad (4.1)$$

Degrees of freedom	12	Beta:	0.90474
Multiple *R*	0.90474	Standard error of *B*:	0.1299
R square	0.81855	*F*:	54.132
Standard error	0.08333		

Income elasticities serve as a growth parameter for the market. Because the level of sales for 1979 and 1980 is very low in comparison with the historic trend, a higher value of income elasticity was chosen for the first few model periods. This decision was made so that the model results would, with the appropriate economic scenarios, replicate the range of available market-trend forecasts, most of which show a sharp increase in automotive sales over the next several years (see figure 5–1, chapter 5). Failing to do so would mean that the model results would have been based on a range of market conditions for the most part very different from those used in other analysis; and quite possibly less representative of the range of uncertainty in the future U.S. automotive market. This result would have lessened the value of this research.

Another alternative would have been to choose a higher level of base sales consistent with some longer-term trend. This alternative would have the effect of overstating 1980 sales, at least, and so distorting current and future firm financial performance, which in reality of course has been adversely affected by the low level of sales.

Instead, for the years 1980–1984, a higher income elasticity of 2.5 was used; afterwards, a value of 0.7 was substituted. A lower value of income elasticity than historical experience indicates is consistent with the possible increasing saturation of the domestic market. Sensitivity analysis indicates that model results are insensitive to the exact choice of income elasticities. Income elasticities are assumed equal for each size class.

Supply Elasticities

To determine what vehicles U.S. and European producers will supply in response to Japanese pricing and marketing moves requires a sophisticated understanding of supplier behavior. Because this question is such a diffi-

Table 4-6
Supply Elasticities

Supply Elasticity	Percent in Sales	Percent in Price
0.1	practically none	practically none
1.0	equal percentage changes	
Infinite	none	all

cult empirical and behavioral one, the analysis simulates a range of price-quantity behavioral responses by U.S. firms. This behavior is defined in the model by the specification of the domestic supply elasticity.

Because of the uncertainty regarding supply response, three alternative specifications of U.S.-European supply elasticity are considered, as specified in table 4-6. These are intended to cover the range of possible responses by the domestic industry.

Consumer Repurchase

Automobiles are characterized by generally high levels of consumer loyalty toward the manufacturer. The purchase of a manufacturer's vehicle significantly increases the probability that a vehicle of the same manufacturer will be purchased in the future. Table 4-7 presents one estimate of repurchase rates of different types of cars.

These future market aspects of current sales introduce a dynamic aspect to market clearing. An automobile sale today carries with it an expected stream of future purchases. If a profit-maximizing producer recognizes this fact, he may choose not to maximize profits based on current sales alone but maximize some measure of life-cycle profits, which include the expected future stream of sales associated with today's sales. Inclusion of these future-market sales may alter pricing strategies.

Analysis of these issues of future-market capture are also important because they highlight the implications of shifting levels of consumer loyalty. While the evidence as to levels of loyalty is unclear, the substantial perceived advantage of Japanese vehicles may mean that future consumer loyalty for Japanese vehicles may be higher than for domestic vehicles.[25] Changes in repurchase rates may have significant effects on the sorts of competitive strategies that are appropriate for each producer. This point will be developed in the chapter on foreign-firm strategies.

The market-clearing mechanism handles these issues of future-market capture by altering the level of profit a manufacturer earns from the current

Table 4-7
U.S. Consumer Repurchase Loyalty, 1979
(percent repurchase same firm)

Type	Percentage
Japanese Cars	26.6
Captive Imports	42.0
U.S. Subcompacts	53.4
U.S. Standards	73.2

Source: Rogers National Research, New Car Buyers Survey, 1979, as cited in U.S. Department of Transportation, *The U.S. Automobile Industry, 1980*, p. 48.

sale of a vehicle to reflect the present value of the stream of profits accruing from future sales "tied" to the current sale. Obviously the present value of this stream of future profits is greater if there is a high repurchase rate. In calculating the present value of the stream of future profit tied to the sale of a vehicle currently, a repurchase cycle of four years and a discount rate of 10 percent are assumed. Chapter 6 analyzes the competitive implications of different rates of consumer repurchase.

Firm Financial Performance

The final section of the model calculates firm financial performance, taking as inputs sales, price, and strategies, and determining manufacturing costs, investment streams, and financial results. The model then generates a complete set of financial statements for each U.S. firm.

Manufacturing Costs

The determination of the variable production costs of each U.S. manufacturer begins with estimates of the 1979 costs of production based on discussions with industry experts (table 4-8). These costs are adjusted to reflect vehicle redesign for fuel economy, productivity improvements, and scale economies. Variable production costs are calculated in constant dollars, with the effects of inflation factored into the final result. Production costs for the Japanese are set through parameters and are one way of representing alternative future states.

It is readily acknowledged that the figures in table 4-8 are only estimates. Sensitivity analysis performed with the model, however, indicated that model results are insensitive to substantial variations in these figures.

Table 4–8
Total Variable Production Costs
(in 1979 Dollars)

Type	General Motors	Ford	Chrysler
Subcompact	3900	4100	4300
Compact	4500	4700	4900
Compact Specialty	4600	4800	5000
Intermediate Standard	4600–4700	4800–4900	5000–5100
Intermediate Specialty	5400	5600	5800
Standard	5600–5700	5800–5900	6000–6100
Luxury Standard	6500–7300	6700–7500	6900–7700

Source: Author's calculations based on discussions with industry experts.
Notes: Includes variable labor (allocated at 100% capacity utilization) and variable material. Excludes plant staff and corporate depreciation allocation (done per direct labor hours). Sensitivity analysis performed showed that model results are insensitive to the choice of these figures.

Changes in U.S. variable production costs resulting from fuel-economy improvements are a function of the base 1979 variable cost, and the variable costs of downsizing, material substitution, front-wheel drive, and other fuel-economy-improving technologies (table 4–3). If the schedule of manufacturer fuel-economy improvement indicates that some of these measures have been incorporated into the current period's vehicle, the variable cost attributable to those measures is added to the total variable cost of the vehicle. This approach assumes that variable costs are additive and equal across all firms and all vehicle classes.

This new variable manufacturing cost estimate is in turn altered to reflect capital and labor productivity advances and scale economies of production. Labor and capital productivity advances are handled in the following fashion. First, vehicle variable manufacturing cost is divided into a capital cost and labor cost. This division of variable cost into capital and labor components is assumed to be in the same proportion as the estimated shares of these factors of production in 1979, as given in the appendix. These capital and labor components are then reduced if there have been corresponding productivity advances. It is assumed that productivity advances are uniform across all vehicle classes.

Scale-economy effects are based on an approximation to table 2–7, chapter 2. Scale economies are calculated on the basis of platforms rather than individual vehicle types; thus, specialty and regular classes, which share common platforms and are differentiated basically by their level of luxury, are aggregated. Production is treated as equal to sales, and unit variable costs are increased if production falls below minimum efficient scale.

Capital Investment

For each U.S.manufacturer, the model calculates capital investment for property, plant and equipment, and tooling. Other items sometimes included in capital-spending figures, such as spending for maintenance, repair and replacement, or research and development, are expensed and so are discussed later. Capital spending for non-U.S. manufacturers is not calculated.

Capital investment for U.S. manufacturers is treated as the sum of capital spending on future fuel-economy improvements, and nonfuel-economy-related capital spending. Nonfuel-economy-related capital investment is assumed constant in real terms; this approach follows an assumption by NHTSA in its analysis.[26]

Fuel-economy-related capital investment for each year is actually a function of the capital investment required by the manufacturer's fuel-economy program for the forthcoming two model periods. It is an industry practice to allocate costs incurred as a result of developments in one year over the preceding two years.[27] To explain how the model calculates fuel-economy-related capital investment for each year, it is first necessary to describe how the capital investment related to a particular year's product program is determined and then how this capital investment is allocated to different years.

The total capital investment, in real terms, incurred as a result of fuel-economy improvements in a given year is a function of three factors: the per-vehicle capital costs of each of the fuel-economy-improvement measures (see table 4–3), the manufacturer's schedule of fuel-economy improvements, and the preexisting manufacturer's production capacity for each of the manufacturer's fuel-economy-improvement measures. For each fuel-economy-improvement measure, if the current model period is the first period in which it has been implemented (for example, 1983 is GM's first year for a second round of downsizing for large basic cars), then fuel-economy capital spending is increased by the product of the total number of the manufacturer's vehicles involved times the per-unit capital cost of the measure. If the current model period is not the first year for that measure (for example, it is now 1984) but sales are greater than capacity (defined by the highest previous level of sales) then those sales in excess of old capacity will also incur a capital charge. If the current model period is not the first year for that measure, and sales are less than capacity, there is no addition to capital spending. The total capital investment for each U.S. producer incurred as a result of fuel-economy improvements in a given year is then the sum of the capital investment required over each fuel-economy measure and vehicle class.

This total capital investment incurred as a result of each period's fuel-economy improvement is then allocated to the previous two years' capital-investment spending: 60 percent in the preceding year and 40 percent in the year before that.[28] These figures are not distorted by inflation, since the calculation of capital investment is done in real terms, with inflation introduced later.

U.S.-firm capital-investment spending in real terms for each model period is therefore the sum of:

Sixty percent of total capacity spending related to next period's fuel improvement.

Forty percent of total fuel-economy-related capital spending for two periods ahead.

Annual nonfuel-economy-related capital spending (constant in real terms).

This approach depends upon several assumptions. First, it assumes that capital spending can be allocated on a per-vehicle basis. While in reality capacity comes in lumps, this approach treats capacity as being highly divisible. Further, it assumes that capital charges per unit are equal across all producers and all vehicle classes. It was not possible to obtain manufacturer-specific estimates of capital costs. Finally, the approach implicitly assumes that capacity is permanent—in other words, once it is there it will never be taken away.

Financial Statements

The model generates detailed financial statements for each domestic producer for each model period. Information generated elsewhere in the model, together with estimated relationships and accounting identities, is used to calculate income, funds flow, balance sheet, and other summary statements.

It is important to keep in mind that the model is concerned only with the financial structure of the U.S. passenger-car operations of GM, Ford, and Chrysler and not with their total operations or even with their complete North American operations. Publicly available financial information does not break out data solely on the segment modeled here, so various public sources were used to develop base financial data for each firm.

Table 4-9
Financial Data: U.S. Passenger-Car Operations

Data	General Motors	Ford	Chrysler
Income-tax rate	.4490	.4490	.4490
Depreciation			
Machinery and equipment	.1161	.1123	.0810
Land and buildings	.0400	.0300	.0300
Amortization (tooling)	.6345	.2686	.2375
Interest rate	.0500	.0530	.1010
Nonfuel-economy investment			
Machinery and equipment	766.3000	481.8000	137.5000
Land and buildings	578.0000	125.8000	99.6000
Tooling	1475.5000	612.5000	304.3000
Retirement	736.9000	468.7000	264.2000

Source: Author's calculations based on Securities and Exchange Commission filings and analysts' reports.

Note: All figures in 1979 dollars (millions) except percentages.

Table 4-10
Balance Sheet: U.S. Passenger-Car Operations, 31 December 1979
(in millions of 1979 dollars)

Item	General Motors	Ford	Chrysler
Machinery and equipment	3235	1005	524
Land and buildings	3794	2128	642
Tooling	629	1062	509
Other assets	7322	2151	1246
Total	14980	6346	2921
Debt	1805	1580	1599
Equity	1237	348	1005
Retained earnings	11938	4418	317
Total	14980	6346	2921

Source: Author's estimates based on Securities and Exchange Commission filings and analysts' reports.

Assets are divided into four categories: land and buildings, machinery and equipment, tooling, and other assets. *Other assets* are essentially a proxy for working capital. Working-capital requirements increase with inflation but are otherwise constant. The book value of real assets is revised by new capital investment and by depreciation and amortization.

Capital investment is allocated among the categories of assets according to prespecified shares that reflect historical experience. Of total capital investment spending, based upon historic allocation of funds, 5 percent is allocated toward land and building, 35 percent is allocated toward machinery and equipment, and 60 percent is allocated toward tooling. The effects of inflation are also introduced here, because capital investment was calculated in real terms.

Each category of asset is depreciated or amortized on a straight-line basis. Rates for depreciation of land and buildings, depreciation of machinery and equipment, and amortization of tools were selected to reflect historical experience during the 1975–1979 period.

Liabilities are divided into equity capital, retained earnings, and debt. Firms are assumed to follow strict short-term-debt financing policies; in other words, equity capital remains constant. Short-term debt can be negative, which is equivalent to assuming that excess capital is invested elsewhere (either in securities or other parts of the firm). The cost of debt (or equivalently its return if debt is negative) is a model parameter, which is adjusted to reflect an inflation premium. The cost of debt and the return of excess funds have the same value.

The assumption of pure debt financing is in response to several considerations. Chrysler's poor financial position suggests that it would have difficulty raising equity capital; these same considerations may also apply to Ford. Furthermore, each firm's capital structure is a function of parts of the firm not modeled here. These factors suggest that debt financing may be a good representation of reality.

Dividends to equity owners are excluded from the analysis. The role of dividends is at best unclear in both practical and theoretical discussions. Financial theory, under strict assumptions, shows that dividend policy is irrelevant to firm valuation.[29] Furthermore, it is inappropriate to model the discretionary dividend decision on the basis of only one part of a larger multinational enterprise. Since ultimately the concern is with the long-term profitability of domestic operations, a reasonable approach is first to analyze performance without dividends, and later to introduce dividend considerations if it appears they would affect the conclusions of the analysis.

A simple income statement is presented in table 4–11. Sales revenue is calculated as the product of the manufacturer selling price of the car less dealer discount (15 percent uniform) times number of cars sold. The uniform dealer discount accords with recent industry developments. Selling and administration, research and development, and maintenance, repair, and replacement are treated as semivariable, with both a fixed and variable component. Nonincome taxes are a function of sales revenue. Retirement costs are assumed constant in real terms for each manufacturer.

Table 4-11
General Motors: Income Statement for Year 1981

Item		In Millions of Current Dollars
Sales revenue		38793.8
Variable costs		23062.8
Fixed costs		
Selling and administration	2051.0	
Research and development	1362.1	
Maintenance, repair, and replacement	2399.5	
Retirement	928.4	
Nonincome tax	1438.7	
Depreciation	1013.5	
Amortization	3584.5	
Interest	0.0	
		12777.7
Pretax income		2953.3
Income tax		1326.1
After-tax income		1627.3

Source: Output of model described in chapter 4.

Income tax is calculated as a percentage of net profit before tax. The tax rate is constant. If net income before taxes is negative, a tax credit is provided. A justification for treating losses as tax credits is that U.S. passenger-car operations of General Motors, Chrysler, and Ford are only one part of a much larger operation. Net losses generated in U.S. operations here can be used to offset profits earned elsewhere, which is equivalent to a negative income tax. In the case of Chrysler, which has divested many of its other operations, this treatment may tend to understate the magnitude of losses. It will also tend to understate losses if they are both extraordinarily large and persistent.

The generation of balance sheet, cash flow, and other summary statements is a straightforward application of accounting and other identities.

Making Some Assumptions Explicit

In describing the structure of the model, some assumptions that deserve further explanation have been rather lightly touched on.

One critical assumption of the model is that the Japanese producers set price in the U.S. market. While this approach obviously ignores the complexities and judgmental inputs that go into price determination, there is no attempt in this analysis to represent market behavior in a detailed fashion that would capture short-term fluctuation, so-called hot models, or specialty niches. On a more aggregate level, the assumption of Japanese price leadership reflects the developing realities of the U.S. market. As domestic and foreign vehicles become increasingly similar in size and function, the basis for product differentiation and pricing independence between imports and the greater part of the U.S. product line disappears. The substantial Japanese cost and perceived quality advantage suggest that Japanese producers enjoy a substantial competitive advantage in the U.S. market, one that will not disappear with the retooling of the domestic industry. It has been suggested, for instance, that without significant trade restrictions, and barring major disruptions such as a currency devaluation, there appear to be very few barriers to a virtually complete displacement of the U.S. auto industry by foreign production.[30] These considerations argue for Japanese price leadership in the domestic market.

The exact manner in which Japanese producers establish price in the U.S. market is a complex behavioral and empirical issue. Events not only in the United States but in Japan and elsewhere will presumably affect the sorts of pricing behavior observed. Furthermore, behavioral patterns of price setting and market clearing may change in the future in response to evolving corporate strategies and other developments.

It is therefore necessary to evaluate several alternative Japanese behavioral models. In doing so, an important issue considered is the linkage between developments elsewhere, as, for example, changes in domestic policy and shifts in the pattern of Japanese market behavior. The analysis speculates on the sorts of conditions that will likely result in various behavioral patterns and then uses the model to delineate their effects.

The blurring of the nationality of vehicles is a problem for any model of the automobile industry. The operations of Volkswagen of America may be a harbinger in this regard: with local assembly and local content, but with a far lower degree of integration than is found in the operations of GM, Ford, or Chrysler, the issue facing the modeler is whether such production should be classed with domestic production or as an import. The decision to treat such local assembly as imports, while admittedly judgmental, is based on the low level of local content and the control of such production by a foreign-based firm that may also be a substantial importer.

Quality as a competitive dimension presents another difficulty. Imported vehicles in general and Japanese vehicles in particular are considered by many consumers to be superior in quality to North American vehicles.[31] Including quality as a competitive dimension in the formulation is difficult because of the lack of any appropriate definition of quality, although the issue may be indirectly addressed through the rate of consumer repurchase. The issue is further complicated by the distinction between *real quality* and *perceived quality* in the minds of consumers.

Another point regards the dynamics of the issues being examined. Decision makers do not face a single decision point but are continually revising their actions over the entire period of the model in the face of a continuous stream of information about industry developments. The structure of strategic and policy decision making is too complex and too little understood to be modeled as such. Furthermore, the full structure of firm and government decision making is not necessary to examine the issues of interest here. The model analysis merely need incorporate the sorts of responses that decision makers might choose. Incorporating these responses is handled through conditional predictions of industry development based on a priori specifications of the actions of strategy and policymakers. To examine the range of developments, alternative specifications are examined.

Model Validation

The problem of validation is perhaps the most elusive of the unresolved methodological problems associated with computer simulation.[32] In spite of these difficulties, model validation is central to this analysis. Without some validation, the modeling effort is simply a hypothetical exercise. Validation allows the conclusions of the model to be linked to actual developments in the auto industry.

The validity of a simulation effort is not an either or preposition but is more effectively thought of as being a matter of degree.[33] Accordingly, model validation involves several steps.[34]

This chapter has already outlined the theoretical structure of the model and attempted to demonstrate that that structure is a reasonable and adequate representation of the real system. The discussion has also tried to demonstrate the relevance of the model parameters to the future, either because other factors suggest that the parameters will remain at historic values in the future, or the model results are insensitive to the parameter value, or through reliance upon outside expert sources.

A second test of validity is a demonstration of the *face validity* of the model results. Face validity refers to the reasonableness of the results and the agreement of specific model results with outside expert predictions when the same set of inputs is used. This test is not strictly a test of validity, but a way of developing further confidence in the model. Issues of face validity will be discussed with the results.

A third test is a demonstration of the face validity of the model components. If each component of the model can be shown to capture the underlying reality, then a greater degree of confidence can be had in the insights that the model results provide—especially if on the surface these results contradict generally accepted thinking.

A test of the validity of model components is their ability to replicate the history of the real system. The ability of the model to replicate a single historical realization is not in itself a strong test and is further limited when the relevant historical record is itself limited. It is nonetheless another weak indication of model validation.

Since the automobile industry has been undergoing structural change, the length of the historical record the model is designed to replicate varies with the parameter. Several different tests of historical replication are therefore performed.

The first set of results is designed to test the validity of the model regarding the internal financial structure of the domestic firms—in other words, how well the model actually represents each firm's cost and financial structure. To test this measure of model validity, the model was run over the 1970–1980 period, with all the initial parameters recalculated to reflect 1969 values. Instead of having the model generate a sales and price stream, however, actual U.S. market sales by firm and vehicle class were input. Since a detailed price record by vehicle class is not available, it was assumed that vehicle prices in real terms remained constant over this period. The results generated by the model for capital expenditures and before tax profit were compared with the estimates of the actual values for these operations. These results are presented in figures 4–3 and 4–4.

A second test is of the model's ability to reproduce changes in vehicle-fleet fuel economy and weight. To test, the model was run over the 1976–1980 period, using the schedule of manufacturer-specific measures to improve vehicle fuel economy and with actual vehicle scale broken down by class as an input. Before 1976 the model is no longer valid, because substantial fuel-economy shifts resulted from the switch to catalytic converters, and earlier from other antipollution measures and the introduction of domestic subcompacts. Figure 4–5 compares model and actual results for fleet fuel economy. Fleet average-weight figures are also available and compared for General Motors (figure 4–6).

A third test is the model's ability to replicate the automobile market. Since the model is constructed to reflect the developing realities of the U.S. auto market, especially the substantial role of Japanese imports, its relevance to past market developments is limited only to recent years. Accordingly, the model was used to replicate the U.S. auto market over the period 1975–1980. A careful study was made to estimate the starting parameters. Income and demand elasticities were the same as for when the model was used to study the post-1980 period, but initial prices and sales levels were changed, and environmental parameters (income changes, gasoline prices, and such) correspond to historical developments. The driving parameter was the requirement that Japanese import share had to equal its actual value. The results of this exercise are given in figures 4–7 and 4–8.

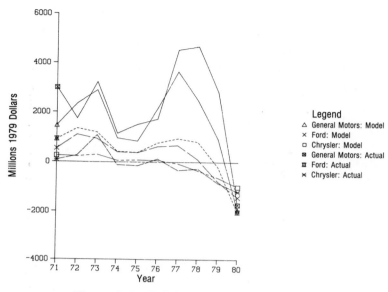

Figure 4-3. Validation: Operating Income

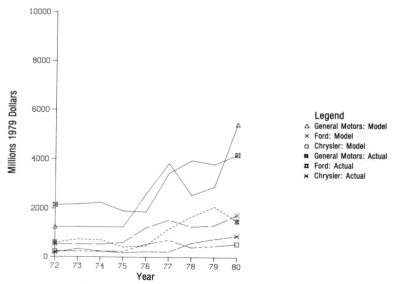

Figure 4-4. Validation: Capital Investment

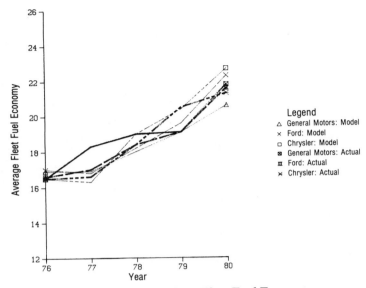

Figure 4–5. Validation: Fleet Fuel Economy

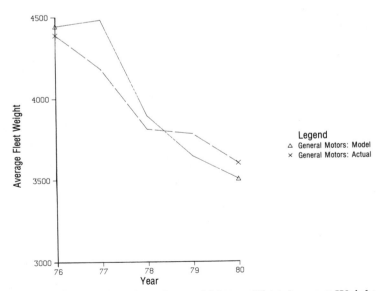

Figure 4–6. Validation: General Motors Fleet Average Weight

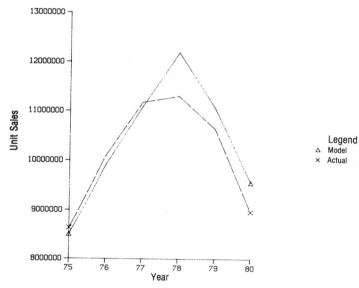

Figure 4-7. Validation: Market Sales

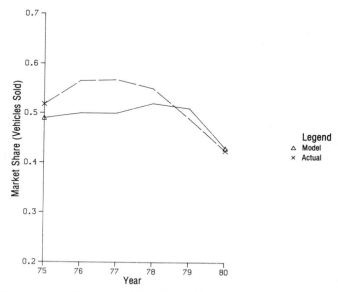

Figure 4-8. Validation: Percent Share Large Basic Cars

Conclusion

The purpose of this model is to link a wide range of possible future developments in markets, strategy, policy, and other dimensions to the performance and structure of the auto industry. The model addresses these issues by relating the forces for structural change to their impact on the financial structure of the three major U.S. producers, and, to a lesser extent, on the Japanese.

To do so, the model first calculates market sales and prices in a manner that takes into account both macroeconomic factors and the strategies of individual firms. It then updates the implications of market developments, the choice of strategy, and government policy on the financial performance of individual firms. The model is designed to handle a variety of different issues in each of these dimensions that may influence the future evolution of the industry.

Notes

1. Raymond S. Hartman, K. Bozdogan, and R.M. Nadkarni, "The Economic Impacts of Environmental Regulations on the U.S. Copper Industry," *The Bell Journal of Economics,* Autumn 1979, p. 613.

2. For a discussion of the use of scenarios see Herman Kahn and Anthony J. Wiener, *The Year 2000: A Framework for Speculation on the Next Thirty-three Years* (New York: Macmillan, 1967), pp. 6, 263; and George A. Steiner, *Strategic Planning: What Every Manager Must Know* (New York: Free Press, 1979), p. 237.

3. U.S. Department of Transportation, Transportation Systems Center, "Role of the Motor Vehicle in the U.S. Economy: Quarterly Economic Indicators," 30 September 1980, as cited in U.S. Department of Transportation, Office of the Assistant Secretary for Policy and International Affairs, *The U.S. Automobile Industry, 1980: Report to the President from the Secretary of Transportation* (Washington, D.C.: January 1981), p. 4.

4. U.S. Department of Transportation, National Highway Traffic Safety Administration, "Rulemaking Support Paper Concerning the 1981–1984 Passenger Auto Average Fuel Economy Standards," July 1977.

5. Richard H. Shackson and H. James Leach, *Maintaining Automobile Mobility: Using Fuel Economy and Synthetic Fuels to Compete with OPEC Oil* (Arlington, Va.: Mellon Institute [1980]).

6. Ibid.

7. U.S. Department of Transportation, "Rulemaking Support Paper."

8. The market-clearing model described here is an expansion of current work being done by Profs. Robert A. Leone and Tony Gomez-Ibanez of Harvard University, and Stephen O'Connell of Massachusetts Institute of Technology. The author is indebted to them for their assistance in developing the approach.

9. Robert R. Nathan Associates, Inc., Attachment 1 to Brief of Tanaka, Walders, and Ritger, on behalf of the Japan Automobile Manufacturers Association before the United States International Trade Commission, " Washington, D.C., 1 October 1980, p. 61; U.S. Department of Transportation, *The U.S. Automobile Industry, 1980,* p. 69; Nissan Motor Corp. et al., "Before the United States International Trade Commission, Motor Vehicles and Certain Chassis and Bodies Thereof, Prehearing Brief, Nissan Motor Corp. in U.S.A.," Washington, D.C., 1 October 1980, p. 53.

10. Wharton Econometric Forecasting Associates, Inc., *An Analysis of the Automobile Market: Modelling Long-run Determinants of the Demand for Automobiles,* report prepared for the U.S. Department of Transportation, Transportation Systems Center, February 1977.

11. Robert R. Nathan Associates, Inc., p. 12; J.P. Stucker et al., *Evaluating Fuel Economy Mandates: An Exploratory Cost-Benefit Analysis* (Santa Monica, Cal.: Rand, [February 1980]), pp. 100–101.

12. U.S. International Trade Commission, *The Gas-Guzzler Tax Proposal: A Comparison of its Impact with that of the Fuel Efficiency Incentive Tax Proposal upon the Future of the U.S. Passenger Automobile Industry* (Washington, D.C.: U.S. Government Printing Office, 1977), pp. 125, 174–178; Robert R. Nathan Associates, Inc., p. 26.

13. See the Wharton model and the work by Stucker, for example.

14. Robert A. Leone et al., *Regulation and Technological Innovation in the Automobile Industry* (Washington: U.S. Congress, Office of Technology Assessment, [July 1980]), pp. 3.37–3.40.

15. The reader should be aware of the limits this assumption imposes on the analysis. In particular, it may cause the model to understate the differentials in performance among U.S. firms by imposing fixed market shares.

16. Stucker, p. 94.

17. The methodology described here was based on the work by Messrs. Leone, Gomez-Ibanez, and O'Connell. However, a similar methodology was employed in at least one other automobile model. (See J.P. Stucker et al., *Evaluating Fuel Economy Mandates: An Exploratory Cost-Benefit Analysis* (Santa Monica, Ca.: Rand, [February 1980].)

18. Testimony of George C. Eads, Council of Economic Advisers, in U.S. Committee on Ways and Means, *World Auto Trade,* p. 248.

19. Discussions with industry experts.

20. Eric J. Toder, Nicholas S. Cardell, and Ellen Burton, *Trade Policy*

and the U.S. Automobile Industry (New York: Praeger Publishers, 1978), p. 47.

21. Nissan Motor Corp. et al., p, 76.

22. Stucker, p. 94.

23. Discussions with industry experts.

24. U.S. Department of Transportation, *The U.S. Automobile Industry, 1980.* p. 6.

25. Ibid., p. 47.

26. U.S. Department of Transportation, Transportation Systems Center, "Disaggregated Financial Data and Analysis for the Domestic Motor Vehicle Manufacturers," July 1977.

27. Statement of Chrysler Corporation, table D.2–24, before the Subcommittee on Economic Stabilization in U.S. Congress, Senate, Committee on Banking, Housing, and Urban Affairs, *Government Regulation of the Automobile Industry, Hearings before the Subcommittee on Economic Stabilization,* 26 April 1979, p. 220.

28. Ibid.

29. For a discussion of these issues see Sasson Bar Yosef and Richard Kolodny, "Dividend Policy and Capital Market Theory," *The Review of Economics and Statistics* 58 (May 1976).

30. Statement of William Abernathy, *Automotive News,* 12 May 1980.

31. U.S. Department of Transportation, *The U.S. Automobile Industry, 1980,* p. 44.

32. Thomas H. Naylor and J.M. Finger, "Verification of Computer Simulation Models," *Management Science* 14 (October 1967):B–92.

33. Robert E. Shannon, *Simulation: The Art and Science* (Englewood Cliffs, N.J.: Prentice Hall, 1975), p. 208.

34. These tests are based upon Naylor and Finger; and James R. Emshoff and Roger L. Sisson, *Design and Use of Computer Simulation Models* (New York: Macmillan, 1970), p. 204.

5

Base Case of the Future of the U.S. Automobile Industry

An essential question in analyzing issues of future structural change is whether current industry structure is viable. To address this issue, a base case of the future of the U.S. auto industry is developed. The base case presents a view of the industry future without major structural change. It evaluates firm performance under a continuation of past conditions, except for the retooling and cost reductions that are part of the 1980–1985 plans of the domestic producers.

In the base case the strategies of domestic producers remain unchanged except for fuel-economy improvements through 1985 and possible manufacturing cost reductions. Government policy and the market share of non-U.S.-chartered firms remain at their initial values. Industry performance is analyzed against alternative economic scenarios designed to reflect the range of demand conditions the industry might reasonably expect to face in the future. Varying assumptions about the cost structure of domestic producers are also examined. The result is an assessment of the exposure of each firm to economic risk, as measured by the effects of alternative economic scenarios and manufacturing risk represented by the structure of manufacturing costs.

Base-Case Scenarios and Strategies

Three alternative economic scenarios, nominal, optimistic, and pessimistic, are considered in the base case. Firm performance is then evaluated under two different sets of cost structures for the domestic producers.

The nominal economic scenario is described in table 5–1, partially based on projections by Data Resources (DRI).[1] Real personal-consumption expenditures grow at an annualized rate of about 3.1 percent without any business cycles. The percentage of personal-consumption expenditures devoted to user-operated transportation remains constant. In real terms fuel prices rise, but without any major disruptions.

Two alternative economic scenarios are considered, both also based on DRI projections. One describes conditions that are generally more favorable to the industry as a whole than the nominal scenario, the other scenario describes less favorable conditions.

Table 5-1
Nominal Economic Conditions

	Inflation	Consumer Income[c]	FRAUTO[b]	Fuel Prices[c]	Domestic Productivity Increase	
					Labor	Capital
1980	13.5	0.0	.127	0.0	a	a
1981	11.0	1.2	.127	1.9	a	a
1982	10.5	2.9	.127	9.3	a	a
1983	10.0	2.6	.127	7.1	a	a
1984	8.5	3.2	.127	7.1	a	a
1985	8.1	4.2	.127	3.2	a	a
1986	8.2	3.3	.127	2.9	2.0	2.0
1987	8.0	2.9	.127	2.4	2.0	2.0
1988	8.0	2.8	.127	2.4	2.0	2.0
1989	8.0	2.6	.127	2.5	2.0	2.0
1990	7.8	2.1	.127	2.6	2.0	2.0
1991	7.8	2.1	.127	2.6	2.0	2.0
1992	7.8	2.1	.127	2.6	2.0	2.0
1993	7.8	2.1	.127	2.6	2.0	2.0
1994	7.8	2.1	.127	2.6	2.0	2.0
1995	7.8	2.1	.127	2.6	2.0	2.0
1996	7.8	2.1	.127	2.6	2.0	2.0
1997	7.8	2.1	.127	2.6	2.0	2.0

Source: Inflation, consumer income, and fuel prices based on TRENDLONG 1280 forecast, Data Resources Inc., *U.S. Long-Term Review,* Winter 1980–1981. Other figures are author's estimates.
a Two rates of 1980–1985 domestic productivity increase are considered: an historic rate (2%) and an accelerated rate (7%). See text.
b *FRAUTO:* Fraction of consumer disposable income allocated to user-operated transportation.
c Real dollars.

In the pessimistic scenario, personal-consumption expenditures are reduced by about 0.5 percent annually from the nominal scenario, the inflation rate is higher, and fuel prices rise at a rate 25 percent greater in the nominal scenario. Vehicle spending as a percentage of personal-consumption expenditures drops over time to slightly below its historic level over the 1960–1980 period,[2] representing a gradual societal disinvestment from automobiles.

The optimistic scenario represents a state of conditions much more favorable to the industry as a whole. Economic growth is at a rate 0.4 percent higher than in the nominal scenario, fuel prices increase at a rate 25 percent below the nominal-scenario rate, and inflation is lower. The percentage personal-consumption expenditures for vehicles rises to its historic high of 13.5 percent.

Table 5–2
Pessimistic Economic Conditions

	Inflation	Consumer Income[c]	FRAUTO[b]	Fuel Prices[c]	Domestic Productivity Increase	
					Labor	Capital
1980	13.5	0.0	.127	0.0	a	a
1981	11.1	0.9	.125	2.4	a	a
1982	10.6	2.2	.123	11.6	a	a
1983	10.1	2.0	.121	9.0	a	a
1984	8.7	2.9	.119	4.8	a	a
1985	8.3	3.8	.117	4.0	a	a
1986	8.5	2.8	.113	3.6	2.0	2.0
1987	8.4	2.4	.113	3.0	2.0	2.0
1988	8.5	2.3	.111	3.0	2.0	2.0
1989	8.5	2.1	.109	3.1	2.0	2.0
1990	8.4	1.6	.107	3.3	2.0	2.0
1991	8.4	1.6	.105	3.3	2.0	2.0
1992	8.4	1.6	.103	3.3	2.0	2.0
1993	8.4	1.6	.101	3.3	2.0	2.0
1994	8.4	1.6	.101	3.3	2.0	2.0
1995	8.4	1.6	.101	3.3	2.0	2.0
1996	8.4	1.6	.101	3.3	2.0	2.0
1997	8.4	1.6	.101	3.3	2.0	2.0

Source: Inflation and consumer income based on LOWTREND 1280 forecast, Data Resources Inc., *U.S. Long-Term Review,* Winter 1980–1981. Other figures are author's estimates.

[a] Two rates of 1980–1985 domestic productivity increase are considered: an historic rate (2%) and an accelerated rate (7%). See text.

[b] *FRAUTO:* Fraction of consumer disposable income allocated to user-operated transportation.

[c] Real dollars.

In the base case, there are no changes in government policy, and the Japanese producers retain between 20 and 25 percent of the market. Japanese production costs in U.S. dollars decline at 3 percent yearly, roughly the historic rate of productivity improvement.[3] This rate also assumes no significant changes in the yen-dollar exchange ratio.

The strategies of domestic producers are assumed to remain unchanged except for fuel-economy improvement over the 1980–1985 period. The manufacturer-specific schedules for implementing fuel-economy-improvement measures are given in tables 5–4 and 5–5, based on public documents.

This analysis excludes several other options for improving fleet fuel economy. No vehicle-mix restrictions, such as limitations on the sale of larger vehicles, or pricing to make fuel-efficient vehicles more attractive, are considered. Domestic producers supply to meet market demand. This assumption is consistent with the view that market forces have superseded

Table 5–3
Optimistic Economic Conditions

	Inflation	Consumer Income[c]	FRAUTO[b]	Fuel Prices[c]	Domestic Productivity Increase	
					Labor	Capital
1980	13.5	0.0	.127	0.0	a	a
1981	10.9	1.5	.128	1.4	a	a
1982	10.4	3.3	.129	7.0	a	a
1983	9.9	2.9	.130	5.3	a	a
1984	8.4	3.5	.131	2.8	a	a
1985	7.9	4.5	.132	2.4	a	a
1986	7.9	3.7	.133	2.2	2.0	2.0
1987	7.9	3.3	.134	1.8	2.0	2.0
1988	7.6	3.1	.135	1.8	2.0	2.0
1989	7.5	2.9	.135	1.9	2.0	2.0
1990	7.3	2.5	.135	2.0	2.0	2.0
1991	7.3	2.5	.135	2.0	2.0	2.0
1992	7.3	2.5	.135	2.0	2.0	2.0
1993	7.3	2.5	.135	2.0	2.0	2.0
1994	7.3	2.5	.135	2.0	2.0	2.0
1995	7.3	2.5	.135	2.0	2.0	2.0
1996	7.3	2.5	.135	2.0	2.0	2.0
1997	7.3	2.5	.135	2.0	2.0	2.0

Source: Inflation and consumer income based on HIGHTREND 1280 forecast, Data Resources Inc., *U.S. Long-Term Review,* Winter 1980–1981. Other figures are author's estimates.

[a] Two rates of 1980–1985 domestic productivity increase are considered: an historic rate (2%) and an accelerated rate (7%). See text.

[b] *FRAUTO:* Fraction of consumer disposable income allocated to user-operated transportation.

[c] Real dollars.

regulations in increasing fleet fuel economy.[4] Another possible means of improving fuel economy is through further reductions in vehicle performance, but this alternative is considered unlikely, and is not modeled.

After 1985, U.S. manufacturers revert back to normal levels of capital investment, and there is no additional extraordinary retooling to reduce vehicle size or improve fuel economy. This assumption is consistent with industry views that the post-1985 fleet will remain competitively viable through the mid-1990s.[5] Otherwise, over the 1980–1985 period, U.S. manufacturers are assumed to follow product strategies that are continuations of those strategies followed in 1979. The product breadth of each manufacturer remains unchanged. In particular, this view assumes that U.S. manu-

Table 5-4
Schedule for Downsizing, Front-Wheel-Drive Conversion, and Material Substitution

	Subcompact	Compact Regular	Compact Specialty	Large Regular	Large Specialty
Downsizing (1st round)					
General Motors	1981	1979	1981	1976	1976
Ford	1981	1977	1980	1978	1979
Chrysler	1977	1981	—	1978	1978
Downsizing (2nd round)					
General Motors	—	—	—	1983	1984
Ford	—	1983	—	1985	1984
Chrysler	—	—	—	1986	1986
Front-wheel drive					
General Motors	1981	1979	rear wheel drive[a]	1984	1984
Ford	1981	1983	rear wheel drive[a]	1985	1984
Chrysler	1977	1981	—	1986	1986
Material substitution (1st round)					
General Motors	1981	1979	1981	1976	1976
Ford	1981	1977	1980	1978	1979
Chrysler	1977	1981	—	1978	1978
Material substitution (2nd round)					
General Motors	1986	1985	1985	1985	1984
Ford	1984	1983	1985	1985	1984
Chrysler	1983	1986	—	1986	1986

Source: Adapted from trade journals, manufacturer announcements, and discussions with industry experts. See especially: U.S. Department of Transportation, National Highway Traffic Safety Administration, *Automotive Manufacturing Assessment System; Vol. I: Master Product Schedules,* November 1979.

[a] Remains rear-wheel drive.

facturers do not begin the domestic production of minicars, although it does not preclude their marketing captive imports under domestic label.

In the base-case analysis, the performance of the U.S. producers is evaluated under two sets of cost conditions. In the first, the manufacturing cost structure for Ford, General Motors, and Chrysler remains unchanged except for productivity improvements at the historic rate of roughly 2 percent.[6] Table 4-8, chapter 4 gives variable manufacturing cost estimates for each producer.

Some observers, however, expect that U.S. manufacturing costs will be lower in the future as a result of changing labor practices and improvements in productivity resulting from substantial capital investment.[7] A second case is also considered, in which U.S. producers reduce these costs.

Table 5-5
Schedule for Efficiency Improvements

	Aerodynamic Drag Reduction	Rolling Resistance	Improved Lubrication	Accessories	Manual Transmission	Automatic Transmission	Engine-operating Parameters	New Gas Engine	Turbocharging	Diesel	Brayton	Stirling
1980												
General Motors	.6	.2	.2	.2	.07	.6	.05	.1	.0	.05	.0	.0
Ford	.6	.2	.2	.2	.05	.25	.05	.1	.0	.0	.0	.0
Chrysler	.3	.2	.2	.0	.0	.0	.05	.1	.0	.0	.0	.0
1981												
General Motors	.7	.4	.4	.4	.07	.4	.15	.2	.0	.10	.0	.0
Ford	.7	.4	.4	.4	.07	.4	.15	.2	.0	.0	.0	.0
Chrysler	.6	.4	.4	.2	.05	.1	.15	.2	.0	.0	.0	.0
1982												
General Motors	.8	.6	.6	.6	.07	.65	.35	.3	.0	.15	.0	.0
Ford	.8	.6	.6	.6	.15	.5	.35	.3	.0	.0	.0	.0
Chrysler	.7	.6	.6	.4	.15	.15	.35	.3	.0	.0	.0	.0

1983

General Motors	.8	.8	.8	.07	.9	.55	.4	.0	.20	.0
Ford	.8	.8	.8	.15	.75	.55	.4	.0	.05	.0
Chrysler	.8	.8	.6	.15	.7	.55	.4	.0	.05	.0

1984

General Motors	.8	1.0	.8	.07	.93	.75	.5	.0	.25	.0
Ford	.8	1.0	.8	.15	.85	.75	.5	.0	.10	.0
Chrysler	.8	1.0	.8	.15	.85	.75	.5	.0	.05	.0

1985

General Motors	.8	1.0	.8	.07	.93	.95	.55	.0	.25	.0
Ford	.8	1.0	.8	.15	.85	.95	.55	.0	.15	.0
Chrysler	.8	1.0	.8	.15	.85	.95	.55	.0	.05	.0

Source: Adapted from U.S. Department of Transportation, NHTSA, *Rulemaking Support Paper Concerning the 1981–1984 Passenger Auto Average Fuel Economy Standards*, July 1977; Richard H. Shackson and James H. Leach, *Maintaining Automotive Mobility: Using Fuel Economy and Synthetic Fuels to Compete with OPEC Oil*, (Arlington, Va.: Mellon Institute, 1980).

While the magnitude of potential cost reductions is unclear, comparisons with the Japanese automotive industry provide some evidence to guide the analysis. Currently, estimates by the U.S. Department of Transportation and by Abernathy et al. indicate that U.S. producers require approximately 125 hours, including management and engineering, to produce a subcompact car. The comparable figure for the Japanese is roughly 90 hours.[8] One guideline is to examine the consequences of improvements in U.S. labor productivity that equalize the labor content of domestic and Japanese production. To do so by 1985, concurrent with the end of domestic retooling, requires an annual 1980–1985 improvement in labor productivity of roughly 7 percent.

An analysis by Abernathy, Harbour, and Henn also indicates the difference in U.S. and Japanese capital costs. Based on the figures in their analysis, it is assumed that U.S.-produced per-vehicle capital costs could be reduced by $272. This reduction corresponds to a 3.5 percent annual 1980–1985 capital productivity improvement for all U.S. producers.[9]

There are other possible cost reductions that this analysis does not consider. Wage rates may be reduced through shifts to nonunion or low labor cost regions, or through renegotiations of union contracts.[10] Changes in component sourcing, particularly increased dependence upon foreign components, might also reduce costs. There is little evidence to guide the inclusion of these and other manufacturer-specific measures in the analysis, and so they are excluded here, though they are considered later.

Results

Predictions of future auto sales and price by model are sensitive to the choice both of scenario and U.S. supply elasticity. Figure 5–1 compares predictions by the model under the case where domestic producers hold their real prices constant over time (infinite supply elasticity) with other published market predictions. The infinite supply-elasticity specification most closely corresponds with historic industry pricing patterns, which have kept the real average price of automobiles almost constant for two decades.[11] Market predictions under the alternate scenarios are intended to encompass the wide range of market forecasts and reflect the uncertainty about future market developments.

Market forecasts also change with the supply-side response specification. Under lower supply-elasticity specifications, the market shows less unit growth because domestic producers absorb increased demand through higher prices rather than increased unit sales.

Table 5–6 shows price changes for different vehicle classes under different supply responses. Price increases are highest under the 0.1 supply elasticity. In this case, U.S. producers increase prices and keep volume

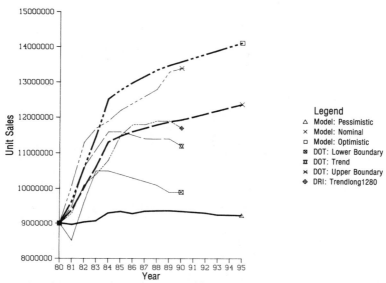

Sources: Data Resources, Inc. (DRI), *U.S. Long-Term Review,* Winter 1980–1981; Transportation Systems Center demand forecasts as cited in U.S. Department of Transportation (DOT), *The U.S. Automobile Industry, 1980* (Washington: [January 1981]).

Figure 5–1. Market Sales: Model and Other Forecasts

almost constant rather than accepting increased unit sales. Under the specifications of the base case, Japanese producers raise their prices over time to maintain share at 25 percent. This price increase is greatest for small luxury vehicles, reflecting the less price-sensitive nature of their demand. Under a low supply elasticity domestic producers respond by increasing prices rather than accepting a greater unit volume; this posture forces Japanese producers to increase their prices even more. When domestic producers maintain constant prices Japanese firms only increase prices slightly. Average price remains constant over time, and demand is reflected in increased unit sales, which is consistent with a continuation of historic market patterns.

Price shifts are also sensitive to the choice of scenario. As expected, price increases are lower under the pessimistic scenario and higher under the optimistic scenario, reflecting the underlying growth in demand.

Table 5–7 summarizes the shift in vehicle mix that occurs in the cases examined. Again, the resulting mix depends both upon the choice of scenario and the supply response. Under an infinite supply elasticity, the share of large basic cars increases with higher demand (for example, optimistic scenario). This trend is consistent with the intuition that with improved economic conditions, more people are likely to prefer larger over smaller

Table 5-6
Price Shifts under Different U.S. Supply Elasticities, Nominal Scenario
(1979 dollars)

	1980	*1985*	*1990*	*1995*
0.1				
Japanese small basic cars	6344.9	9812.0	10423.3	10741.9
Japanese small luxury cars	7863.1	15169.2	16823.0	17889.3
U.S. small basic cars	6070.5	8848.2	9188.0	9305.9
U.S. small luxury cars	8524.2	12851.9	13313.4	13468.7
U.S. large basic cars	9513.3	10958.5	10798.1	10504.5
U.S. large luxury cars	12534.8	16741.3	17130.8	17233.6
1.0				
Japanese small basic cars	6282.0	8465.9	8380.3	8378.7
Japanese small luxury cars	7922.3	12776.9	12960.5	13365.2
U.S. small basic cars	6044.8	7743.2	7747.3	7669.7
U.S. small luxury cars	8508.1	11077.5	11041.9	10893.4
U.S. large basic cars	9508.2	10583.7	10327.3	9974.8
U.S. large luxury cars	12516.6	15110.6	15102.9	14950.2
Infinite				
Japanese small basic cars	6171.6	6297.2	6505.0	6462.0
Japanese small luxury cars	8118.2	8571.9	9623.6	9986.4

Note: U.S. prices unchanged under infinite supply elasticity.

Table 5-7
Market-Mix Shifts: Base Case

	Small Basic Cars	*Small Luxury Cars*	*Large Basic Cars*	*Large Luxury Cars*
1980	.33	.31	.32	.04
1995				
Nominal Scenario				
0.1 supply elasticity	.30	.35	.31	.04
1.0	.33	.34	.29	.04
Infinite	.36	.32	.28	.05
Optimistic Scenario				
0.1	.28	.37	.30	.04
1.0	.33	.35	.28	.04
Infinite	.34	.30	.32	.05
Pessimistic Scenario				
0.1	.31	.32	.33	.05
1.0	.32	.31	.32	.05
Infinite	.39	.34	.23	.05

cars, prices held constant. Under the lower supply elasticities, the opposite result holds true. In this case, U.S. producers price so as to maintain almost constant volume (under the 0.1 supply elasticity). As a result, all the unit growth in the market takes place in the small-car segments, where the Japanese are positioned; under better economic conditions, this growth in small-car unit volume is higher, and therefore the share of large cars is smaller.

Manufacturer fleet fuel-economy improvements as a result of retooling and mix shifts are shown in figure 5–2. Changes in mix between the cases examined contribute little to fuel-economy shifts, so only one case is shown. Consistent with widespread predictions, all of the producers exceed the mandated CAFE standards for every year and achieve average fuel-economy levels of around thirty miles per gallon by 1985.

Capital investment in constant dollars for each manufacturer is shown in figure 5–3. Over the 1980–1985 period, aggregate capital spending by the three domestic producers, excluding research and development, preproduction and launch, and maintenance, repair, and replacement spending, is estimated at 50 billion 1979 dollars. This figure is consistent with a U.S. Department of Transportation estimate of 56 billion dollars for comparable spending over the 1979–1985 period.[12] After 1985, capital spending declines to historic levels with the end of extraordinary retooling to improve fuel economy.

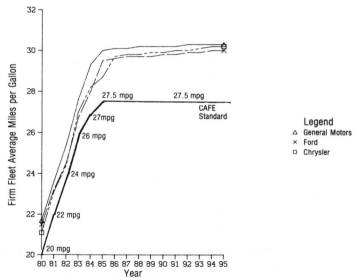

Figure 5–2. Average Fleet Fuel Economy, Nominal Scenario, Infinite Supply Elasticity

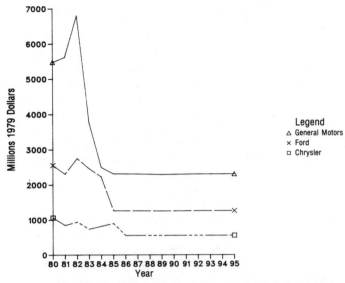

Figure 5-3. Capital Investment, Nominal Scenario

Financial Performance: Nominal Scenario

This section analyzes the financial performance of the domestic producers under the nominal scenario and different supply elasticities and cost conditions.

Domestic Producers Do Not Raise Prices (infinite supply elasticity)

In the case where U.S. producers do not raise vehicle prices (infinite supply elasticity), and without major cost reductions, the domestic industry as a whole performs quite badly. General Motors does not earn a positive profit until 1989. Its retained earnings are negative for several years. Ford and Chrysler perform even more poorly. They continue to experience losses throughout the period examined. Ford's losses begin to decrease slightly after 1990, although its retained earnings position continues to worsen as a result of negative cash flows that persist even after net income begins to increase. Chrysler's losses plateau after 1990, but its position does not improve.

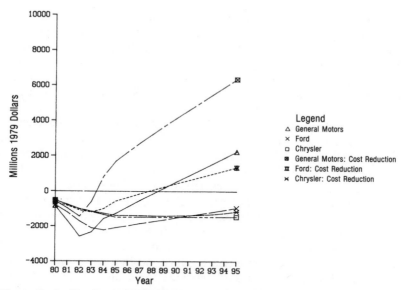

Figure 5–4. Net Income, Nominal Scenario/Infinite Supply Elasticity

With cost reductions, each firm's performance is improved, although there are wide differences between the firms. General Motors emerges financially healthy in this case. It becomes profitable by 1984, and by 1987 its real retained earnings regain their initial level. Its debt ratio peaks at 0.7 in 1983 as a result of high levels of capital investment in fuel economy and rapidly declines after that, so that by 1989 it has eliminated all debt. Ford sustains substantial losses peaking in 1983, and becomes profitable by 1988. During this period, even with cost reductions it is severely weakened financially, so that for a number of years it has negative retained earnings, and very high levels of debt. Its debt ratio peaks in 1986 at 1.2. After the late 1980s it regains financial strength, although Ford still has a very high debt level in 1995.

Chrysler remains in a clearly untenable position, with continued losses (though of smaller magnitude than in the case without cost reductions) and negative retained earnings throughout.

These results raise several crucial policy and managerial concerns. First, they suggest that a more viable future industry structure may have General Motors U.S. operations and foreign-chartered or U.S.-controlled foreign production as the principal participants, with the domestic operations of Ford and Chrysler playing a much smaller role. These developments may require new thinking by government policymakers accustomed to dealing with the U.S. auto industry as a self-contained and homogeneous whole.

For Ford, these results may also pose a challenge. While the analysis indicates that Ford U.S. operations eventually regain their profitability, until the late 1980s they incur large losses. It is a relevant managerial issue to question whether maintaining a presence in U.S. manufacturing is worth the substantial financial drain on the rest of Ford's worldwide manufacturing system, and the possibility of missed strategic opportunities elsewhere.

The relative performance of the three firms in these cases is explained by differences in their relative manufacturing cost structure, debt loads (and financing charges), and market position. General Motors has the lowest-cost manufacturing position, lower debt loads and cost of capital, and has the greatest share of the large car market, with its higher unit variable margin. Chrysler's poor performance is due to its poor position along each of these dimensions. Ford lies somewhere in between.

This analysis suggests that, contrary to some current thinking, the U.S. operations of Ford and Chrysler are poorly positioned to face the future. While General Motors emerges as a strong, financially viable producer, the other two domestic manufacturers are weak performers.

These results are of note in that they suggest that there is a significant potential for structural change in the auto industry in the future. A continuation of historic conditions—in other words, constant real auto prices and sales consistent with other predictions—does not lead to a return of historic financial results for two of the three domestic producers. While General Motors does quite well after a brief period of losses, assuming that it can reduce its costs, Ford remains at best a marginal producer, and Chrysler clearly would require restructuring.

Domestic Producers Raise Prices (0.1 and
1.0 supply elasticities)

The domestic industry performs best under the nominal scenario when they respond to demand shifts by raising prices (0.1 elasticity). This supply response results in the highest per-unit variable margin. The increased per-unit revenues more than compensate for the decrease in unit volume compared to the infinite-supply-elasticity response considered before.

Figure 5–5 presents net income for the three domestic firms under this case. Without major cost reductions, General Motors regains profitability in 1983 and Ford in 1984. Chrysler, however, continues to incur losses until 1989. By 1985, General Motors' retained earnings are at their initial levels in real terms. Ford is more seriously weakened—1985 real retained earnings are half of initial values—but it recovers rapidly. Chrysler's position does not improve until the 1990s.

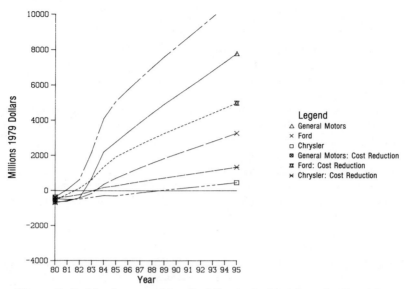

Figure 5-5. Net Income, Nominal Scenario/ 0.1 Supply Elasticity

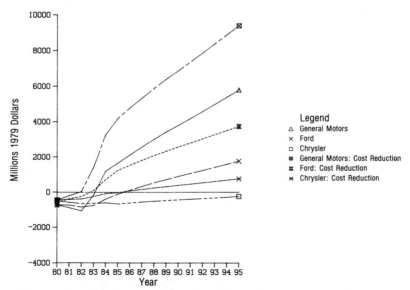

Figure 5-6. Net Income, Nominal Scenario/1.0 Supply Elasticity

As in the case without price increases, cost reductions markedly improve the industry performance. GM becomes profitable in 1981, Ford in 1982, and Chrysler in 1984. Chrysler experiences negative retained earnings for several years, although they bottom out in 1983 and become positive in 1986. In this case, each of the firms does very well, although they retain their relative rankings in terms of financial performance.

These results, however, must be interpreted in the context of the extreme price increases that occur, which have the effect of keeping demand virtually stagnant. Whether such pricing policies would be politically acceptable remains an open question.

What this outcome indicates is that future industry structure under conditions equivalent to those of current demand projections will evolve in ways very different from much of current thinking. The choices for policymakers are not easy—maintenance of the current industry structure may mean that the market for automobiles changes drastically as cars become more expensive, while a move to an industry dominated by GM and foreign production would require a complete rethinking of industry policy and an acceptance of employment losses and a weakened trade position.

Financial Performance: Optimistic and Pessimistic Scenarios

This section analyzes domestic firm performance under the optimistic and pessimistic scenarios. The results for fuel economy and capital investment have already been discussed.

Optimistic Scenario

Figure 5–7 shows net income and retained earnings for each producer under the optimistic scenario in the case where prices are kept constant (infinite supply elasticity). Roughly speaking, this scenario corresponds to the instance where demand grows at a much higher level than expected in current demand projections, and domestic producers react as they have historically by keeping average prices constant. Even in this case, without cost reductions the industry performs badly. General Motors' retained earnings decline until 1986 and are negative for several years; it is not until 1993 that it regains its initial financial strength. The positions of Ford and Chrysler worsen throughout the period examined.

With cost reductions, GM is profitable by 1984, and Ford in 1987. Chrysler again does not make a profit. GM's position is weakened for several years; in 1983, its debt ratio has risen to 0.7, and real retained earn-

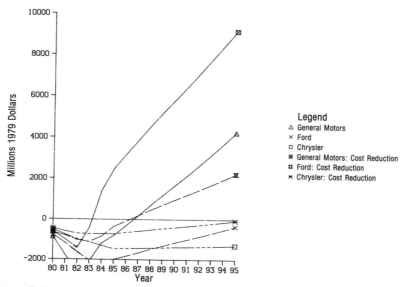

Figure 5-7. Net Income, Optimistic Scenario/Infinite Supply Elasticity

ings are half their initial value. Ford, meanwhile, suffers negative retained earnings for several years. By the 1990s, however, both producers are again in very strong financial positions. Chrysler continues to be in an untenable position.

This position suggests that a policy goal of maintaining the traditional three domestic competitors as viable producers without accepting significant structural change may be unrealistic. A return to a high level of demand from the current depressed market conditions will not, according to this analysis, save the industry. Chrysler especially is in a very weak position.

Assuming very high price increases (0.1 supply elasticity) (figure 5-8), both Ford and General Motors are in excellent financial strength, both doubling their retained earnings by 1985. Chrysler becomes profitable in 1983 or 1984, depending upon whether it reduces costs successfully. As noted earlier, however, these excellent financial results must be interpreted in light of very high price increases that occur.

This result suggests that the viability of the current structure of the domestic industry depends upon dramatic changes in the market pricing. This need for higher prices establishes a clear conflict between the interests of producers, consumers, and workers that effective policy will have to resolve.

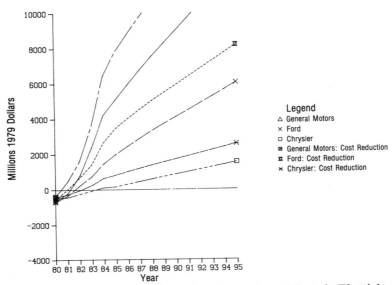

Figure 5–8. Net Income, Optimistic Scenario/0.1 Supply Elasticity

Pessimistic Scenario

With the pessimistic scenario and constant real prices (figure 5–9), sales remain between nine and ten million units over the period of the model. In this case, without cost reductions none of the producers earns a positive profit. Paradoxically, Chrysler does relatively better than the other producers in this case in the sense that it has lower losses; Chrysler's performance changes relatively less with respect to the scenario examined—because a proportionately smaller part of Chrysler's costs are fixed as compared with Ford and GM. Ford and GM are hence much more sensitive to changes in total revenue, since high fixed costs induce large shifts in relative profitability. Chrysler's poor but relatively more stable performance is due to higher variable productions costs and a mix emphasizing smaller, less profitable cars.

With cost reductions, GM becomes profitable by 1985. Ford and Chrysler continue to experience losses: Ford's losses decrease after 1984, but Chrysler's position does not improve at all.

Hence, the future viability of Ford as a domestic producer in the case without structural change depends critically upon the level of demand. While GM is profitable under all levels of demand, the uncertainty about future demand and Ford's critical exposure to this dimension makes Ford's position as a U.S. producer very risky.

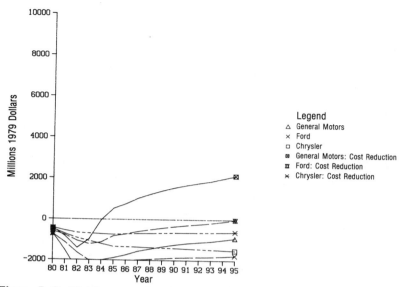

Figure 5–9. Net Income, Pessimistic Scenario/Infinite Supply Elasticity

Under high price increases (0.1 supply elasticity) (figure 5–10), without cost reductions again none of the producers shows a positive profit for the period examined. With cost reductions, General Motors becomes profitable by 1985. Although retained earnings drop to half their initial value by 1983, GM recovers by 1988. Ford becomes profitable in the late 1980s, although it is financially very weak for the entire period of the model. Chrysler continues to suffer losses even with cost reductions.

This outcome reinforces the point just made about Ford's high level of risk exposure. With just a perceived possibility of low demand, these results again suggest that an appropriate managerial concern for Ford is whether it wishes to continue its exposure to the chance of very poor financial results from its North American operations. This issue is particularly relevant because of its link to the broader competitiveness of Ford's worldwide strategic position.

Conclusion

This chapter has examined firm performance under the case where there are no major structural or environmental changes, and in which industry conditions return to so-called business as usual. These base-case conditions are similar to the view that the problems of U.S. industry are those only of tran-

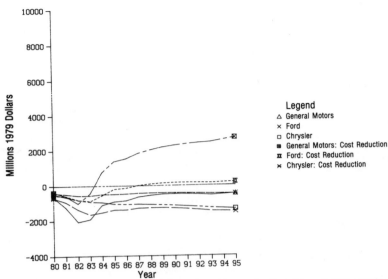

Figure 5–10. Net Income, Pessimistic Scenario/0.1 Supply Elasticity

sition to a higher level of fuel economy, rather than being indicative of more fundamental shifts.[13]

The reality suggested by this analysis is quite different, however. The critical reality this chapter has identified is that a return to business as usual for the U.S. auto industry is not a viable option. Under a continuation of historic pricing practices, even with cost reductions, Ford remains a marginal producer, and Chrysler is competitively unviable. These results are not significantly altered under the optimistic scenario in which demand is greater than expected. Levels of sales consistent with historic expectation do not lead to a return of historic levels of profitability.

To the extent that the present firm strategies are accurately reflected in the base case, these results indicate that the current structure of the U.S. industry is unstable. This observation serves as a preface for the next several chapters, which examine some of the forces for structural change in the U.S. auto industry.

Notes

1. Data Resources, Inc., *U.S. Long-term Review, Winter 1980–1981* (Lexington, Mass.: DRI, 1980).

2. U.S. Department of Transportation, Transportation Systems Center, "Role of the Motor Vehicle in the U.S. Economy," 30 September 1980, as cited in U.S. Department of Transportation, Office of the Assistant Secretary for Policy and International Affairs, *The U.S. Automobile Industry, 1980: Report to the President from the Secretary of Transportation* (Washington: January 1981), p. 4.

3. William J. Abernathy, James E. Harbour, and Jay M. Henn, *Productivity and Comparative Cost Advantage: Some Estimates for Major Automotive Producers,* Report to the Transportation Systems Center, Department of Transportation (Cambridge, Mass.: December 1980), p. 68.

4. Donald A. Hurter, *The Changing World Automotive Industry Through 2000* (Cambridge, Mass.: Arthur D. Little, January 1980), p. 2.

5. U.S. Department of Transportation, *The U.S. Automobile Industry, 1980,* p. 72.

6. Abernathy, Harbour, and Henn, p. 2.

7. Abraham Katz, "Statement of Abraham Katz, Assistant Secretary of Commerce for International Economic Policy, prepared for the Subcommittee on Trade of the House Committee on Ways and Means," 18 March 1980. (Typewritten.)

8. U.S. Congress, House, Committee on Ways and Means, *World Auto Trade: Current Trends and Structural Problems, Hearings Before the Subcommittee on Trade,* 36th Congress, 7, 18 March 1980, p. 318; Abernathy, Harbour, and Henn, pp. 60–67.

9. Abernathy, Harbour, and Henn.

10. Ibid., pp. 13–14.

11. U.S. Department of Transportation, *The U.S. Automobile Industry, 1980,* pp. 4–6.

12. Ibid., pp. 64–65.

13. See, for example, the statement of Ambassador Robert D. Hormats, Deputy U.S. Trade Representative, in U.S. Congress, House, *World Auto Trade: Current Trends and Structural Problems,* pp. 173, 186–191; also statement of Thomas Murphy, GM chairman, calling the domestic industry "viable" and "aggressive." *Automotive News,* 12 May 1980, p. 38.

6

The Role of Japanese Firms in the Future U.S. Industry

The strategic choices by foreign-based auto firms are a critical factor influencing future developments in the U.S. market, and the domestic performance of Ford, Chrysler, and General Motors. This chapter will attempt to link the choice of foreign-firm strategies in the U.S. market both to domestic developments and also to the dynamics of the international industry. The effects of various trade policies on the performance of the domestic industry and the strategic choices of foreign firms will be analyzed.

The analysis will focus on the Japanese industry, since it will probably remain the predominate foreign-chartered participant in the U.S. market over the period examined.

In chapter 3, possible future developments in non-U.S. markets were discussed, and the implications for future strategic change, especially in the Japanese industry, were considered. Because there is great uncertainty about future foreign-firm strategies and competitive developments, this chapter considers a multiplicity of cases representing a range of possible developments.

The first case examines the consequences of the Japanese acting so as to collectively maximize their short-term profits in the U.S. market. In the second case, the Japanese expand their U.S. market share at a rate greater than they would under profit maximization. The reasons why the Japanese might behave in one or another of these fashions are also discussed. In the third case, the Japanese industry loses its cost advantage over domestic producers, so that by the late 1980s the production costs of the two industries are equal. For each of these cases, the consequences of trade policy and different levels of underlying demand are evaluated.

Japanese Profit Maximization

This situation analyzes the case in which the Japanese industry maximizes its collective short-term profit from the U.S. market. As in the base case, Japanese costs decline at 3 percent yearly, and U.S. producers are assumed to attain significant reductions over the 1980–1985 period. In other respects, the strategies of U.S. producers are the same as those in the base case.

Instead of the analysis looking at all three supply responses by the domestic industry, this and subsequent chapters generally will discuss only the results for the supply response under which the domestic industry performs the best. In this chapter, this supply response was usually the case in which domestic producers increase prices rather than respond to demand shifts through changes in unit volume (0.1 supply elasticity). Other results are discussed where appropriate. It is readily acknowledged that in some instances the results of these supply responses might be politically or socially unacceptable. The broader point, however, consistent with the focus of this book on financial performance, is that these results indicate the *best* that the industry can do, not necessarily what will happen.

Future-Market Capture and Perceived Product Quality

An important though subtle dimension of competitive strategy concerns the degree of future market capture—that is, the extent to which a firm takes into account the linkage between potential future sales and current actions. These linkages to future market sales are important in the auto industry because of the generally high rates of consumer loyalty and repurchase. It is particularly relevant here because of its link to the perceived quality advantage of Japanese vehicles. This perceived superior quality may change rates of consumer repurchase.

Four cases are considered—one in which the Japanese maximize profit from current sales, and three cases in which Japanese pricing reflects different probabilities of repurchase for Japanese vehicles: 30 percent, 50 percent, and 80 percent.[1] For the last three cases, future-market-capture effects are handled by altering the model so that the profit from the sale of a Japanese vehicle includes the expected present value of profit from future sales as well. (See chapter 4 for a discussion of how the model is changed to capture this effect.)

Figure 6-1 portrays Japanese market-share changes under different economic conditions, assuming current profit maximization. While under the base case Japanese market share was limited by assumption to approximately its 1980 level, in this analysis Japanese share in all except the pessimistic cases continues to increase over time. The share of small luxury cars in the Japanese mix increases quickly from 40 percent to 55 percent. The price of Japanese cars—especially small luxury cars—rises rapidly.

What this situation suggests is that retooling of the domestic industry for improved fuel economy will not result in a decrease in the share of Japanese vehicles; in fact, quite the opposite may happen. It also suggests that Japanese producers may increase their competitive threat to the traditional domestic producers in the future, as Japanese firms increasingly compete

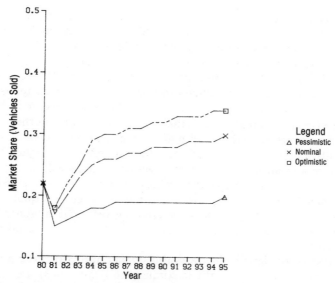

Figure 6–1. Japanese Market Share, Profit Maximization/0.1 Supply
Elasticity

with small luxury vehicles instead of remaining at the bottom end of the
market.

These conclusions become even more appropriate if the Japanese set
prices to reflect the present value of profits from future sales, as well as
current sales. The direct effect of taking into account future market capture is to reduce current Japanese prices and increase Japanese sales and
market penetration. Table 6–1 shows how price changes in these cases.

Table 6–1
**Annualized Percentage Change in Selling Prices under Different Levels
of Japanese Future-Market Capture, 1980–1990**

Japanese Repurchase Rate	Japanese Small Basic Cars	Japanese Small Luxury Cars	U.S. Small Basic Cars	U.S. Small Luxury Cars	U.S. Large Basic Cars	U.S. Large Luxury Cars
0	4.4	6.9	4.0	4.3	1.2	3.1
.3	3.8	5.9	3.7	4.1	1.2	2.9
.5	3.3	5.0	3.5	3.9	1.1	2.8
.8	2.1	3.1	3.1	3.5	1.1	2.7

The lower prices and higher sales occur because a current sale is worth more when the stream of future purchases tied to it are taken into account. Because the stream of small luxury vehicle sales is more profitable than an equivalent stream of small basic-vehicle sales, Japanese luxury-car prices are reduced, and sales increased, proportionately more. Hence, the inclusion of future-market-capture dimensions in pricing strategies tends to shift upwards the mix of vehicles and increase market share (figure 6-2).

These effects are greater for higher repurchase rates. In other words, if Japanese producers price to reflect high rates of consumer loyalty, the sorts of competitive effects injurious to the domestic industry—higher Japanese market share and an increasing shift upwards in mix—will be heightened. This effect is crucial because of the probable link between perceived quality and consumer loyalty. If consumers continue to perceive a quality advantage in Japanese vehicles, and this perception is reflected in higher levels of consumer loyalty, the result could be a worsened competitive position for domestic firms.

The next set of figures illustrates this impact upon domestic producers. The results under current profit maximization (figure 6-3) are not materially different from those discussed in the base case. Because the inclusion of future market dimensions reduces Japanese prices, domestic-producer profitability is reduced (figure 6-4).

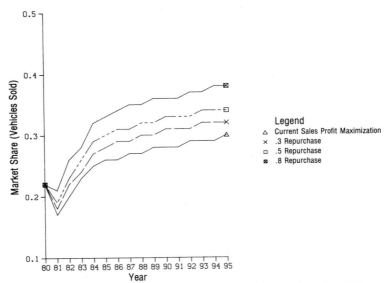

Figure 6-2. Japanese Market Share under Different Levels of Future Market Capture, Nominal Scenario/0.1 Supply Elasticity

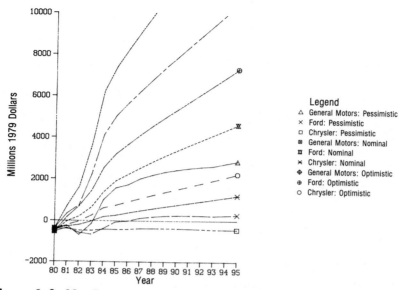

Figure 6-3. Net Income under Japanese Profit Maximization, Different Scenarios/0.1 Supply Elasticity

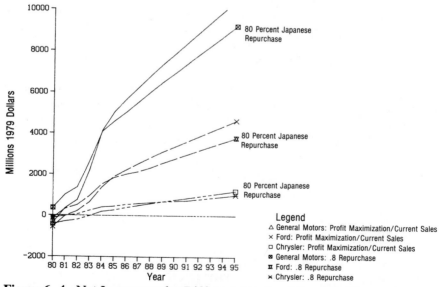

Figure 6-4. Net Income under Different Levels of Japanese Future Market Capture, Nominal Scenario/0.1 Supply Elasticity

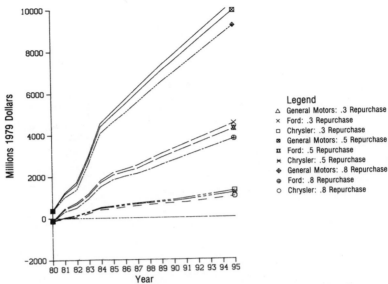

Figure 6–5. Net Income under Alternative Levels of Japanese Future Market Capture, Nominal Scenario/0.1 Supply Elasticity

The level of domestic profitability is quite sensitive to the degree of future market capture (figure 6–5). If Japanese pricing reflects a high level of consumer repurchase and future market capture instead of just current profit maximization, 1990 net income of GM drops by 10 percent, that of Ford by 15 percent, and Chrysler by 17 percent.

The importance of these results stems both from their delineation of another dimension of strategy and also from their link with issues of quality. If consumer-loyalty rates in the future respond to the perceived quality advantage of Japanese vehicles—or even just if Japanese producers act as if they will—then there may be major effects upon U.S. producers. Note further that there is nothing in this discussion about sales "lost" by domestic auto makers. The impact stems solely from the perception of future developments.

Trade Policy

The above results suggest that Japanese manufacturers will remain a major competitive threat to domestic producers in the future. For managers, the analysis indicates the importance of future market capture—which is probably linked to perceived quality—in improving domestic profitability.

For policymakers, trade restrictions may be an important policy tool for addressing these concerns. In the following analysis, four different trade policies are considered:

1. *Uniform quota:* A quota of 1.68 million Japanese vehicles yearly, the sales restraint of a recent policy action, is evaluated.
2. *Luxury-car quota:* Japanese luxury-car sales are restricted to 800,000 yearly, their 1979 level, while leaving unrestricted the number of small basic cars that can be imported.
3. *Uniform tariff:* A tariff rate of 20 percent on the selling price is set so as to compensate, at initial prices, for the Japanese production cost advantage.
4. *Luxury-car tariff:* A 35 percent tariff on luxury cars is designed as a punitive measure.

Each of these trade measures is imposed for the period 1981–1995.

The effects of these measures on Japanese market position can be both dramatic and strategically significant (figures 6–6 through 6–8 and tables 6–2 and 6–3). Quotas more severely restrict Japanese volume than tariffs.

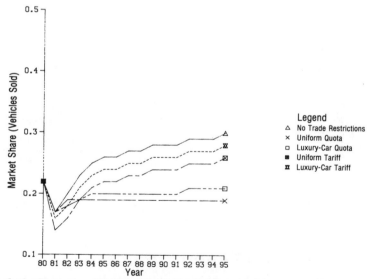

Figure 6–6. Japanese Market Share under Different Trade Policies, Nominal Scenario

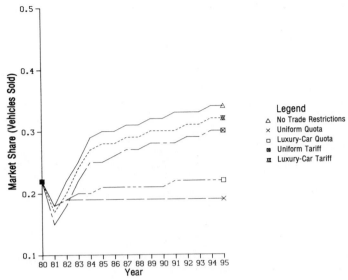

Figure 6-7. Japanese Market Share under Different Trade Policies, Optimistic Scenario

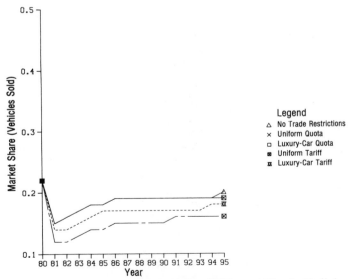

Figure 6-8. Japanese Market Share under Different Trade Policies, Pessimistic Scenario

Uniform quotas are the most restrictive; under the case evaluated Japanese share remains at under 20 percent. Trade restrictions also change Japanese pricing and mix. Table 6–2 presents the share of luxury cars in the Japanese mix under the different restraints. A uniform quota increases the share of luxury vehicles the most. This greater shift upwards is as expected, because under a volume constraint profit is increased by selling a greater proportion of luxury vehicles. A uniform tariff also encourages a shift upwards, because a tariff effectively increases either or both the production cost or price of Japanese vehicles, making sales of small basic cars less desirable to the producer than the proportionately more profitable luxury class.

All of the trade restraints increase average vehicle prices, although a luxury-car quota decreases the price of Japanese small basic cars. Quotas have a greater price effect than do tariffs, because Japanese producers absorb about half of the tariff, rather than passing it along in price increases.

The effects of trade policies upon the net worth of the Japanese position in the domestic market are shown in table 6–4. Quotas have less effect upon Japanese net worth than do tariffs—a uniform quota only reduces the net worth of the Japanese position by 11 percent, even though it severely restricts their share. This differential between quotas and tariffs results

Table 6–2
Japanese Mix: Percent Small Luxury Cars

	1980	1985	1990	1995
Japanese profit maximization	.40	.55	.55	.55
Uniform quota	.40	.63	.66	.68
Luxury-car quota	.40	.46	.43	.42
Uniform tariff	.40	.59	.59	.59
Luxury-car tariff	.40	.39	.40	.41

Table 6–3
Japanese Vehicle Prices: Small Luxury Cars

	1980	1985	1990	1995
Japanese profit maximization	7863.1	14886.3(5)	15395.5(5)	15720.9(5)
Uniform quota	7863.1	17935.3(2)	19399.8(2)	20377.1(2)
Luxury-car quota	7863.1	19001.6(1)	20501.9(1)	21332.8(1)
Uniform tariff	7863.1	16733.8(4)	17283.8(4)	17598.1(4)
Luxury-car tariff	7863.1	17726.3(3)	18310.8(3)	18612.8(3)

Table 6-4
Japanese Vehicle Prices: Small Basic Cars

	1980	1985	1990	1995
Japanese profit maximization	6334.9	9678.7(4)	9752.5(4)	9726.2(4)
Uniform quota	6334.9	11113.9(1)	11626.7(1)	11896.5(1)
Luxury-car quota	6334.9	7726.8(5)	7375.0(5)	6996.2(5)
Uniform tariff	6334.9	10591.5(2)	10644.8(3)	10584.7(3)
Luxury-car tariff	6334.9	10474.7(3)	10752.4(2)	10880.4(2)

Table 6-5
**Net Present Value of Japanese Profit: 1980-1995; Nominal
Scenario, Japanese Profit Maximization**
(in billions of 1979 dollars)

Trade Policy	Net Present Value	
Japanese profit maximization	131.9	(100%)
Uniform quota	118.0	(89%)
Luxury-car quota	113.5	(86%)
Uniform tariff	92.3	(70%)
Luxury-car tariff	88.9	(67%)

because under a uniform quota there is a greater shift toward more profitable luxury vehicles, while under a luxury-car quota, a scarcity premium is obtained for these cars. Tariffs, on the other hand, have less effect upon market volume, but because Japanese producers under this formulation absorb part of the tariff burden, they have greater effect upon the profitability of the Japanese position. The luxury-car tariff most reduces Japanese profitability both because the tariff acts as a "tax" on that segment and because prices for Japanese basic vehicles are lower in this case.

These results suggest the sometimes ambiguous effects of trade policy. Uniform quotas, for example, while they reduce the net worth of the Japanese position in the United States, also encourage increased mix shift upwards and so may work to the long-run competitive disadvantage of U.S. firms. Trade restrictions also increase prices; a relevant policy concern is whether any improvements in the financial performance of domestic firms are worth the higher prices that consumers face.

Figures 6-9 to 6-12 present the net income of domestic producers under different trade policies. The most important observation is how little impact trade restrictions have upon domestic-firm financial performance.

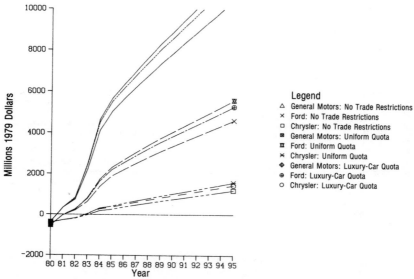

Figure 6-9. Net Income under Imposition of Quotas, Nominal Scenario/ 0.1 Supply Elasticity

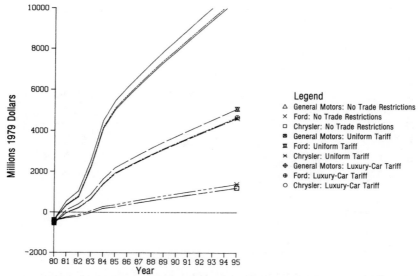

Figure 6-10. Net Income under Imposition of Tariffs, Nominal Scenario/ 0.1 Supply Elasticity

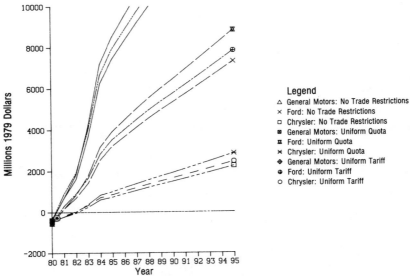

Figure 6-11. Net Income under Different Trade Policies, Optimistic
        Scenario/0.1 Supply Elasticity

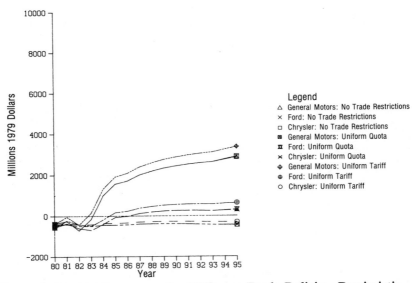

Figure 6-12. Net Income under Different Trade Policies, Pessimistic
        Scenario/0.1 Supply Elasticity

Uniform quotas have the greatest effect, but there is little immediate improvement under any of the trade restraints.

These results can be explained by noting that price increases are greatest under the uniform quota. The Japanese absorb much of the burden of tariffs. With quotas, however, initial price increases over the case of no trade restraints are modest, because the quotas are not severely restrictive at that point. These modest initial price changes do little to improve domestic-firm financial results. Furthermore, price increases also reduce market volume, which works against any improvement in financial performance.

The conclusion from this analysis is that trade restrictions under these conditions may be an ineffective policy tool. They may even be harmful to the domestic industry in the long run, as with quotas encouraging a shift upwards in Japanese mix.

Japanese Expansion

In the second case examined, the Japanese expand their aggregate market share at a rate greater than that under profit maximization, so that Japanese share grows to 40 percent of the total market by 1990.

Whether Japanese behavior will in fact more closely resemble short-term profit maximization or expansion depends both upon the time horizon of the Japanese industry and upon its ability to collude effectively. Japanese expansion can be viewed as a form of long-run profit maximization, in which continued growth in market share above the short-term profit-maximizing level improves the perceived long-run net worth of the Japanese position. This result is consistent with the results of the last section, which showed that Japanese share is greater when dimensions of future market capture are taken into account.

Whether the Japanese industry in aggregate will pursue profit maximization or expansion may also depend upon the ability of the Japanese to coordinate their behavior effectively. Profit maximization, of course, has a higher value for the Japanese than does share expansion. If the Japanese industry is unable to develop patterns of coordination allowing joint profit maximization, the strategic imperatives of the Japanese industry suggest that in aggregate it may continue to expand in foreign markets at higher than a profit maximizing rate. As discussed in chapter 3, with slowing growth in the domestic Japanese market, the smaller firms are under pressure to expand through exports to maintain competitive volumes. Isuzu's recent attempt at growth in the U.S. market is an example. Efforts at coordination and profit maximizing may be complicated by such differences within the Japanese industry in outlook and distribution of benefits. Smaller Japanese producers in particular may have more to gain through continued expansion than through coordination. The interests of each individual firm, driven by the needs of the smaller producers to increase volume, may dictate that the industry in aggregate continues to expand volume at a higher rate than joint profit maximization would dictate.

Financial Impact of Japanese Expansion

Figures 6–13 and 6–14 compare the net income of Ford, Chrysler, and General Motors under Japanese expansion and profit maximization. Japanese expansion reduces domestic-firm profitability, with Ford and Chrysler affected proportionately more than General Motors. Total undiscounted net income for General Motors under Japanese expansion is 74 percent of the comparable value under Japanese profit maximization. The figure for Ford is 41 percent of the comparable figure, while Chrysler's losses over the period increase 270 percent.

The reason for these results is that Japanese expansion results in generally lower prices than Japanese profit maximization. Accordingly, prices, especially for small domestic cars, are lower than under profit maximization. These lower small-car prices affect Chrysler and Ford more than General Motors because they are more strongly positioned at the small end of the market.

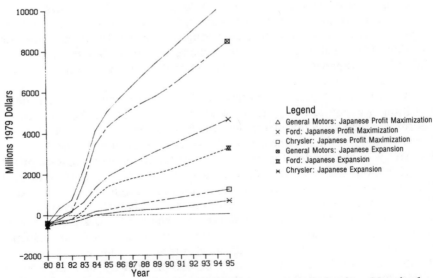

Figure 6–13. Net Income under Different Japanese Behavior, Nominal Scenario

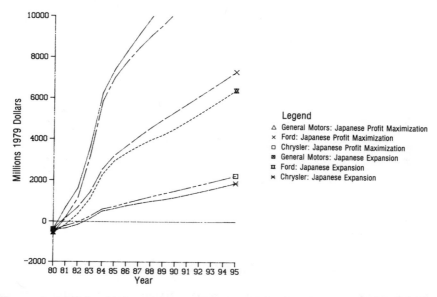

Figure 6–14. Net Income under Different Japanese Behavior, Optimistic
Scenario

The net worth of the Japanese position in the United States is lower
under share expansion than under profit maximization by 20 percent (105.6
billion versus 131.9 billion). This decrease results both from lower prices
and from the larger share of small basic cars (which are less profitable) in
the Japanese fleet under expansion.

These results illustrate the manner in which changes in the structure and
behavior of the Japanese industry can have a profound impact on the viability of U.S. producers. Effective analyses must be cognizant of these sorts
of relationships. The results also suggest that it is in the interest of the
domestic auto producers to shift the Japanese away from an expansion
strategy. The high level of dependence Japanese firms have on U.S. sales
argues that domestic policymakers may have significant indirect leverage on
influencing structural change in the Japanese industry. Effective policy
analysis may wish to consider the variety of ways in which it can shape the
sorts of strategies that Japanese producers choose to follow.

Policy Responses

To do so, however, may be a difficult policy task. Figures 6–15 through
6–18 illustrate this by presenting the effects of different trade policies upon
domestic producer net income. The only trade restraint that has any appre-

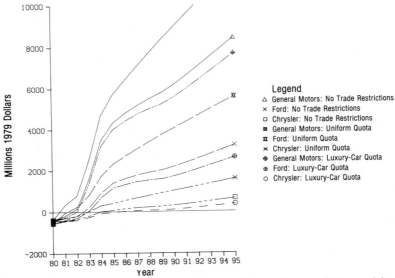

Figure 6–15. Net Income under Japanese Expansion and Imposition of Quotas, Nominal Scenario

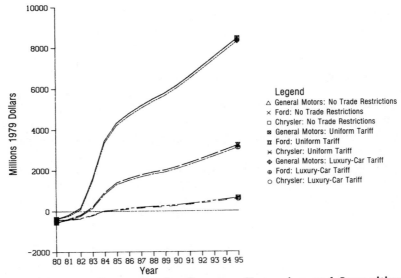

Figure 6–16. Net Income under Japanese Expansion and Imposition of Tariffs, Nominal Scenario

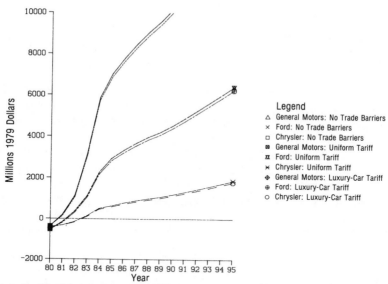

Figure 6-17. Net Income under Japanese Expansion and Imposition of Tariffs, Optimistic Scenario

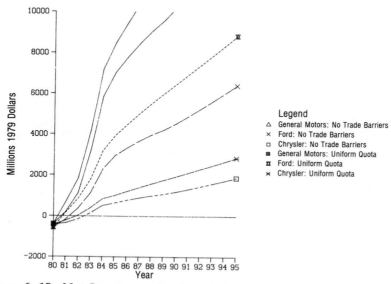

Figure 6-18. Net Income under Japanese Expansion and Imposition of Quotas, Optimistic Scenario

ciable effect is the uniform quota. Tariffs have little effect given Japanese expansion because the Japanese absorb most of the tariff rather than increasing prices. Luxury-car quotas result in price reductions for small basic vehicles, which counteract the effects of any price increase in the constrained luxury-car class.

A uniform quota has the greatest impact because it effectively bars Japanese expansion. Under it the Japanese are forced to profit maximize a constrained volume and to increase prices sharply to ration the limited supply. These actions benefit domestic profitability.

Table 6–6 shows how trade restrictions affect the value of the Japanese position in the United States. Tariffs most reduce Japanese net worth under share expansion because their cost is mostly taken out of Japanese profits. A uniform quota, however, actually increases Japanese profitability from the case of no trade restraints, by forcing Japanese mix toward small luxury cars. While high rates of expansion result in less than profit-maximizing

Table 6–6
Net Present Value of Japanese Profit: 1980–1995; Nominal Scenario, Japanese Expansion
(in billions of 1979 dollars)

Trade Policy	Net Present Value	
Japanese expansion[a]	105.6	(100%)
Uniform quota[b]	118.0	(112%)
Luxury-car quota	76.8	(75%)
Uniform tariff	63.6	(60%)
Luxury-car tariff	68.5	(65%)

[a]Eighty percent of profit maximization
[b]In this case the Japanese are limited to 1.68 million units and so by definition cannot expand.

Table 6–7
Japanese Mix: Percent Small Luxury Cars

	1980	1985	1990	1995
Japanese expansion	.47	.51	.48	.49
Uniform quota	.47	.63	.66	.68
Luxury-car quota	.47	.24	.17	.17
Uniform tariff	.47	.51	.49	.50
Luxury-car tariff	.47	.42	.43	.44

returns, the interfirm dynamics of the Japanese industry may block joint profit maximization. A quota may increase Japanese profitability by eliminating some of these strategic options.

What this analysis does not consider is how changes in the net worth of the Japanese position in the United States—say, as a result of the imposition of tariffs—may in itself engender strategic change. Tariffs, by virtue of removing much of the profit from Japanese exports to the United States, may encourage Japanese producers to change their product mix or production locale. Alternatively, a quota, by increasing Japanese profitability and blocking certain types of strategies, may encourage further industry coordination.

A dilemma of sorts is indicated by this analysis. On one hand, quotas appear to be an effective policy tool in the event that Japanese producers are following an expansion strategy, improving the profitability of domestic producers. On the other hand, the net worth of the Japanese position in the United States is actually increased by the imposition of quotas, and Japanese mix is shifted upwards. Neither of these latter developments are desirable to the United States, either from a broad national point of view, or in terms of the long-term competitive threat Japanese production poses to the three domestic manufacturers.

This situation illustrates several points. First, it is necessary to balance short- and long-term interests. While quotas improve domestic-firm performance in the short run, the long-run consequences must also be understood; the cordination between Japanese producers may be improved as a result, or Japanese firms may be encouraged to dominate the profitable small luxury-car market, leaving domestic producers with the less profitable low end of the market. Second, it illustrates how important it is that the formulation of policy take into account the strategies of industry participants and the manner in which policy may alter them. According to this analysis, quotas have a very different impact when the Japanese are pursuing profit-maximizing strategies than when they are pursuing an expansion strategy.

Japanese Cost Increase

In the third case considered, Japanese production costs rise so that by the late 1980s total unit production costs for Japanese and the most efficient U.S. producer (GM) are roughly equal. Such a loss of competitive advantage could arise in several ways. One source of cost shifts could be changes within the Japanese industry. For example, with the greater maturity of the Japanese industry there may be less opportunity for additional scale economies, while labor costs may increase due to seniority practices. A second source of relative cost shifts are those that originate outside of the industry.

Changes in yen-dollar exchange rates can quickly alter the profitability of U.S. sales. Local-content requirements, especially if they require a high level of value added, are a policy tool for exogenously imposing such cost changes.

Distinguishing between different causes of cost shifts is important because cost changes accompanying structural change within the Japanese industry may lead to very different responses than cost changes imposed exogenously. It may be, for example, that cost changes that result from structural change within the Japanese industry will more quickly encourage greater intraindustry coordination than exogenously imposed cost shifts that are not accompanied directly by structural change.

In the case of exchange-rate shifts, there is a more direct reason. If the yen appreciates, laws against dumping insure that a rise in yen must be passed through into an increase in the dollar price of Japanese cars.[2] These higher dollar prices might discourage continued high rates of Japanese expansion in the U.S. market.

Local-content requirements might nullify more than just a portion of the Japanese cost advantage. To the extent that perceived product quality is the result of country-specific factors such as labor attitudes and supplier infrastructure, local-content requirements might reduce both Japanese cost and perceived quality advantages. Local-content requirements might also disrupt existing Japanese manufacturing and managerial structures, and hence may have even greater consequences than just to shift costs.

While the behavioral implications of cost shifts are a complex issue, preliminary analysis by the model indicates that Japanese expansion with reduced cost advantage greatly lowered the net worth of the Japanese position in the United States, resulting in negative profits in some cases. These results appear extreme; hence, this section will assume that the Japanese profit maximizes under a reduced cost advantage.

This result in itself is significant because it suggests that cost changes are one dimension with which policymakers may be able to shape the sorts of strategies Japanese producers follow, if the right policy tool can be found. Local-content requirements, to the extent that they would destroy the existing Japanese cost advantage, are one possible policy option.

Figures 6-19, 6-20, and 6-21 compare Japanese market share at reduced competitive advantage with the cases examined earlier. The effect of a reduction in competitive advantage is to lower Japanese market share from what it would be otherwise. Japanese prices are also higher, and there is a large shift upwards to luxury vehicles in the Japanese mix. In spite of these responses, the net worth of the Japanese position declines to 78 percent of the case with retained competitive advantage in the nominal scenario.

The loss of Japanese competitive advantage benefits U.S. producers (figures 6-22, 6-23, 6-24), mostly as a result of the higher market prices.

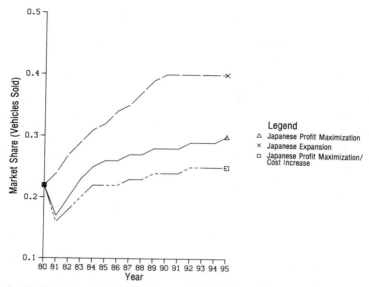

Figure 6–19. Japanese Market Share under Different Japanese Behavior, Nominal Scenario

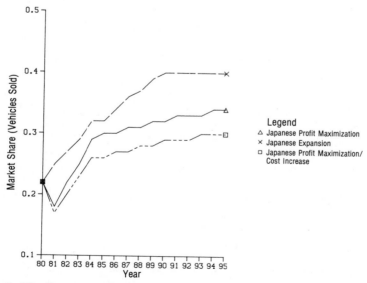

Figure 6–20. Japanese Market Share under Different Japanese Behavior, Optimistic Scenario

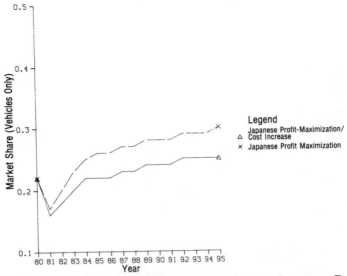

Figure 6-21. Japanese Market Share under Different Japanese Behavior, Pessimistic Scenario

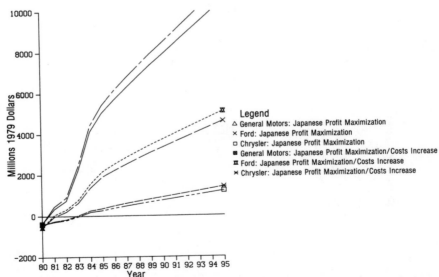

Figure 6-22. Net Income under Different Japanese Behavior, Nominal Scenario

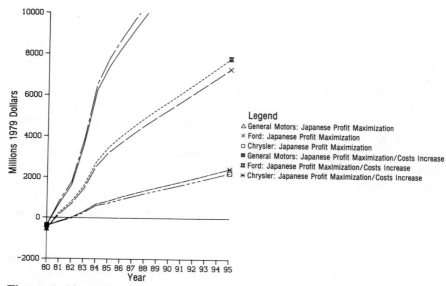

Figure 6-23. Net Income under Different Japanese Behavior, Optimistic Scenario

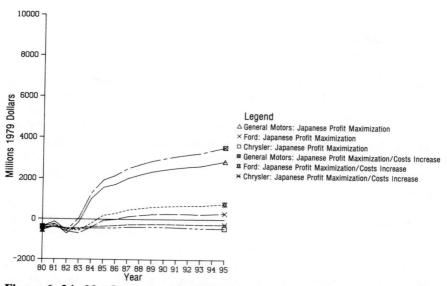

Figure 6-24. Net Income under Different Japanese Behavior, Pessimistic Scenario

The greatest improvement in financial performance occurs under the pessimistic scenario. In this case, there is little market growth and hence little opportunity for Japanese volume gains. The Japanese response in this scenario is to increase prices and shift mix upwards even more than under the nominal scenario and so reduce share. While the upward-mix shift does not benefit domestic firms, the increase in prices does.

Ford particularly benefits under the pessimistic scenario in this case. Its retained earnings are almost triple those under the case in which Japanese costs do not rise. Ford benefits proportionately more than GM because price increases are greatest for small cars, where Ford is more strongly positioned than GM. In large basic cars, where GM is most strongly positioned, reduced Japanese competitive advantage raises prices very little. While Chrysler's revenues increase under this case even more than Ford's, Chrysler's poor manufacturing cost position and high level of financing charges mean that it does not benefit proportionately as much as Ford.

These results reinforce the conclusion that a reduction in Japanese competitive advantage may be a relevant goal for U.S. policymakers concerned with the viability of domestic producers. Local-content requirements have already been discussed. Quotas may also increase Japanese costs if they slow the rate of growth for the Japanese industry, resulting in reduced opportunities for experience effects and burdening the industry with overcapacity.

Indirect Implications of Quotas and Orderly Marketing Agreements

Quotas, or voluntary export restraints (for example, orderly marketing agreements), have figured prominently both in this analysis and also in recent policy actions by the U.S. government. Considering their importance, this section will discuss some of the possible indirect effects of these policy tools that the model analysis does not present. These indirect effects are important to understand because they relate to the way in which policymakers can influence the strategies of foreign competitors—an important theme of this chapter.

While the level of trade restraint may be the same under both quotas and voluntary export restraints, the ultimate effects may differ.[3] Voluntary export restraints are usually administered by the exporting country's government or industry, while quotas are administered by the importing country. The establishment of an administrative apparatus by the exporting industry for restraint and coordination has a number of consequences. First, it may complicate enforcement, since an exporting industry or country may not really wish to restrain exports. More important, however, may be the distributional effects. The imposition of a quota or export restraint generates a revenue equal to that of a hypothetical tariff of exactly the same market effect. However, with a quantitative unit restraint on imports, this tariff-equivalent revenue does not go to the government, and its distribution is indeterminate. The ability of the exporting industry to allocate market share and administer the trade restraint may help to improve its ability to capture a greater share of this revenue.

Furthermore, the administrative structure necessary to enforce a voluntary export restraint may also encourage increased industry cartelization or coordination. The allocation of export quotas among exporting firms and the increased communication between industry participants are both mechanisms for increasing industry coordination. Quotas or trade restraints also reduce the uncertainty of export markets and increase the power of exporting firms over price, again encouraging increased industry coordination.

In the case of automobiles, a quota or voluntary export restraint may have other substantial effects outside of strictly economic consequences. These effects include the following:

1. Quotas might help to restrain industry overcapacity both by reducing the uncertainty inherent in future market expansion and by improving intraindustry coordination. This outcome is of particular importance for the Japanese industry in the face of possible worldwide overcapacity in small cars by the mid-1980s.

2. Quotas encourage a shift upwards in product mix, a move consistent with Japanese strategy as discussed in chapter 3.

3. Quotas may remove some of the political pressure that Japanese producers face in the U.S. market.

4. The administrative position of MITI vis-a-vis the Japanese industry may be improved by quotas. This effect occurs because MITI has taken the responsibility for assigning share allocations in the industry, increasing the agency's administrative power over the industry. The greater administrative power of MITI may aid efforts in future industry coordination.

5. Quotas may also encourage Japanese producers to invest in U.S. production facilities. This action may be a force for strategic repositioning by Japanese firms, especially if U.S. production facilities differ in terms of cost or quality from existing Japanese capacity.

The point, of course, is to suggest the extent to which the procedural and indirect consequences of trade policy influence the ultimate outcome of any policy and the importance of looking at them in the choice of effective policy.

Conclusions

The critical reality this analysis has outlined is that the Japanese will remain a significant force for structural change in the domestic industry. Contrary to much current thinking, the results here suggest that Japanese share will probably continue to increase in the future, and the strategies Japanese producers follow will have profound effects upon the profitability and even viability of domestic automobile production.

This chapter has examined the effects of different trade policies and foreign-firm strategies on the U.S. industry. Several observations can be drawn from these results.

1. Dimensions of future market capture and consumer repurchase rates are a subtle but dynamic and significant factor for the future viability of the domestic industry. To the extent that these issues are linked with perceived vehicle quality, this analysis indicates the importance of that competitive dimension—and expectations of future consumer behavior—to the domestic industry.

2. Given a particular Japanese strategy, the analysis has indicated that the effects of trade restraints as such, without changes in foreign-firm strategy, contribute little to the competitive viability of the U.S. manufacturers.

3. Improvements in domestic-manufacturer financial performance stem primarily from differences in Japanese strategy, especially in the early 1980s.

4. Trade policy can significantly alter the net worth and strategic value of the Japanese position in the U.S. market. These effects include both the dollar value of the current and future profits derived from that competitive position, and also the "fit" between developments in the domestic market and global strategies of Japanese firms.

For policymakers, an important conclusion stemming from these results is that effective policy should concern itself with ways in which it can influence the strategies Japanese producers choose to follow. The role of the U.S. as a central market for automobiles gives domestic policymakers a subtle but potentially powerful influence over the strategies and structure of foreign automobile exporters.

Notes

1. The evidence as to what the real rate of consumer repurchase is appears to be somewhat muddled: note, for example, the seeming contradiction between table 11, chapter 3, and table 7, chapter 4. The supposed significantly higher consumer repurchase rates for U.S. vehicles (see, for example, U.S. Department of Transportation, *The U.S. Automobile Industry, 1980,* p. 47) also run counter to both the widespread perception of high Japanese quality and the continual growth of Japanese market share.

To avoid confusion, the analysis here chooses three representative values to indicate the significance of future market issues.

2. Nissan Motor Corporation, et al., *Before the United States International Trade Commission, Motor Vehicles and Certain Chassis and Bodies Thereof, Appendix to Prehearing Brief, Nissan Motor Corp. in U.S.A.,* 1 October 1980, p. 132.

3. The discussion of the general effects is taken from C. Fred Bergsten, "On the Non-Equivalence of Import Quotas and 'Voluntary' Export Restraints," in *Toward a New World Trade Policy: The Maidenhead Papers,* ed. C. Fred Bergsten (Lexington, Mass.: Lexington Books, D.C. Heath and Co., 1975), pp. 239–271.

7

Oil Shocks,
Energy Policy, and
Fuel-Economy-Related
Issues

The experiences of the past decade suggest that the United States and other major oil-consuming nations are vulnerable to unpredictable interruptions in petroleum supply. Concerns about the domestic auto industry's ability to cope with such changes, and with broader national goals of energy conservation, have already prompted several regulatory proposals for additional post-1985 fleet fuel-economy standards.[1]

New regulatory actions and the uncertainty in petroleum markets suggest that the domestic industry may again face the need to improve overall fuel economy radically. This chapter evaluates the impact of such developments on the U.S. automotive market and the firms competing in it. To do so, different scenarios are examined that cover a multiplicity of possible future developments in both energy and firm strategies. These include scenarios of future oil shocks such as were experienced during the past decade, reductions in the real price of petroleum, and different rates of smooth increase in oil prices. Trade and energy policies, as well as the consequences of different firm strategies, are evaluated against these cases.

Background to the Analysis

Before presenting the analysis, it is necessary first to describe the sorts of strategies that manufacturers may follow to increase fuel economy, and second, to describe more fully future market conditions that may drive demand for increased fuel economy.

By 1985 U.S. automobile producers are expected to have fleet fuel economies averaging thirty to thirty-five miles per gallon, a figure consistent with the analysis of previous chapters. This manufacturing capability should give domestic manufacturers sufficient flexibility to meet most changes in demand composition.[2]

Post-1985 improvements in fleet fuel economy may result either from improvements in vehicle fuel efficiency or from mix shifts within the fleet. By the mid-1980s, further rounds of downsizing while holding constant the vehicle concept will not be possible.[3] Many of the other measures used to improve vehicle fuel efficiency in the 1977–1985 period will have been

almost entirely implemented by then. Post-1985 improvements in vehicle
fuel economy will depend more upon weight reduction through material
substitution and the increased use of more efficient engines such as turbo-
charged diesels.[4] The use of these technologies, however, may be constrained by safety or emissions regulations.

Other more radical technologies, including electric cars and advanced
engines like the Brayton and Stirling, might have significant effects on fleet
fuel economy. Because of long production lead times, it is unlikely that any
of these technologies will penetrate the market significantly before 1995,
and so are excluded from this analysis.[5]

Tables 7–1 and 7–2 present estimates of the measures used by manufacturers to improve post-1985 fuel economy. These measures consist principally of increased penetration of diesel engines and further rounds of
material substitution. These strategies are similar to those projected by a
Congressional Budget Office study.[6] It should be noted that these technology schedules are highly speculative, since there exist no public predictions
by manufacturers of the measures they would use to improve fuel economy.

A second source of fleet fuel-economy improvement is mix shifts.
Future increases in fuel prices will likely encourage further shifts to smaller

Table 7–1
**Manufacturer-Specific Schedules for Post–1985 Fuel-Economy
Improvements**

	Subcompact	Compact Regular	Compact Specialty	Large Regular	Large Specialty
Material substitution (3rd round)					
General Motors	93	91	89	87	87
Ford	93	91	89	87	87
Chrysler	93	91	89	87	87
Front-wheel-drive conversion					
General Motors	81	79	89	84	84
Ford	81	83	89	85	84
Chrysler	77	81	89	86	86

Source: Adapted by author's calculations from Richard R. John, "Transition to the Post–1985
Motor Vehicle" (Cambridge, Mass.: Transportation Systems Center, [31 October 1979])
(Mimeographed.); Bruce Rubinger, "Improving Automobile Energy Efficiency in the Post-
1985 Period" (Cambridge, Mass.: Transportation Systems Center, [May 1980]) (Typewritten);
Richard H. Shackson and James H. Leach, *Maintaining Automobile Mobility: Using Fuel
Economy and Synthetic Fuels to Compete with OPEC Oil* (Arlington, Va: Mellon Institute
1980).

Table 7-2
Schedule for Post-1985 Efficiency Improvements

	Aerodynamic Drag Reduction	Rolling Resistance	Improved Lubrication	Accessories	Manual Transmission	Automatic Transmission	Engine-operating Parameters	New Gas Engine	Turbocharging	Diesel	Brayton	Stirling
1986												
General Motors	.85	.85	1.0	.85	.07	.93	.95	.65	.05	.30	0	0
Ford	.85	.85	1.0	.85	.15	.85	.95	.65	.05	.20	0	0
Chrysler	.85	.85	1.0	.85	.15	.85	.95	.65	.01	.10	0	0
1987												
General Motors	.9	.9	1.0	.9	.07	.93	1.0	.70	.10	.35	0	0
Ford	.9	.9	1.0	.9	.15	.85	1.0	.7	.1	.25	0	0
Chrysler	.9	.9	1.0	.9	.15	.85	1.0	.7	.05	.15	0	0
1988												
General Motors	.95	.95	1.0	.9	.07	.93	1.0	.75	.20	.45	0	0
Ford	.95	.95	1.0	.9	.20	.85	1.0	.75	.20	.35	0	0
Chrysler	.95	.95	1.0	.9	.15	.85	1.0	.75	.10	.25	0	0
1989												
General Motors	1.0	1.0	1.0	1.0	.07	.93	1.0	.8	.3	.50	0	0
Ford	1.0	1.0	1.0	1.0	.15	.85	1.0	.80	.30	.40	0	0
Chrysler	1.0	1.0	1.0	1.0	.15	.85	1.0	.8	.15	.40	0	0

Table 7-2 continued

	Aerodynamic Drag Reduction	Rolling Resistance	Improved Lubrication	Accessories	Manual Transmission	Automatic Transmission	Engine-operating Parameters	New Gas Engine	Turbo-charging	Diesel	Brayton	Stirling
1990												
General Motors	1.0	1.0	1.0	1.0	.07	.93	1.0	.9	.4	.50	.0	.0
Ford	1.0	1.0	1.0	1.0	.15	.85	1.0	.9	.4	.4	.0	.0
Chrysler	1.0	1.0	1.0	1.0	.15	.85	1.0	.9	.4	.4	.0	.0
1991												
General Motors	1.0	1.0	1.0	1.0	.07	.93	1.0	1.0	.50	.50	.0	.0
Ford	1.0	1.0	1.0	1.0	.15	.85	1.0	1.0	.40	.40	.0	.0
Chrysler	1.0	1.0	1.0	1.0	.15	.85	1.0	1.0	.40	.40	.0	.0

Source: Adapted by author's calculations from Richard R. John, "Transition to the Post-1985 Motor Vehicle" (Cambridge, Mass.: Transportation Systems Center, [31 October 1979]) (Mimeographed); Bruce Rubinger, "Improving Automobile Energy Efficiency in the Post-1985 Period" (Cambridge, Mass.: Transportation Systems Center, [May 1980]) (Typewritten); Richard H. Shackson and James H. Leach, *Maintaining Automobile Mobility: Using Fuel Economy and Synthetic Fuels to Compete with OPEC Oil* (Arlington, Va.: Mellon Institute 1980).

cars, although the magnitude of these mix shifts may be less than those seen during the 1970s, both because all of the so-called easy switches will have already been made, and because improvements in vehicle fuel efficiency may partially mitigate the consequences of rising fuel prices.[7]

Predictions of future petroleum prices are highly speculative for reasons both geological and political. A review of major studies of future oil supplies and prices shows substantial uncertainty about future forecasts of demand, non-OPEC supply, and OPEC production.[8] While scenarios used elsewhere in this analysis have shown fuel prices rising smoothly, the experience of the past decade suggests that future fuel prices may experience abrupt changes in response to political or economic changes throughout the world. Accordingly, table 7–3 presents an oil-shock scenario. This scenario, based originally upon analysis done in another Congressional Budget Office

Table 7–3
Oil-Shock Economic Conditions

Year	Inflation	Consumer Income	FRAUTO[a]	Fuel Prices	Domestic Productivity Increase	
					Labor	Capital
1980	13.5	0.0	.127	0.0	7.0	3.5
1981	11.0	1.2	.127	1.9	7.0	3.5
1982	10.5	2.9	.127	9.3	7.0	3.5
1983	10.0	2.6	.127	7.1	7.0	3.5
1984	28.5	− 3.4	.127	34.1	7.0	3.5
1985	14.8	0.9	.127	3.2	7.0	3.5
1986	10.7	0.9	.127	2.9	2.0	2.0
1987	10.5	0.7	.127	2.4	2.0	2.0
1988	8.0	2.8	.127	2.4	2.0	2.0
1989	8.0	2.6	.127	2.5	2.0	2.0
1990	30.2	− 5.2	.127	28.6	2.0	2.0
1991	21.2	− 2.3	.127	2.6	2.0	2.0
1992	12.3	0.6	.127	2.6	2.0	2.0
1993	7.8	2.1	.127	2.6	2.0	2.0
1994	7.8	2.1	.127	2.6	2.0	2.0
1995	7.8	2.1	.127	2.6	2.0	2.0
1996	7.8	2.1	.127	2.6	2.0	2.0
1997	7.8	2.1	.127	2.6	2.0	2.0

Source: Inflation, consumer income, and fuel prices are author's calculations based on analysis by U.S. Congressional Budget Office, *The World Oil Market in the 1980s: Implications for the United States;* other figures are author's estimates.

[a] *FRAUTO:* Fraction of consumer disposable income allocated to user-operated transportation.

Table 7-4
Oil-Price-Reduction Economic Conditions

Year	Inflation	Consumer Income	FRAUTO[a]	Fuel Prices	Domestic Productivity Increase	
					Labor	Capital
1980	13.5	0.0	.127	0.0	7.0	3.5
1981	11.0	1.2	.127	1.9	7.0	3.5
1982	10.5	2.9	.127	9.3	7.0	3.5
1983	10.0	2.6	.127	7.1	7.0	3.5
1984	8.5	3.2	.127	7.1	7.0	3.5
1985	8.1	4.2	.127	3.2	7.0	3.5
1986	8.2	3.3	.127	-3.0	2.0	2.0
1987	8.0	2.9	.127	-3.0	2.0	2.0
1988	8.0	2.8	.127	-3.0	2.0	2.0
1989	8.0	2.6	.127	-3.0	2.0	2.0
1990	7.8	2.1	.127	-3.0	2.0	2.0
1991	7.8	2.1	.127	-3.0	2.0	2.0
1992	7.8	2.1	.127	-3.0	2.0	2.0
1993	7.8	2.1	.127	-3.0	2.0	2.0
1994	7.8	2.1	.127	-3.0	2.0	2.0
1995	7.8	2.1	.127	-3.0	2.0	2.0
1996	7.8	2.1	.127	-3.0	2.0	2.0
1997	7.8	2.1	.127	-3.0	2.0	2.0

Source: Author's estimates.

[a] *FRAUTO:* Fraction of consumer disposable income allocated to user-operated transportation.

study, posits temporary 20 percent reductions in oil supplies in 1984 and 1990, resulting in higher fuel prices, higher rates of inflation, and lower levels of economic activity. The result is fuel costing about $3.50 per gallon (1979 dollars) by 1995, as compared to around $2.00 in the scenarios considered earlier.[9]

Two other scenarios will also be analyzed. Table 7-4 presents an oil-price-reduction scenario, in which real petroleum prices decline slightly after 1985. The third is the nominal scenario based on DRI forecasts, which has been described previously.

The Risk Exposure of Fuel Economy

Uncertainty is a prominent characteristic of future petroleum markets. For the automobile industry, this uncertainty is a source of risk exposure. Manufacturers unprepared for abrupt shifts in the market demand for fuel economy can be competitively disadvantaged. On the other hand, a manufacturer may be financially penalized if the cost of fuel-economy improvements is in excess of market demand. This risk exposure may vary depending upon the strategies of different firms.

This section examines the risk exposure of the industry by analyzing the consequences of firms' retooling or failing to retool in the face of an uncertain future environment, as represented by the oil-shock, oil-price-reduction, and nominal scenario. These scenarios are intended to represent the range of future fuel-price conditions facing the industry, and so define the exposure of individual firms to developments along this dimension.

Figure 7–1 presents the effects of a second round of retooling on manufacturer fleet fuel economy under the nominal scenario. Improvements in fleet fuel economy under the nominal scenario principally result from improvements in vehicle fuel economy, rather than mix shifts. Under the nominal scenario, mix shifts are minor. Without further mix shifts but with retooling, fleet averages around thirty-seven miles per gallon result; mix shifts add two to three miles per gallon more. These results are consistent with those of other analysis.[10]

Capital investment by Ford, GM, and Chrysler under retooling is shown in figure 7–2. With a second round of retooling, total industry capital spending for the post-1985 period, including maintenance, repair, and

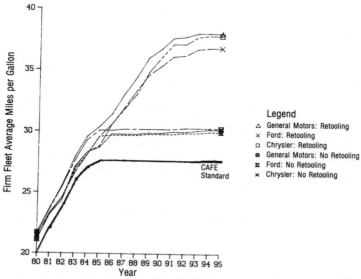

Figure 7–1. Firm Fuel Economy: Post-1985 Retooling versus No Retooling

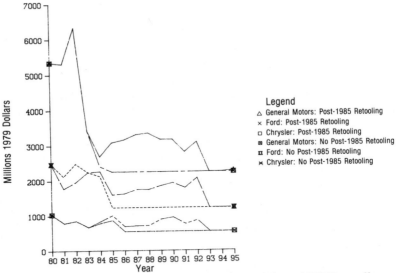

Figure 7-2. Capital Investment: Effects of Post-1985 Retooling

replacement, is estimated at $73 billion (1979 dollars). This figure compares with an estimate by the Congressional Budget Office of $78.5 billion.[11]

Market Impacts of Different Energy Futures

The effects of different energy futures on the U.S. automotive market are presented in figures 7-3 and 7-4. For each scenario, only the supply response under which the domestic industry performs best is generally shown. Except under the oil-shock scenario, the domestic producers performed best when they responded to demand shifts primarily through price instead of volume shifts (0.1 supply elasticity). Under these scenarios and this supply response, domestic prices rise over time. In the case of oil shocks, demand is so reduced that prices would have to decline under this supply response. In the case of oil market disruptions, therefore, the best domestic supply response is to change volume rather than price (infinite supply elasticity). In effect, the domestic pricing response puts a floor but not a ceiling on sales prices—in other words, prices can increase but not decline.

Not surprisingly, the oil-shock scenario has the most severe impact upon sales, as a result both of higher gasoline prices and lower levels of economic activity. Sales are higher with post-1985 retooling because in-

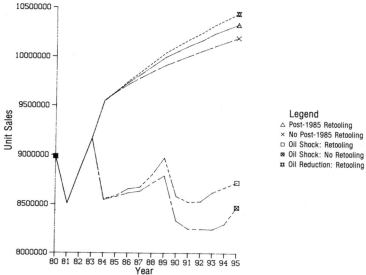

Figure 7-3. Total Sales under Nominal, Oil-Shock, Oil-Price-Reduction Scenarios—Effects of North American Retooling

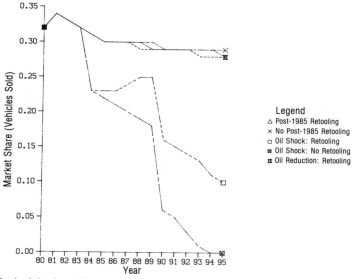

Figure 7-4. Market Share Large Basic Cars under Nominal, Oil-Shock, Oil-Price-Reduction Scenarios—Effects of North American Retooling

creased fuel economy decreases the consumer cost of ownership, making the vehicles less expensive. Part of this decrease in operating costs is captured as an increase in intensive demand by auto makers, but a portion also accrues to consumers. For a similar reason, sales are highest under the oil-price-reduction scenario.

Figure 7–4 shows the consequences of these developments on the share of large basic cars. Under the nominal and oil-price reduction scenarios, post-1985 retooling has little effect upon the share of large cars because U.S. producers absorb any differences in demand between more and less fuel-efficient large cars in terms of price instead of unit sales. In the oil-shock scenario, however, further fuel-economy retooling makes a significant difference. Each oil shock causes a sharp drop in the share of large cars; without retooling, large basic cars completely disappear as a class by 1995. With retooling, large cars still retain a small market segment; increased fuel efficiency reduces the effective consumer price, and so increases the demand for this class of vehicles over what it would be without retooling.

It needs to be emphasized that by 1985 large basic cars in the model are not the "gas guzzlers" of recent memory but are instead vehicles with fuel-economy ratings of twenty-four to twenty-seven miles per gallon. With a second round of retooling, fuel economy for this class is in excess of thirty miles per gallon. Mix shifts under the oil-shock scenario occur in spite of these substantial fuel-economy improvements.

Japanese market share increases dramatically under the oil-shock scenario, a result consistent with the experience of the past decade (figure 7–5). The increase in Japanese share results from an increase in the share of small cars in the overall market rather than from a relative gain within a size class by the Japanese. This increase is similar to what has occurred in past oil disruptions. Japanese penetration is lower if U.S. producers retool, because retooling reduces the market shift to smaller cars.

In fact, this analysis may understate the growth of Japanese market share, especially if Japanese producers increase their penetration of the small luxury-car market. Such increased penetration is consistent with the strategic shifts of Japanese producers discussed in chapter 3.

The increase in Japanese market share is mirrored by a decrease in General Motor's share as a result of the almost complete disappearance of the large basic-car segment that GM historically has dominated. These results suggest that if GM is to maintain its competitive strength under this scenario, it will have to increase its relative share in the smaller vehicle classes, instead of merely redefining vehicle classes downward.

Based on these results, and the analysis of chapter 3, one implication that emerges is that General Motors and Japanese producers may be competing head-on in the same market segments in the future. A strategic im-

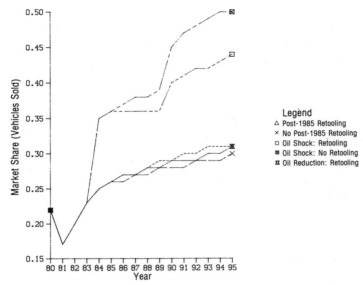

Figure 7-5. Japanese Market Share under Nominal, Oil-Shock, Oil-Price-Reduction Scenarios—Effects of North American Retooling

perative of Japanese producers is to shift their mix upwards in response to changing market and cost conditions. General Motors' dominant position in large basic cars is shown here to be especially vulnerable to future oil shocks. A reasonable managerial response to this exposure might be to shift mix toward smaller vehicles. In fact, of course, General Motors is shifting toward smaller cars with its downsizing program. What the results of this analysis show, however, is that such downsizing and fuel-economy improvement may still be insufficient to prevent major changes in market segmentation in the event of future oil-supply disruptions. In that case, GM may have to further strengthen its position in small cars to reduce its risk exposure.

Japanese Profitability under Different Energy Futures

The net worth of the Japanese position in the United States (table 7–5) is unaffected in the nominal and oil-price-reduction scenarios by the strategies of domestic firms. The oil-shock scenario reduces the value of the Japanese position, but only by about 15 percent from the nominal scenario. The Japanese net worth actually declines by a smaller amount if the domestic

Table 7-5
Net Present Value of Japanese Profits: 1985, 1990, 1995; Nominal,
Oil-Shock, Oil-Price-Reduction Scenarios
(in billions of 1979 dollars)

	1985	1990	1995
Nominal scenario			
No post–1985 retool	47.2	95.8	131.9
Post–1985 retool	47.3	97.8	136.5
Oil shock			
No post–1985 retool	44.5	88.1	127.2
Post–1985 retool	44.6	83.7	115.2
Reduced energy prices			
No post–1985 retool	47.2	97.0	135.3
Post–1985 retool	47.3	98.7	139.3

industry does not retool, because Japanese producers benefit more than the domestic firms from the downward shift in market classes that occurs in the oil-shock scenario.

Strategic Risk Facing Domestic Producers

The impact of these fuel-economy-related developments on General Motors, Ford, and Chrysler is more complex, determined both by the scenario that obtains and the choice of strategy—whether the firm engages in a second round of retooling or not. While the issue of which scenario obtains is largely beyond the control of the firm, the choice of whether to engage in a second round of retooling is a managerial decision conditioned by government policy.

It is important to distinguish between these areas of control because they define at least two of the dimensions of risk exposure of each firm. First is the strategic risk of retooling—that is, given a particular scenario, the consequences of investing or failing to invest in post-1985 fuel-economy improvements. In essence, this risk is the strategic *cost of being wrong*—the difference in performance that results from the firm's pursuing the less appropriate strategy. The other dimension of exposure is economic risk: given the firm strategy, how the choice of scenario affects performance. The exposure of firms to these two sources of risk may be very different. If so, these differential consequences may condition the responses of managers and policymakers.

These dimensions of risk exposure are of particular importance in this discussion because of the long product lead times associated with substantial fuel-economy improvements and the high level of environmental uncertainty. These factors mean that firms must commit themselves to a strategy without knowing the future economic conditions critical to that strategy's success.

Figures 7-6 through 7-9 show how the profitability of Ford, Chrysler, and General Motors is affected by the decision to retool or not under a given scenario. Under both the nominal and pessimistic scenarios, retooling has the effect of increasing manufacturer selling prices while volume and mix remain basically unchanged (table 7-6). This price shift implies an increase in the intensive demand facing automobile manufacturers, as producers capture a portion of the consumer dollar that previously went to operating costs. The absolute price increase due to retooling is slightly higher under the pessimistic scenario because fuel prices are higher. While the dollar-price changes due to retooling differ only slightly between the optimistic and pessimistic scenarios, because prices are lower under the pessimistic case the percentage price increases and, hence, the impact upon profitability is greatest. Price shifts also differ among vehicle classes. Prices for large basic and small luxury cars increase about twice that for other classes in both absolute and percentage terms.

Table 7-6
Price Changes due to Post-1985 Retooling
(from case with no post-1985 retooling—1990 selling price)

	U.S. Small Basic Cars	U.S. Small Luxury Cars	U.S. Large Basic Cars	U.S. Large Luxury Cars
Oil-Price Reduction				
Percent	3.2	5.6	5.1	3.6
Dollars	291.9	761.1	575.5	620.3
Oil Shock	Not significant because U.S. producers hold price constant (infinite-supply response).			
Nominal				
Percent	3.7	6.7	6.1	4.2
Dollars	332.8	867.9	656.3	707.9
Pessimistic				
Percentage	5.4	10.1	7.5	5.8
Dollars	353.3	921.9	697	751.9

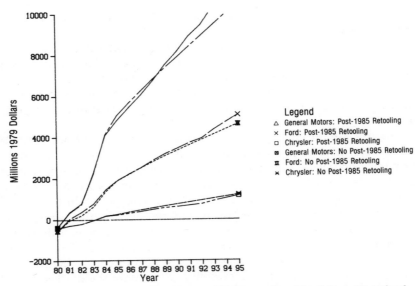

Figure 7-6. Net Income under Post-1985 Retooling Decision, Nominal Scenario/0.1 Supply Elasticity

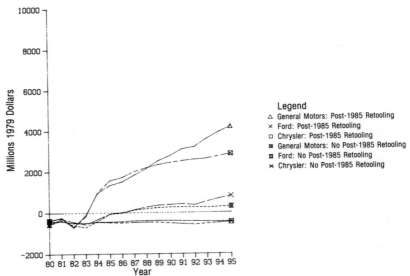

Figure 7-7. Net Income under Post-1985 Retooling Decision, Pessimistic Scenario/0.1 Supply Elasticity

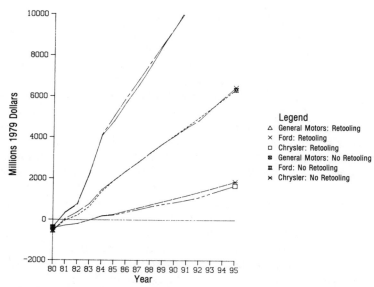

Figure 7–8. Net Income under Post-1985 Retooling Decision, Oil-Price-Reduction Scenario

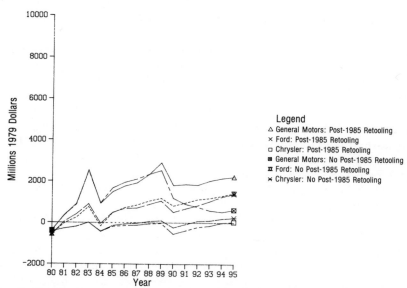

Figure 7–9. Net Income under Post-1985 Retooling Decision, Oil-Shock Scenario

General Motors and Ford are better positioned in these segments to benefit from the price increases than Chrysler, and accordingly their net income with retooling is higher than without retooling. During the mid-1980s retooling reduces General Motors' profitability because a second round of retooling increases GM's capital spending while the benefits of retooling in terms of manufacturer prices are still several years away. Ford's capital spending in relation to its financial structure is such that these effects are less severe, although still evident.

Chrysler performs worse with retooling than without, for two reasons. First, Chrysler is poorly positioned in the market to benefit from the larger price increases due to retooling, which are greatest in luxury and large-car segments. Second, Chrysler's financial structure is so weakened from the first round of fuel-economy improvement that the additional capital spending required greatly increases its debt load. By 1990, for example, under the nominal scenario, retooling has the effect of decreasing General Motors' surplus funds by 6 percent from the case without retooling, and Ford's by 11 percent, but Chrysler's debt increases 360 percent. The resulting debt level is impossibly high by industry standards, and in reality under such conditions it is likely that Chrysler would have to restructure its operations. Chrysler therefore has a very high risk exposure to competitive or regulatory developments that would require post-1985 retooling.

The results under the oil-price-reduction scenario are similar (figure 7-9). As expected, price increases resulting from retooling under this scenario are smaller than under scenarios with higher fuel prices, because with lower fuel prices the potential for operating cost reductions is reduced.

The exposure of individual firms and the impact of a second round of retooling is most vividly illustrated in the oil-shock scenario. The best U.S. supply response under the oil-shock scenario is constant selling prices (if prices were adjusted, they would move downwards because of the reduction in demand). As a result, retooling creates no appreciable difference in manufacturer selling prices. However, the consumer price is higher under the case without retooling, and sales consequently are slightly lower because operating costs are higher. The biggest effect of the scenario, noted earlier, is to reduce the share of large basic cars. Without retooling, large basic cars as a class disappear by 1994; with retooling, their share shrinks to a third of its former size.

General Motors is uniquely exposed by these changes, which reduce the size of the market segment it has historically dominated.

In contrast, Ford and Chrysler are better off because of their stronger position in the smaller-car segments. With retooling, both Ford and Chrysler improve their relative position vis-a-vis General Motors, and Ford exceeds GM's return on sales. Under the case without retooling, Ford's absolute profitability exceeds GM's. This result comes about not so much from an improvement in the profitability of Ford and Chrysler as from a sharp drop in GM's earnings and suggests the high degree of exposure that General Motors has to changes in its dominant position in large basic cars.

The exposure of General Motors to petroleum disruptions is in contrast to analysis in earlier chapters, in which GM has emerged by far the strongest domestic producer. This fact again reinforces the point first made in the base-case analysis—a critical reality facing industrial policymakers and managers is that the domestic industry may experience significant structural change in the future. It further illustrates how the form of this structural change depends upon a range of uncertain, or difficult to predict, events.

Economic-Risk Exposure of Domestic Producers

So far, this section has analyzed the exposure of firms to strategic risk—that is, the consequences of further improvements in vehicle fuel efficiency given a particular scenario. The next step is to analyze economic risk and address the question of which source of exposure is more critical to each firm.

Figures 7–10 and 7–11 contrast net income for the three domestic producers under the case in which they all engage in post-1985 retooling. Figures 7–12 and 7–13 do the same for the case in which there are no further rounds of retooling. From these figures, it is evident that the negative consequences of the oil-shock scenario for domestic earnings are more serious than the exposure created by the decision whether to retool or not given a particular scenario. By contrast, the improvement in performance under the oil-price-reduction scenario (which is more favorable to the industry) is minor.

From these results, two conclusions can be drawn. First, in terms of environmental risk, the "upside" potential of the oil-price-reduction scenario is minor in comparison with the "downside" potential of future oil shocks. This situation implies that the domestic industry as a whole has a significantly negative exposure as a result. Second, environmental risk tends to swamp the strategic risk. The change in performance that results from the decision whether to retool in the post-1985 period or not is much less significant than the impact upon performance that results from which scenario obtains. This result suggests the extent to which managers have less control and influence over the future performance of their firms than is sometimes supposed, since developments largely outside of their control have a greater influence on earnings.

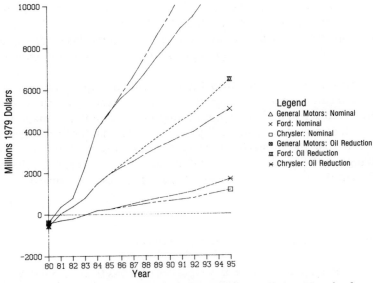

Figure 7–10. Net Income under Post-1985 Retooling—Nominal versus Oil-Price-Reduction Scenarios

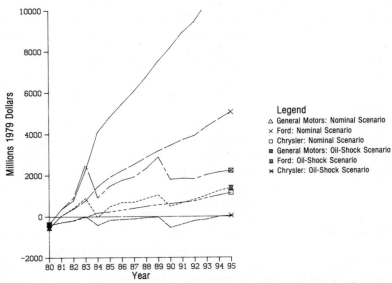

Figure 7–11. Net Income under Post-1985 Retooling—Nominal versus Oil-Shock Scenarios

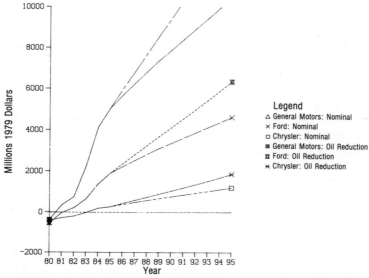

Figure 7–12. Net Income under No Post-1985 Retooling—Nominal versus Oil-Price-Reduction Scenarios

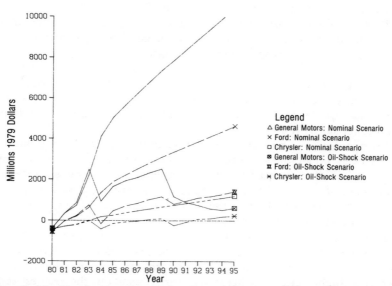

Figure 7–13. Net Income under No Post-1985 Retooling—Nominal versus Oil-Shock Scenarios

Trade Policy

This section evaluates the effects of trade restrictions within the context of the scenarios and strategies outlined above. There are two important reasons why evaluating the consequences of trade policies is critical to this analysis.

First, trade policies represent an important set of instruments available to policymakers for responding to the consequences of future oil shocks. Restraints upon the rapid and dramatic increase in Japanese market share that occur under the oil shock is one policy response. It is particularly necessary to relate this analysis to what has been revealed about the risk exposure of firms, since a critical question of policymakers is the degree to which trade policy alters the exposure of domestic firms. Since trade policy has a much shorter lead time than the lead time required for a second round of retooling, it or similar policy instruments may represent a flexible policy option for aiding the industry.

Second, it may be that trade policies were already imposed for some other reason and were part of the policy environment when an oil-market disruption occurred. In that case, the unexpected environmental change defines the risk exposure that the policies have created, not only for the firms in the industry but also for the policy itself and its intended consequences. It is important to understand these effects as well, because they illustrate the unintended consequences of policy that are oftentimes ignored.

To study these issues, this section examines the consequences of four trade-policy alternatives first examined in the context of the previous chapter within the context of the oil-shock scenario.

Figure 7–14 shows how Japanese market share changes under the different trade policies. As expected, quotas restrict Japanese expansion the most. As a result, sales by General Motors, Ford, and Chrysler are much higher under quotas than they are under other trade restraints, even though total market sales are lower than with tariffs.

Price increases as a result of trade restraints (table 7–7) are greatest for U.S. vehicles under the uniform tariff. For Japanese vehicles, the price increase is initially greatest for a tariff, but later quota-induced price hikes exceed those of tariffs. U.S. prices do not respond accordingly because for most of the model period under the oil-shock scenario the best U.S. supply response is constant vehicle prices.

Tariffs reduce the net worth of the Japanese position (table 7–8) the most. As in earlier analysis, this reduction occurs because much of the tariff burden is absorbed by the Japanese producers rather than being passed on in terms of higher prices. A luxury-car tariff results in the greatest reduction. This outcome is not entirely unexpected since small luxury cars are more profitable for the Japanese.

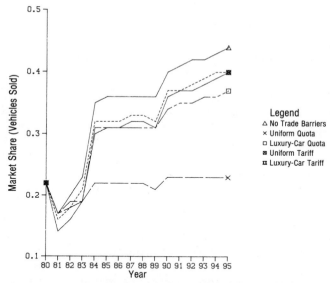

Figure 7-14. Japanese Market Share under Different Trade Policies, Oil-Shock Scenario/Post-1985 Retooling

Table 7-7
Price Changes due to Trade Policy
(in percent, from case with no trade restraints—1990 selling price)

	Japanese Small Basic Cars	Japanese Small Luxury Cars	U.S. Small Basic Cars	U.S. Small Luxury Cars	U.S. Large Basic Cars	U.S. Large Luxury Cars
Uniform quota	27.1	42.3	3.1	2.8	0.5	1.4
Luxury-car quota	3.3	36.3	2.4	2.8	0.4	1.2
Uniform tariff	12.5	13.5	3.6	3.2	0.6	1.6
Luxury-car tariff	-0.2	20.9	0.1	1.4	0.1	0.4

Regardless of whether domestic producers retool or do not retool, uniform quotas most improve domestic earnings (figures 7-15 through 7-17). Unlike the cases examined in the previous chapter, the effects of trade restrictions are significant. This improvement in domestic perfor-

Table 7-8
Net Present Value of Japanese Profits: 1985, 1990, 1995; Oil-Shock
Scenario and Trade Policy
(in billions of 1979 dollars)

	1985	1990	1995
Oil shock, uniform quota	40.8	71.6	94.1
Oil shock, luxury-car quota	42.6	78.5	105.9
Oil shock, uniform tariff	31.3	58.9	82.1
Oil shock, luxury-car tariff	30.5	56.3	77.9
Oil shock, no retooling, uniform quota	40.8	73.9	100.2
Oil shock, no retooling, uniform tariff	31.2	62.5	91.6

mance comes from two effects of the quota. First, the quota, by limiting
Japanese sales, prevents a large shift in unit volume away from the domestic
industry that would otherwise occur under the oil shock. In addition, the
quota increases domestic sale prices, increasing manufacturer revenue. A
uniform tariff also improves domestic prices, but is less effective in prevent-
ing volume shifts, which are critical to domestic profitability.

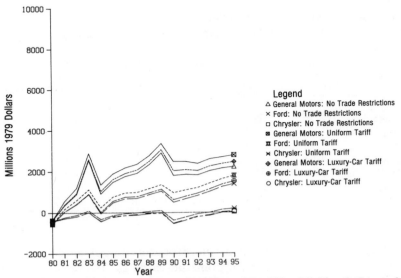

Figure 7-15. Net Income under Imposition of Tariffs, Oil-Shock Scenario/
Post-1985 Retooling

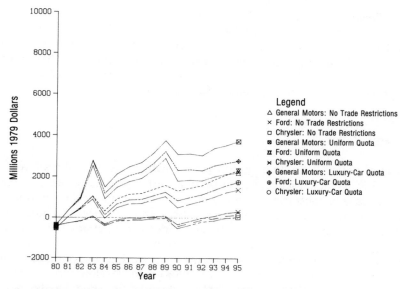

Figure 7–16. Net Income under Imposition of Quotas, Oil-Shock Scenario/Post-1985 Retooling

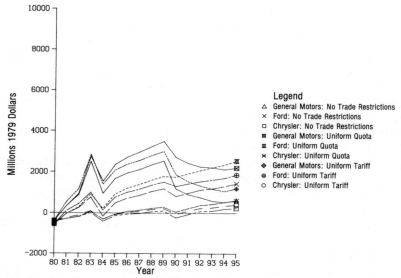

Figure 7–17. Net Income under Different Trade Policies, Oil-Shock Scenario/No Retooling

These results are much the same under the case with no post-1985 retooling. In this case, a uniform quota is especially effective in reducing GM's exposure. GM's performance relative to Ford's is most improved under a quota, suggesting that GM benefits relatively more than the other two producers in this case. This outcome is as expected, since GM is most exposed to volume losses under these conditions.

Energy Policy

Energy policy is another option government decision makers have in responding to the critical concerns of an uncertain energy future. The energy-policy case is contrasted with the oil-shock scenario by the smoothness of the transition to higher fuel prices. Although fuel prices ultimately rise to about the same level that they would under the oil-shock scenario, in the energy-policy scenario prices rise in a smooth manner. Furthermore, the economy is assumed to adjust to rising energy prices without a reduction in economic performance. Such a scenario could develop fortuitously, as a result, say, of OPEC policies. More directly, it could be the result of national policies designed to smooth out the bumps occasioned by oil shocks. The scenario envisioned is described in table 7–9. In the analysis that follows, two cases are presented, in which the domestic industry either does or does not retool.

Under the energy-policy scenario and best U.S. supply response (in which U.S. producers raise prices rather than accepting demand shifts (0.1 supply elasticity)), market sales and the mix of vehicles are similar to the nominal scenario, although sales are slightly lower. Japanese market share is also comparable to the nominal scenario. Manufacturer selling prices for vehicles (table 7–10) are lower under this scenario than under the nominal scenario, while the consumer cost (selling price plus operating cost) is almost constant. The consequence of higher fuel prices under the energy-policy scenario is to reduce the intensive demand of auto makers; manufacturers must compensate for higher fuel prices and consequently higher operating costs by restraining selling-price increases. These results apply whether manufacturers retool or not, although with retooling manufacturer selling prices are higher because the operating costs of more fuel-efficient vehicles are lower.

Figures 7–18 and 7–19 compare the net income for General Motors, Ford, and Chrysler under the energy-policy scenario with results for the oil-shock scenario. While performance under the energy-policy scenario is worse than under the nominal scenario as a result of reduced selling prices, it is significantly improved over the oil-shock scenario. Performance is improved because both unit sales and vehicle prices are higher under the

Table 7–9
Energy-Policy Scenario

Year	Inflation	Consumer Income	FRAUTO[a]	Fuel Prices	Domestic Productivity Increase	
					Labor	Capital
1980	13.5	0.0	.127	0.0	7.0	3.5
1981	11.0	1.2	.127	6.5	7.0	3.5
1982	10.5	2.9	.127	6.5	7.0	3.5
1983	10.0	2.6	.127	6.5	7.0	3.5
1984	8.5	3.2	.127	6.5	7.0	3.5
1985	8.1	4.2	.127	6.5	7.0	3.5
1986	8.2	3.3	.127	6.5	2.0	2.0
1987	8.0	2.9	.127	6.5	2.0	2.0
1988	8.0	2.8	.127	6.5	2.0	2.0
1989	8.0	6.5	.127	6.5	2.0	2.0
1990	7.8	2.1	.127	6.5	2.0	2.0
1991	7.8	2.1	.127	6.5	2.0	2.0
1992	7.8	2.1	.127	6.5	2.0	2.0
1993	7.8	2.1	.127	6.5	2.0	2.0
1994	7.8	2.1	.127	6.5	2.0	2.0
1995	7.8	2.1	.127	6.5	2.0	2.0
1996	7.8	2.1	.127	6.5	2.0	2.0
1997	7.8	2.1	.127	6.5	2.0	2.0

Source: Author's calculations

[a] *FRAUTO:* Fraction of consumer disposable income allocated to user-operated transportation.

Table 7–10
U.S. Vehicle Price Changes under Energy-Policy Scenario
(in percent, from nominal scenario)

	U.S. Small Basic Cars	U.S. Small Luxury Cars	U.S. Large Basic Cars	U.S. Large Luxury Cars
Energy policy and retooling				
Percent	−3.5	−3.6	−6.0	−3.3
Dollars	−324.2	−496.8	−680.3	−583.8
Energy policy and no retooling				
Percent	−4.6	−5.5	−7.9	−4.5
Dollars	−409.3	−718.1	−847.4	−763.4

energy-policy scenario. General Motors benefits the most from these developments, largely because it retains its profitable position in large basic cars. The improvement is most dramatic in the case without retooling.

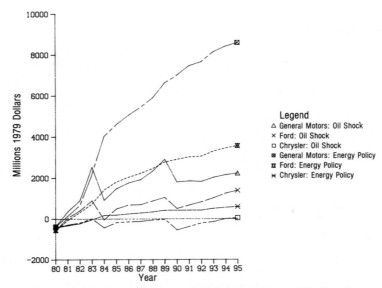

Figure 7-18. Net Income under Post-1985 Retooling—Oil-Shock/
Energy-Policy Scenarios

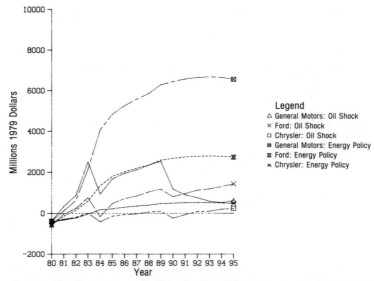

Figure 7-19. Net Income under No Post-1985 Retooling—Oil-Shock/
Energy-Policy Scenarios

It is clear from these results that high fuel prices by themselves are not fatal to the domestic industry; rather, it is the combined economic effects of an oil shock that are so injurious. While under the energy-policy scenario, domestic firms can adjust to shifts in demand through pricing and technology, the combination of events in the oil-shock scenario is too extreme for such a response to maintain their market positions. For policymakers, this fact suggests that they have available alternative policies.

Conclusions

The analytical results of this chapter may be summarized as follows:

1. Achieving higher levels of post-1985 fleet fuel economy appears to be both technologically and economically feasible for the domestic industry. While the level achieved depends upon the extent of mix shifts, fleet fuel economies of thirty-seven to forty-two miles per gallon appear practical, a result consistent with other analysis.

2. Domestic firms are exposed in very different ways to the risks of post-1985 retooling. General Motors is particularly exposed to the consequences of future oil shocks in the event that it does not retool in the post-1985 period. For both Ford and GM in general, a second round of fuel-economy improvements appears to improve performance under all of the cases examined. For Chrysler, however, the high capital costs of retooling increase its debt load so as to make retooling financially impossible.

3. The U.S. industry faces a critical downside exposure to environmental risk. Future oil shocks reduce profitability more than any other single development. Again, General Motors is particularly exposed to such developments. The Japanese industry does not share this exposure; in the case of oil shocks the net worth of its position is only modestly reduced.

4. There is a multiplicity of policy instruments, including quotas and energy policy, that appears to reduce the domestic industry's exposure to the consequences of oil shocks. These policies differentially affect domestic firms. General Motors most benefits from an energy policy, which preserves its position in large basic cars. Quotas are the most effective trade policies under an oil shock, forcing the preponderance of small-car sales onto U.S. firms. Ford and Chrysler are better positioned to benefit from this trend than GM.

A few further observations can be made about these results. First, as a caveat, these results may be sensitive to how shifts in market share are modeled. To the extent that consumers, when abandoning large cars for smaller vehicles in the face of increased prices, stay within the same manufacturer's line, the model may have overstated the exposure of the domestic industry to future market-mix shifts. The formulation used, however, is consistent with the market behavior of the past decade, which had seen a rough constancy in manufacturer share within each size class.

The results of this chapter clearly illustrate how the consequences of a particular choice of strategy or policy are critically dependent upon the scenario or on developments in other dimensions. For example, quotas, while not improving domestic-industry performance significantly in the context of an earlier chapter, were effective in the case of an oil shock in improving industry profitability. The effect of post–1985 fuel-economy improvements similarly varied depending on uncertain developments in future energy markets.

This observation is important for two reasons. First, it illustrates a freqently overlooked point—that the concept of risk exposure is relevant to public policy as well as firm strategy. The choice of policy, like the choice of strategy, defines the sorts of conditions that industrial policy is prepared to handle.

Second, although this analysis has examined strategies and policies within the context of a specific scenario, in fact decision makers may have to choose a course of action before they necessarily know what future market, policy, and competitive conditions will be. While the managerial and policymaking imperatives stemming from this problem will be discussed in the concluding chapter, it is clear from this analysis that the cost of being wrong in terms of choosing a strategy or policy inappropriate to the actual industry conditions may be very high.

Notes

1. U.S. Congress, Congressional Budget Office, *Fuel Economy Standards for New Passenger Cars After 1985* (Washington, D.C.: U.S. Government Printing Office, December 1980), pp. 1–3.

2. U.S. Department of Transportation, Office of the Assistant Secretary for Policy and International Affairs, *The U.S. Automobile Industry, 1980: Report to the President from the Secretary of Transportation* (Washington, D.C.: January 1981), p. 72.

3. Donald A. Hurter, *The Changing World Automotive Industry Through 2000* (Cambridge, Mass.: Arthur D. Little, January 1980), p. 2.

4. U.S. Congressional Budget Office, p. xiv.

5. Dr. S. William Gouse, *Seminar on Automobile Fuel Efficiency, Vol. I, Summary of Proceedings* (Washington, D.C.: Mitre Corp., 1978), p. 64; U.S. Congressional Budget Office, p. 5.

6. U.S. Congressional Budget Office, pp. 7–28.

7. Ibid., pp. 29–32.

8. John C. Sawhill, *Energy: Managing the Transition* (New York: The Trilateral Commission, 1978), p. 14.

9. U.S. Congress, Congressional Budget Office, *The World Oil Market in the 1980s: Implications for the United States* (Washington, D.C.: U.S. Government Printing Office), pp. 60–61 passim.

10. U.S. Congressional Budget Office, pp. xiv, 33; Daniel Yagin, ed., *The Dependence Dilemma: Gasoline Consumption and American Security* (Cambridge, Mass.: Center for International Affairs, Harvard University) p. 33; Bruce Rubinger, "Improving Automotive Energy Efficiency in the Post–1985 Period" (Cambridge, Mass.: Research and Special Programs Administration, Transportation Systems Center, May 1980), p. 12. (Type-written.)

11. U.S. Congressional Budget Office, pp. 53–55.

8 Other Government-Policy Initiatives

Government initiatives intended to address perceived social or economic problems associated with the industry are themselves a possible force for structural change. In this chapter some of these policy initiatives not considered in the context of previous chapters are analyzed. These areas include subsidies to the domestic industry, further cost reductions, a merger between Chrysler and Ford, and restrictions on the use of diesel engines. This chapter obviously examines only a fraction of the possible policy initiatives. Rather than attempting to catalog every conceivable consequence, however, the intent of the chapter is to further delineate the critical realities that shape the development of industrial policy through the examination of several policy proposals.

Subsidies

This section examines the consequences of subsidies designed to mitigate the effects of high levels of capital spending imposed upon the industry because of retooling or the achievement of other regulatory goals. Here the case is evaluated where either the government lends, at no interest, capital funds to domestic firms or provides a subsidy to pay for capital charges, so that the domestic firms effectively have a zero cost of capital. The intent of such a policy measure is to mitigate the burden of the extraordinarily high capital-spending requirements that fuel-economy conversion has imposed on the industry.

While this section analyzes the extreme case of an explicit subsidy, this formulation also partially applies to policy or strategic choices that only reduce the firm's cost of capital. Government-guaranteed loans or other factors that change the level of perceived risk facing firms and reduce the firm's effective cost of capital would be relevant here.

The results of this analysis are presented in figures 8-1 through 8-8, which outline the effects of a subsidy under several scenarios. In the nominal scenario, 0.1 supply-elasticity case (figure 8-1), subsidies have the greatest effect over the 1980–1985 period. This result is as expected, since capital-investment requirements and debt loads are highest over this period. Under the optimistic scenario, subsidies have less impact, since domestic firms have higher cash flows from operations, and hence lower debt loads.

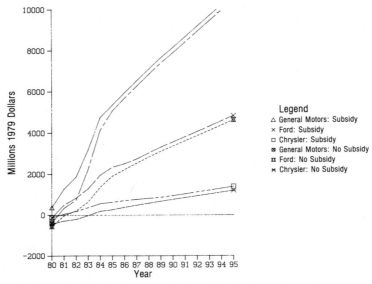

Figure 8-1. Net Income with Subsidies, Nominal Scenario

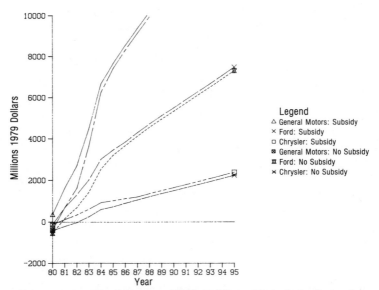

Figure 8-2. Net Income with Subsidies, Optimistic Scenario

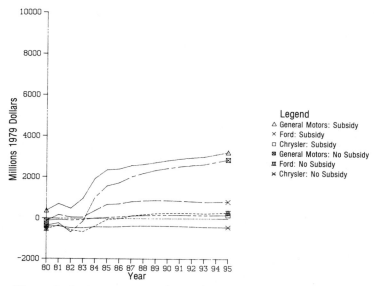

Figure 8–3. Net Income with Subsidies, Pessimistic Scenario

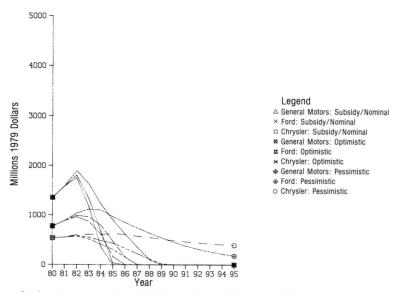

Figure 8–4. Amount of Subsidies to U.S. Firms, Different Scenarios/
0.1 Supply Elasticity

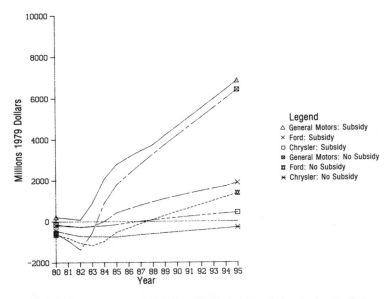

Figure 8-5. Net Income with Subsidies, Nominal Scenario/Infinite Supply Elasticity

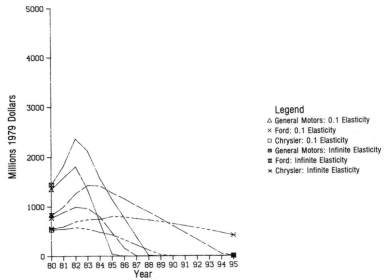

Figure 8-6. Amount of Subsidies to U.S. Firms, Nominal Scenario/ 0.1, Infinite Supply Elasticity

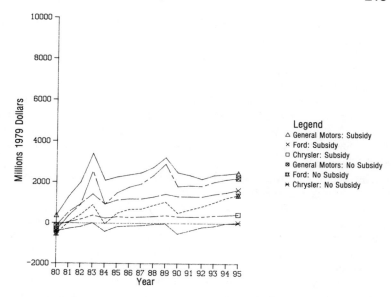

Figure 8-7. Net Income with Subsidies, Oil-Shock Scenario/Post-1985 Retooling

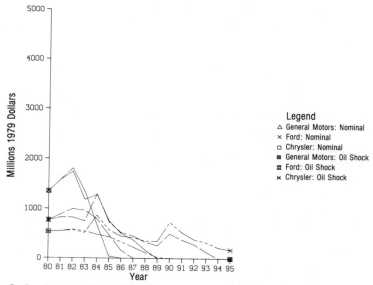

Figure 8-8. Amount of Subsidies to U.S. Firms, Nominal/Oil-Shock Scenarios—0.1 Supply Elasticity

Subsidies have a more dramatic effect when industry conditions are poor (figure 8-3), as with the pessimistic scenario. In this case, a subsidy makes Ford operations financially viable rather than marginal, and Chrysler earns a positive, albeit small, profit. Both Chrysler and Ford benefit proportionately more from the subsidies than does GM. General Motors' greater financial and market strength means that its debt load is proportionately lighter than that of the other two firms. Figure 8-4 shows the magnitude of this subsidy for each firm over time under different economic conditions. Note that while with the nominal and optimistic scenarios the subsidies are only temporary, under the pessimistic scenario both Ford and Chrysler become substantial and seemingly permanent pensioners.

Two points emerge from these results. First is that subsidies of this form are a very inefficient way of improving domestic-firm performance. The magnitude of the subsidy ranges to over $35 billion during the early 1980s. Furthermore, such subsidies are not necessarily temporary measures. If demand is low, subsidies of over $1 billion continue to be payed to Ford and Chrysler.

Figures 8-5 through 8-8 present two further cases delineating the effect of subsidies. In the first (figure 8-5), the industry keeps real average prices constant (infinite supply elasticity), but accepts a subsidy. This case might be considered within the context of policy efforts to reconcile consumer interests in lower prices with policy concerns about industry viability. In other words, in exchange for a subsidy the industry might agree not to raise prices (0.1 supply elasticity). The effects upon General Motors' profitability are significant during the period of retooling but are less so afterwards. For both Ford and Chrysler, subsidies result in a major increase in profitability and viability.

While the shift in pricing response has obvious benefits for consumers in terms of lower prices and higher market sales, it exacts a substantial financial cost, as a comparison of magnitude of the subsidy under the two cases reveals (figure 8-6) substantial subsidies to both Ford and Chrysler. Under restrained industry pricing, subsidies are over five billion dollars yearly in the early 1980s. Perhaps more significant, even under demand conditions consistent with current predictions, subsidies prove not to be just a transitory measure. In 1995, subsidies to Ford have just ended, and Chrysler still requires assistance.

The final case (figures 8-7 and 8-8) examines the effect of subsidies in changing firm exposure to oil shocks. For both Chrysler and Ford, subsidies improve the level of earnings, and perhaps just as significantly, reduce their variance. The net result is to turn one marginal firm and one clearly unviable firm into profitable operations. Proportionately, the two smaller firms benefit more than General Motors, because the reduction in General Motors' earnings reflects more shifts in market segments than the effects of high levels of capital spending.

In conclusion, the net effects of subsidies as formulated here is to reduce the financial exposure of each of the domestic firms, although the smaller firms benefit proportionately more. The analysis suggests, however, that a subsidy of this form would not be merely a transitory measure if future industry conditions do not develop along optimistic lines. Ford and Chrysler especially have the capability of becoming permanent pensioners. The analysis also illustrates how inefficient subsidies of this form are as a means of improving industry performance. Subsidies may be an appropriate policy response if the industry is regarded as undergoing a temporary disruption due to conversion to higher fuel economy. It is less clear that they are an appropriate response to the pressures for long-term structural change.

What is captured in this analysis, however, is not only the effect of subsidies, but, perhaps more importantly, the financial market's valuation of the riskiness of each firm. If policymakers or managers can reduce this perceived risk, then firms may receive some of the same sorts of benefits outlined without the need for explicit interventions.

This point is relevant because, although explicit subsidies may improve financial performance, they may also have the effect of increasing firm exposure to dimensions of political risk. Subsidies are both a highly visible and controversial form of policy intervention, and the political consequences of such a move should be recognized. Other policy or strategic responses that have the same effect without increasing the degree of political exposure may be preferable.

Extreme Industry Cost Reductions

This section evaluates the consequences of a much more extensive reduction of domestic manufacturing costs than has been considered in earlier analyses. Here, domestic-cost reductions by 1985 are such that the real domestic variable labor cost of manufacturing a subcompact car equals the estimated current equivalent Japanese cost (corresponding approximately to a $500 cost reduction in addition to the other cost reductions first included in the base case).[1] These cost reductions are extreme and probably beyond the ability of the individual firms to achieve them. To the extent that such cost reductions are at all possible, they would probably require some form of government intervention. Such reductions could be the result of a variety of developments, including:

Government action to restrain real wages,

Reduction of the regulatory burden,

Redistribution of the social-welfare costs of regulation (for example, through value-added taxes),

Changes in antitrust enforcement to allow shared research and development,

Changes in tax policy (for example, depreciation, amortization, and investment tax credits).

The exact form that the specific cost reductions would take is unspecified.

Comparisons of domestic net income for several different scenarios under these extreme cost reductions and earlier assumptions about cost reductions are given in figures 8–9 to 8–11. The consequences of extreme cost reductions can be easily summarized. Unlike subsidies, cost reductions have a roughly proportional impact upon the profitability of each of the domestic firms. By increasing the general level of earnings, the risk exposure of the industry is reduced under the pessimistic and oil-shock scenarios. However, without industry price increases (that is, noninfinite supply elasticities), extreme cost reductions are still not sufficient to improve Chrysler's position to anything more than a marginal producer.

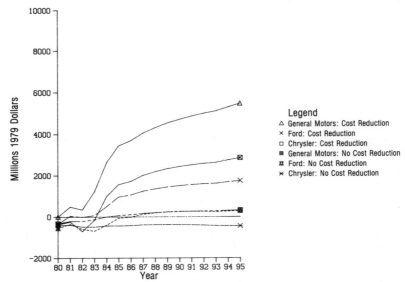

Figure 8–9. Net Income under Extreme Industry Cost Reductions, Pessimistic Scenario/No Post-1985 Retooling

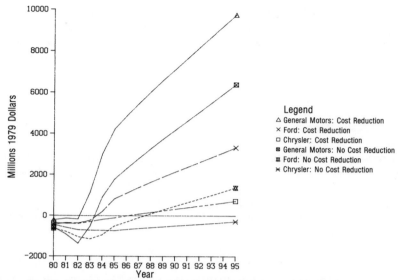

Figure 8–10. Net Income under Extreme Industry Cost Reductions, Nominal Scenario/Infinite Supply Elasticity

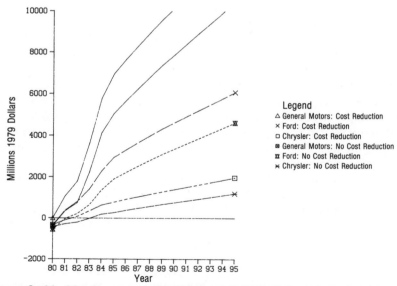

Figure 8–11. Net Income under Extreme Industry Cost Reductions, Oil-Shock Scenario/No Post-1985 Retooling

This result reinforces the conclusion made throughout this analysis that the domestic industry faces the potential for significant structural change. Even with cost reductions far in excess of those considered in the chapter 5 base case, the analysis indicates that the current structure of the industry is still unstable.

Ford-Chrysler Merger

This section evaluates the consequences of a merger between the North American operations of Ford and Chrysler. While earlier analysis suggests that General Motors will remain a profitable industry leader under most circumstances, Ford sometimes appears marginal, and there are serious questions as to Chrysler's viability. The advantages of a combination between the two smaller firms might include greater volume for the combined firm and a more complete and competitive product line, with Chrysler's front-wheel compact filling a gap in the Ford product line. The success of such a merger, however, would be affected by several uncertainties. These uncertainties include the extent to which operating synergies would in fact be achieved, whether the market share of the merged firm would equal the market share of the two firms separately, and the manner in which the financial structures of the operations would be consolidated.

To bound the discussion, two extreme cases are established. In one, a Chrysler-Ford merger results in perfect synergies. Ford gets Chrysler's market share, plus those segments of Chrysler's product line that Ford is currently lacking. The resulting firm has Ford's lower cost position. In the alternative case, there are no synergies; the result of a combination is the same as adding the separate net incomes of the two firms together.

The no-synergy case results in the amalgamation of two smaller losers into one larger loser. This conclusion is obvious from earlier analysis and so is not presented. In fact, to the extent that a merger may increase costs (for example, the need to pension redundant workers), this analysis may underestimate the magnitude of losses.

Under optimal conditions, however (figures 8-12, 8-13, 8-14), a Chrysler-Ford combination is much more profitable than the two firms separately. These results are critically dependent upon the additional volume the combined firm has, more than upon any savings in capital-development costs. A second critical factor that influences these results is the cost structure.

The point of this exercise is not to argue either for or against a Chrysler-Ford merger, as there are numerous other subtleties that have been left out of the analysis. It is important to note, however, the degree to which the success of this merger is a function of the synergies obtained. Policymakers

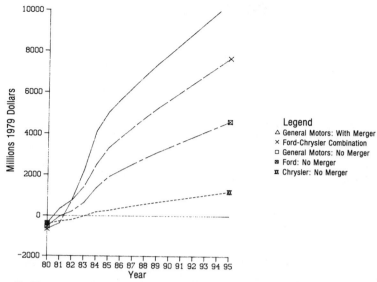

Figure 8–12. Net Income under Ford-Chrysler Merger, Nominal Scenario/
No Post-1985 Retooling

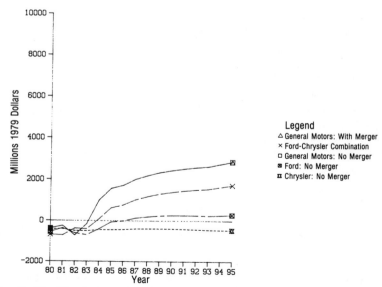

Figure 8–13. Net Income under Ford-Chrysler Merger, Pessimistic
Scenario/No Post-1985 Retooling

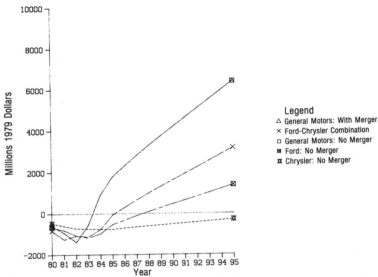

Figure 8-14. Net Income under Ford-Chrysler Merger, Nominal Scenario/ Infinite Supply Elasticity

would certainly have a large role to play in the structuring of any Ford-Chrysler deal, (if only because of the existing loan guarantee) and, hence, in the ability of the combined firm to achieve the necessary synergies. This involvement of policymakers in structuring the merger means that policymakers are implicitly accepting part of the risk of whether the combination will be successful or not. The high degree to which the success of the merger depends upon such synergies suggests that the amount of risk policymakers are exposed to in this case may not be small.

Restrictions on Diesel Engines

Diesel engines are characterized by different emissions from those of the more common gasoline engine, including higher levels of NO_x and particulates. Although the 1977 Clean Air Act Amendments relax NO_x standards to permit the use of diesel-engine technology,[2] concerns about the effects of these emissions, together with the absence of technological advances in diesel engines, could lead to further regulatory limits on diesel engine penetration. To estimate how this regulatory initiative would change the exposure of the industry, this section considers the case in which diesel penetration is limited to 1980 levels, keeping diesel cars at only a small percent of the market.

Such restrictions have minor effects on firm performance (figures 8-15 and 8-16) except in the event that an oil shock precipitates further rounds of fuel economy improvement (figure 8-17). In that case, the effect of a diesel ban is to deny a principal dimension of the strategic responses of firms to the need for increased fuel economy. As a consequence, without extensive diesel penetration average fuel economy with retooling is between thirty-five and thirty-seven miles per gallon instead of thirty-nine to forty-two miles per gallon.

General Motors is the loser from these developments. The improved fuel economy from diesel engines is especially important in increasing both the intensive demand and unit sales of the large basic-car segment. Restrictions on this technological response are therefore similar in effect, although less severe, to a failure to engage in post-1985 retooling.

This example illustrates two themes recurring throughout the analysis. First, it illustrates the manner in which policy proposals alter the risk exposure of the affected sector. In this case diesel restrictions have no negative effects under most of the scenarios examined. It is only in the event of oil shocks and the need for further fuel-economy improvement that the domes-

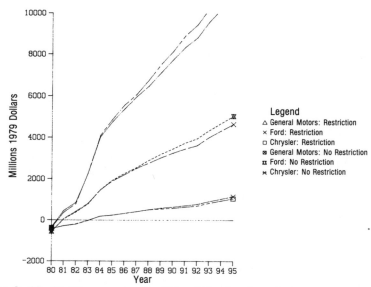

Figure 8-15. Net Income under Diesel-Engine Restrictions, Nominal
Scenario/Post-1985 Retooling

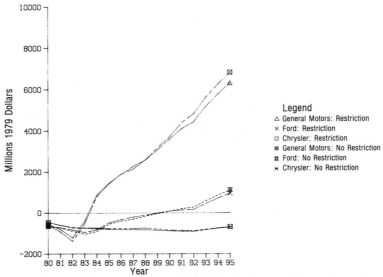

Figure 8-16. Net Income under Diesel-Engine Restrictions, Nominal
Scenario/Infinite Supply Elasticity

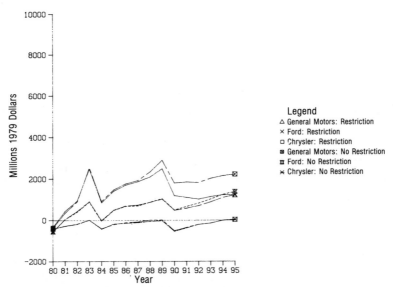

Figure 8-17. Net Income under Diesel-Engine Restrictions, Oil-Shock
Scenario/Post-1985 Retooling

tic industry is exposed as a result of these policy actions. This section further exemplifies the differential impacts of individual policy initiatives. By virtue of its market position in larger cars, which are more sensitive to fuel-economy-related issues, General Motors is uniquely exposed to these policy impacts.

Conclusions

As noted in the introduction, the intent of this chapter has been to further delineate the critical realities that shape the development of industrial policy. Beyond the specifics of each of the policy proposals, three key points emerge from the analysis of these impacts.

First is to note again how the achievement of legitimate social goals can alter the exposure to risk of individual firms. Obviously, by virtue of addressing issues of public health through restrictions on diesel engines there was created a set of exposures in other areas that were quite serious for one producer. More subtly, by employing subsidies to improve industry performance, the result may be an increase in the political exposure of the industry. These effects are dependent upon the unique characteristics of the individual policy. For example, both subsidies and other government-induced cost reductions have the net effect of altering favorably the cost structure of the domestic industry. The sorts of exposure that result from these measures, however, may be very different.

A second and perhaps less obvious point is that reductions or shifts in the locus of risk in themselves form a legitimate goal of government policy. Reductions in the perceived financial risk of firms, for example, may improve industry performance as much as any direct policy intervention. While the manner in which the magnitude and locus of risk may be changed is undoubtedly a difficult and subtle policy problem, this difficulty does not obviate the essential conclusion.

Finally, it is important to recognize how the choice of character of public policy critically determines not only impacts on firms, but also the degree and character of risk facing policymakers. In other words, policymakers face risk as well, and the choice of regulatory initiatives determines their individual exposure. For example, to the extent that cost reductions depend upon successful government intervention, the net effect is to shift some of the risk usually borne by firms onto policymakers. If cost reductions result from lower real wages than the industry would have been able to obtain on its own, government decision makers have in effect assumed a share of the risk normally borne by the individual firms in their labor policies. A second example regards a Ford-Chrysler combination. In this analysis, it has been argued that the effectiveness of such a combination critically depends upon its ability to achieve synergies. The part played by government regulation and policies in influencing or determining the ability of a merged firm to achieve synergies again effectively shifts at least a portion of the risk inherent in the merger onto policymakers. Whether policymakers either wish to or are prepared to accept this risk and the manner in which they respond to it are issues critical to an effective formulation of industrial policy.

Notes

1. William J. Abernathy, James E. Harbour, and Jay M. Henn, *Productivity and Comparative Cost Advantage: Some Estimates for Major Automotive Producers,* Report to the Transportation Systems Center, Department of Transportation (Cambridge, Mass.: December 1980).

2. *Automotive News,* 10 March 1980, p. 2.

9

Implications for Managers and Policymakers

The past decade has witnessed significant change in the domestic auto industry as a result of government policies, the rise of foreign competition, changes in underlying factor costs, and strategic shifts. The results of this analysis indicate that in the future the rapid pace of change may continue. An understanding of these issues of structural change is complicated by the wide range of forces that influence the ultimate results. Nonetheless, increased concerns about the consequences of structural change have challenged policymakers and managers to shape industrial policies and corporate strategies that recognize and respond effectively to these realities.

Earlier chapters have examined the specific impacts of both public policy and firm strategic choices on the structural integrity of the U.S. automotive industry. This chapter summarizes the results and discusses conclusions for policymakers, managers, and analysts.

Future Risk Exposure of the Automobile Industry

This analysis has suggested that, contrary to some current thinking, future changes in industry structure may under the appropriate circumstances be both extensive and radical in scope. The results indicate that a return of future industry conditions to historic levels or trends may not lead to a return of historic levels of profitability. Indeed, under business-as-usual conditions the analysis suggests that an industry structure dominated by General Motors and foreign or U.S.-controlled overseas production appears to be more financially viable than the current structure of the industry.

The form future structural change may take is difficult to predict, since it depends upon numerous uncertain and complex developments. The effects of some of the possible forces for structural change were analyzed earlier, including the future strategies of Japanese firms, uncertainties in petroleum markets, and government regulatory initiatives.

For both managers and policymakers, the potential for significant structural change in such a key sector of the economy poses a number of challenges for the effective choice of strategy and policy. Below are sum-

225

marized some of the possible future developments in the automobile industry that earlier chapters have identified, plus some comments about the sorts of strategies and policies that may be used.

Automobile demand: It is perhaps axiomatic to note, and the results of this analysis confirm, that increased levels of automotive demand improve the performance of the domestic auto industry. These results also indicate, however, that even with high levels of future demand the industry may still have the potential for further structural change.

This seemingly straightforward observation presents policymakers with a complex array of choices as to how best to achieve desired results and recognize the side effects of policy choices. The analysis suggests that improvements in domestic-firm performance are greatest when U.S. producers respond to increasing demand by raising unit prices rather than increasing volume. A possible equity conflict exists between producers, workers, and consumers, in which concerns about the financial viability of the industry argue for pricing policies that are inimical to consumer and worker interests.

The results also suggest that the risk exposure of domestic firms to the uncertain future level of demand varies considerably, assuming that U.S. producers continue to follow the strategies evaluated here. General Motors is financially viable under the range of future demand conditions. Ford's domestic operations are much more exposed to this risk; if demand is low, they incur substantial losses. Under all except the best circumstances, Chrysler sustains prolonged losses.

Fuel economy: Based upon already announced manufacturer plans, domestic firms will achieve fleet fuel-economy averages close to thirty miles per gallon by 1985. With a second round of retooling after that, they can reasonably achieve fleet averages between thirty-seven and forty-two miles per gallon, depending upon fleet mix.

It is frequently argued that post-1985 fuel-economy standards are necessary if domestic producers are to maintain competitiveness with foreign-chartered competitors. This analysis suggests that the consequences of post-1985 fuel-economy improvements involve a complex set of competitive and policy issues.

The set of possible manufacturer fuel-economy-improvement strategies examined here reflects the characteristics of the current CAFE standards, the most prominent characteristic being its focus on average fleet fuel economy. Since average fleet fuel-economy levels depend both upon the fuel-economy ratings of individual vehicles and the composition of fleet mix, shifts in market mix towards less fuel-efficient vehicles can frustrate regulatory compliance. While both this analysis and others indicate that market forces will most likely compliment compliance with the 1985 standards, the post-1985 situation is less clear.

Without post-1985 CAFE standards, manufacturers can respond to the pressures for greater fuel efficiency in several ways. Besides technological increases in fuel economy, manufacturers might instead reduce sales prices to compensate for low gas mileage, so as to keep the total cost to the consumer the same. The financial consequences of these different responses will depend upon the level of future energy prices and the character of market demand. If fuel prices fall, the analysis indicates that post-1985 fuel-economy improvements are financially unrewarding for domestic firms. Alternatively, higher fuel prices compliment a move toward greater vehicle fuel efficiency and so improve financial performance.

The imposition of post-1985 CAFE standards would reduce the strategic options available to firms. It is not necessarily true, however, that this reduction in strategic options is a bad thing. The crux of the issue is what happens to fuel prices. If future fuel prices rise, a second round of CAFE standards would compliment the preferred strategies of U.S. producers. The regulations would also provide a clear signal to the firms as to what strategy they should pursue, a not unimportant issue given long product lead times for fuel-economy improvement. Conversely, if fuel prices fall in the future, further CAFE standards would lock manufacturers into a poor position. The point that emerges, therefore, is that the choice of future fuel economy standards should be closely linked to a consideration of future energy prices and policies.

There are also substantial joint effects between policy actions in energy, fuel economy, emissions, and trade issues. The analysis of emissions-based restrictions on diesel-engine penetration illustrates a direct conflict between the attainment of different regulatory goals. Diesel restrictions reduced attainable average fleet fuel economy by four to five miles per gallon in the post-1985 period, sacrificing energy conservation for emissions reductions. Furthermore, restricting diesels has unintended and adverse impacts on corporate performance. While Ford and Chrysler are unaffected, GM's profitability is reduced dramatically under some but not all sets of future conditions.

Trade policy in the form of quotas was shown to reduce the exposure of domestic firms to the consequences of oil shocks. However, while improving domestic firm financial performance, quotas were clearly inimical to the achievement of a number of other valid policy goals. By limiting Japanese sales, an important source of more fuel-efficient vehicles, quotas might work directly against the achievement of broader energy goals, even if they do not constrain the attainment of firm-specific fuel-economy requirements. By increasing prices, quotas might reduce market sales, possibly discouraging the scrapping of less fuel-efficient vehicles. Higher prices and low vehicle sales may also run counter to broader macroeconomic concerns. The model results may understate these negative effects, particularly if domestic producers are also capacity constrained in smaller vehicles.

Trade policy and foreign-firm strategies: There is a critical need for effective policy analysis to recognize strategic choices as a function both of developments in the domestic market and of the broader international context of the auto industry. In the automobile industry the particular strategies Japanese producers choose to pursue in the U.S. market are a major factor influencing the future viability of domestic production. The analysis suggests that the Japanese producers will remain a significant competitive force in the future U.S. market. Japanese competitive advantage in dimensions of both cost and perceived product quality underlie these analytical results.

These results suggest that further cost reductions and improvements in perceived vehicle quality may form important dimensions of competitive success in the future for domestic producers.

Several different trade policies, including quotas, tariffs, and local-content requirements, were analyzed. While the results are summarized elsewhere, a few significant points stand out. First is to note how critically dependent the results are both on the specific form of the trade policy and on the strategy of Japanese producers. In general, tariffs had little direct impact upon domestic financial performance because the projected Japanese pricing response was to absorb a significant part of the tariff. The effects of tariffs in the analysis may be understated, however, if sharp tariff-based reductions in the profitability of Japanese participation in the U.S. market force strategic change within the Japanese industry.

Uniform quotas had much more impact in the analysis, both in the event of an oil shock and in the case of Japanese share expansion. Local-content requirements had little immediate effect since resulting Japanese cost increases did not occur until the mid-1980s due to the lead times involved in such regulations.

Less straightforward is the manner in which the form of trade policy either compliments or works against the strategies of foreign firms. Uniform quotas, by encouraging a shift towards luxury cars in the composition of the Japanese fleet, compliments evolving Japanese strategies. It is less clear what sorts of responses tariffs may engender, but by reducing the profitability of Japanese exports tariffs indirectly may encourage significant strategic change. Similarly, the analytical results do not capture the potentially wrenching effect U.S. local-content regulation might have on the manufacturing and managerial structure of Japanese firms. Local-content requirements would force the Japanese into a worldwide decentralized manufacturing structure whose effective management would require organizational and managerial skills—to say nothing of a manufacturing infrastructure—that the Japanese auto firms do not currently have.

There are several other issues that, while not dealt with in the analytical results here, are also important to mention. One relates to whether trade restraints are *general* or *country specific*. Country-specific restraints, while more difficult to enforce effectively, also encourage the movement of capacity to other locales. Such diversified manufacturing systems work against the current strategic capabilities of the Japanese auto makers, while complimenting the strategies of U.S.-chartered multinationals. Country-specific trade restraints may also have far less impact on the U.S. market than general restraints, since imports from other than the restrained national industry can substitute for the vehicle imports under restraint. To the extent that the concern centers about Japanese imports rather than all auto imports, policymakers may prefer country-specific actions.

Another issue concerns the timing of trade policy and the distortions that can result from expectation about either the beginning or end of a trade restraint. The level of quotas or voluntary export restraints are frequently based upon recent historical results. A rational response by firms anticipating the imposition of a quota is to increase imports to as high a level as possible so as to better their position under the restraint. The effect of an anticipated quota therefore may be to worsen the perceived problem.

The broader point is that the choice of trade policy to pursue—whether it be trade restraints or benign neglect—must be inextricably tied to the need to recognize both the direct and indirect effects.

Cost reductions and other issues: Two other topics—cost reductions and consolidation of the domestic industry—were discussed. While this set of topics does not by any means exhaust the list of possible developments, it does further illustrate how policy initiatives alter the strategic exposure and risk structure of individual firms.

The analysis considered three different forms of cost reduction: those that other more detailed analysis has considered it possible for the industry to achieve on its own, subsidies in addition to the industry cost reduction, and cost reductions whose achievement would probably require government intervention. The obvious and again almost axiomatic conclusion is that cost reductions improve the financial performance of the domestic manufacturers. The broader issue concerns the exact form that these cost reductions would take and the implications for corporate risk exposure of the industry. For example, subsidies increase the exposure of the industry to political developments, since subsidies by their very nature are both a highly visible and controversial form of government involvement. Should extreme cost reductions result from reductions in real wages greater than those the industry on its own could achieve, government policy has effectively taken over part of the firm's labor policy, traditionally an area of managerial discretion.

The net effect, in these and other cases, is that there is a shifting of risk exposure that is dependent upon the exact form that the cost reductions take. Depending upon the conditions, it may be that cost reductions are not unambiguously favorable to the long-run viability of domestic producers.

The limited analysis done here of a Ford-Chrysler consolidation suggests the extent to which the success of such a venture depends upon how much synergy is possible to achieve. To the extent that these factors are outside of managerial discretion, and concern public policy, risk is shifted onto policymakers.

Implications for Managers and Policymakers

The results presented here challenge both the view that the problems of the U.S. auto industry are transitory and the notion that the disappearance of automotive manufacturing capability in North America is inevitable. The industry's future instead depends upon the numerous dimensions of uncertain developments, many of them outside of any direct influence by either managers or domestic policymakers. While the importance of these exogenous factors to the long-term viability of the industry may lead some observers to conclude either that changes in public policy and firm strategy are not needed, or that they would accomplish little, this analysis suggests that the issues are more complex. The turmoil of structural change the industry is undergoing compel both private and public decision makers to make some fundamental adjustments in the broader framework of their decision making.

Lessons for Managers

A sophisticated understanding of the implications and effects of strategic choice in the process of structural change is crucial if managers are to act in an effective and responsible manner. Such a sophisticated understanding hinges upon the recognition of several key points that this analysis has identified.

First is to note the manner in which strategic and public policy choices define the risk exposure of individual firms. With General Motors, for example, failure to engage in post-1985 retooling exposes the firm to significant risk in the event that future disruptions in petroleum markets occur. Less obvious but also important is that, to the degree that consumer loyalty is linked to perceived quality, the failure by domestic firms to effectively address the perception of poor quality can lead to reduced performance. This concept of exposure also applies to policy developments, where its effects are probably less well recognized and sometimes subtle. For example, subsidies clearly improve firm financial performance, and managers concerned with the extraordinary capital requirements for retooling may find such a temporary measure appealing. However, by virture of their visible and controversial nature, subsidies create a new dimension of political risk exposure for individual firms. A change in political sentiment may result in changes in the level or form of subsidies, for example, or government support may be tied to requirements in other so-called social dimensions of firm performance and behavior. The net effect may be to change the performance or increase the risk of individual firms, perhaps in unexpected ways.

It is important to understand that these issues have nothing to do with normative concerns about the relative merits of various forms of government intervention or free enterprise. The point is that these consequences, though sometimes both subtle and complex, may have very real operating consequences for the firms' performance.

The second point is that these effects may differ among firms in the industry. Strategic choice defines the firms' exposure to risk. For example, by virture of its strong position in the large-car market, General Motors is uniquely exposed to regulatory or economic developments affecting this segment. Chrysler's weak financial position exposes the firm to substantial financial risk if extraordinary post-1985 retooling is required.

Exposure may be positive as well. The results of this analysis indicate, for example, that Ford proportionately benefits the most from quotas or local-content requirements imposed upon Japanese producers. The implication is that, from the managerial perspective, public policy may be viewed as a source of corporate competitive advantage. Separate from its broader social perspective, the differential effects of policy create possible further dimensions of competitive interaction that managers can exploit.

This observation is particularly important because of the manner in which the choice of corporate strategy may influence the determination of policy. In subtle fashion corporate-strategy conditions the success, cost, and focus of government actions. The current product strategies and capital-investment plans of domestic auto makers, for example, may condition the form of future regulatory responses in fuel economy. The multinational nature of U.S.-chartered auto producers may focus policy attention on issues of foreign sourcing and the ultimate competitiveness of domestic manufacturing more rapidly—and in different ways—than if U.S.-chartered firms were strictly domestic. To the extent that policy reacts to developments in the industry, strategic choices may help condition those policy actions. It must be emphasized that these effects are entirely separate from political efforts to influence government action.

The third point is that under some circumstances managers may have little control over the destiny of their firms. Two separate cases in the analysis illustrate this point. The first concerns the future level of vehicle demand. While General Motors' domestic operations performed well under the range of projected demand conditions, the future viability of Ford and

and Chrysler as U.S. producers depended much more critically on the level of demand. There is little that Ford and Chrysler managers can do to influence this situation. The second case relates to uncertainties in future petroleum markets. The change in performance for each of the U.S. firms resulting from the decision to engage or not in post-1985 retooling was far less significant than the impact of alternative energy futures. Petroleum price, and not the managerial decision about product configuration, is the critical factor in this case.

This managerial powerlessness in turn has implications for the degree of corporate risk exposure. Risk is increased if the fate of the firm is largely outside the control of its managers. A relevant managerial issue then becomes whether or not it is desirable to maintain a U.S. manufacturing base if the operations have a very high risk exposure. This concern may be particularly relevant for Ford. The results of the analysis suggest that its U.S. operations may be particularly vulnerable to events outside its managerial control. Within the context of Ford's worldwide structure managers may question whether this high degree of risk exposure is desirable.

Lessons for Policymakers

Efforts to develop effective policy responses to structural change must be conditioned by a recognition of the substantial strategic implications of industrial policy. Whatever choices of policy are made should be cognizant of the following critical realities that shape the choices that can and cannot be made effectively.

First, the choice of policy can have substantial indirect and differential impacts upon the performance of individual firms. For example, efforts to address legitimate social concerns about air pollution through restrictions upon diesel engines have a profound and negative impact upon General Motors' profitability, and even viability, if future oil shocks occur. Trade policies designed to restrict Japanese imports so as to improve domestic-firm performance may in fact encourage strategic shifts within the Japanese industry that work to the long-run detriment of domestic production.

The second critical reality of industrial policy is that it shifts and changes the composition of risk, not only between firms but also between the private and public sectors. For example, the limited analysis of a Ford-Chrysler merger illustrates how risk associated with the success of such a venture may end up being shifted from managers onto public policymakers. Subsidies, a highly visible and politically controversial form of support for the industry, increase the political exposure of the industry. If extensive industry cost reductions are partially achieved through government encouragement of real wage reduction, then policymakers have implicitly accepted part of the risk traditionally accepted by firms in their labor policies.

Both of these points are particularly important because of the political sensitivity to equity concerns. This research has illustrated under numerous guises the manner in which choices of public policy create winners and losers—sometimes dramatically—within the industry. What also emerged is how policy measures designed to improve industry viability affect outside groups. For example, industry pricing practices that most improve profitability also result in sharply higher consumer prices. To the extent that the political process is not equipped to make the sorts of hard choices that may be required, an industrial policy attempting to resolve these conflicts at best may prove ineffective.

A third issue is the extent to which policymakers may under some circumstances be the controlling force of industry developments. Just as managers may sometimes be powerless, the choice of policy may be a much more critical dimension than is generally supposed.

For example, the existence of an energy policy smoothing the transitional pressures of an oil-market disruption appears to be the determining factor in domestic-industry performance regardless of what fuel-economy strategies the firms pursue.

This point emphasizes how critical the effective choice of policy can be to the future viability and evolution of the domestic industry. The results of this analysis suggest that there are certain dimensions along which policymakers should play an active and dynamic role if they are to be effective in aiding the future viability of the domestic industry.

A final lesson for policymakers is that a legitimate goal of policy may be to encourage strategic shifts within foreign firms. The analysis suggests that changes in Japanese strategy, and not trade policy itself, ultimately affect domestic-industry performance. Trade policy is most effective only as a means of changing strategy. With most Japanese auto makers heavily dependent on exports to the U.S., the ability of U.S. policymakers to control access to this market implicitly gives the substantial leverage on the strategies that foreign firms pursue. The results of this research suggest that the use of such influence may play a significant role in improving the viability of domestic producers.

Risk Exposure and Risk Hedging

A broad theme of this analysis is the extent to which uncertain or unpredictable developments in other dimensions affect the success of policy and strategic choices. For example, quotas are far more effective in improving domestic-industry performance in the event of an oil-supply disruption than they are under other possible future conditions. A strategy of post-1985 retooling similarly has dramatically different results depending upon conditions in oil prices and supplies.

This point is crucial because of its implications for the choice of effective policy and strategies. Effective strategies and policies should be robust under a wide range of different conditions—in other words, the choice of strategy or policy should be responsive to the full range of possible risks that it faces. The analysis here has examined selected strategies and policies against well-defined scenarios. In fact, however, decision makers face a generally uncertain future environment. This uncertainty results not only from uncontrollable exogenous events (for example, oil-market disruptions) but also from the actions of other industry participants. To the extent that both policy and strategy have inherent in them a degree of momentum, either due to institutional or physical factors, neither governments nor firms can instantaneously alter their positions to fit a new set of circumstances. For example, long product lead times mean that several years may elapse before a manufacturer can respond to the demand for increased vehicle fuel economy. In government policy, political or institutional factors may similarly limit the flexibility of policy actions.

This statement implies that effective policy or strategy should perform well under the range of different conditions that they may likely face. In practice, this approach may mean that firms or governments choose courses of action that hedge the risk they face by selecting a strategy that reduces the risk exposure under a wide variety of possible developments. For example, risk hedging for General Motors may involve post-1985 retooling; according to the results of this analysis the negative exposure of not retooling in the event of oil shocks far outweighs the reduced financial performance if GM retools and fuel prices then decline.

The concept of risk hedging also applies to government policy. Energy policy designed to smooth the disruptions of future oil shocks is one example; such a policy reduces the negative consequences if oil prices rise sharply, but alternatively may be both an unneeded and possibly costly policy tool if oil prices decline in the future.

The important point is that risk hedging, either by governments or corporations, is not costless. Reducing risk exposure under one set of conditions generally means foregoing a better course of action under at least some other circumstances. Returning to the example of General Motors and fuel economy, reducing GM's exposure to the uncertainties of future oil supplies implies that it may forego the opportunity of benefiting from not retooling if fuel prices in fact are stable.

Policymakers can respond to this reality by attempting to reduce the risk firms must hedge against. Energy policy is one example of such risk reduction. Policies designed to ensure high and stable levels of automobile demand are another. Consistent and coherent policy formulation reduces the risks and burdens that firms face in trying to adapt to inconsistent regulatory initiatives. By reducing the level of risk that firms face, the costs of strategic risk hedging in terms of competitive performance can be reduced.

Framework for Dealing with Structural Change

The most basic conclusion is that understanding how the strategic choices of private firms and policy decisions of public officials are conditioned by each other is critical if managers and policymakers are to respond effectively to challenges of structural change. Below are summarized some general conclusions for managers and policymakers based on the example of the future U.S. automobile industry.

1. *Acknowledge the multiplicity of ways in which government policy can affect firm performance and industrial evolution:* Ultimately, effective managerial action depends upon an appreciation of the complexities and subtleties of the strategy-policy interaction. The imperatives of increased foreign competition and a heightened pace of environmental and policy change not only in automobiles but also in other basic sectors argues for a sophisticated managerial view of the process.

2. *Recognize that public policy can be a source of competitive advantage:* Managers should be aware that the achievement of the broader social goals of policy carries with it possibly substantial competitive consequences. These impacts may be a legitimate source of competitive advantage; indeed, the achievement of broader policy goals may depend upon the willingness and ability of private industry to exploit these effects.

3. *Carefully distinguish between long- and short-term effects:* This analysis has illustrated several cases where longer-term strategic shifts that a policy may engender act counter to the short-run effects. Managers should be aware of the broader implications in time of both strategic and policy actions.

4. *Perform expanded policy analysis:* Effective policy formulation requires identifying the total effects of policy initiatives. This analysis has identified three areas to which more analytic attention should be devoted. First are the indirect effects of policy, those effects that result from the more subtle or longer-term fashion in which the choices of strategic planners are shaped. Second are the joint or multiplicative effects of policy, the "fit" of individual initiatives with the broader context of the goals and characteristics of industrial policy. While in both these areas of expanded analysis the effects are not necessarily clear-cut, it is clear from looking at their potential affect on the auto industry that they are very important.

The equity implications of policy are a third area for expanded analysis. The results presented here demonstrate the dramatic ability of policy choices to create winners and losers among the impacted sector, as well as their redistributive effects between the industry and other groups. Explicitly recognizing this reality is crucial if policy is to deal effectively with the consequences of these differential impacts.

5. *Exhibit constancy and consistency in policy formulation:* Sudden changes in public policy can destroy the internal coherence of a corporate strategy. At times, of course, this effect may be desired, as in some cases of trade policy. More generally, however, public policy should strive to recognize the momentum that is a product of the choice of corporate strategy.

In addition to constancy, consistency is a second needed attribute of effective policy. By consistency, policy should provide a clear mix of signals to firms across the broad range of dimensions.

6. *Share risk:* This research has shown in numerous forms the manner in which policy initiatives alter both the magnitude of risk and who bears it. Policymakers should recognize this reality and accept where it is appropriate a share of the risk.

The analytical results presented here, dealing with only a limited number of policies, strategies, and exogenous states, can only suggest the range of outcomes that might occur and the complexity of the underlying process. While individual policies may successfully address narrowly defined issues, the interactions among different regulatory initiatives may in turn induce unexpected and perhaps counterproductive effects. In other words, attention has to be paid not only to the specifics of individual government initiatives but also the fit of these actions to the broader context of policy and strategy. The joint effects of policy, which transcend the consideration of individual initiatives, may ultimately shape the strategic decisions of individual firms in unexpected manners.

These observations suggest the extent to which the strategic implications of industrial policy are as yet poorly understood. This ignorance of the underlying process is underscored when the inherently uncertain and dynamic elements of industrial evolution are taken into account. The joint effects of policy measures, the role of expectations in the face of an uncertain future environment, and the dynamics of strategic change introduce additional complexities into the analysis that are little understood. This fact suggests that at the current level of knowledge it may be analytically presumptuous to think that policymakers can somehow *manage* the process of structural change.

These observations also reinforce the conclusion that strategic adaptation by firms to the challenges of environmental and policy change is not a trivial problem. A strategy of responding piecemeal to one policy challenge after another may bring disaster. Market demands and regulatory requirements may differ significantly. There is a need for managers to think strategically about the political environment, the behavior of groups wielding political power, and the competitive implications of government actions.

Strategy must reflect regulatory as well as market realities if it is to meet regulatory requirements while being consistent with market demands and corporate goals.

Concluding Observations

The importance of the auto industry as a vital part of the U.S. industrial base has challenged concerned managers, policymakers, and analysts alike to develop effective responses to its current problems and to revise, explicitly or implicitly, the national industrial policy for automobiles. While only some of these responses have been analyzed in any detail here, all of them must confront the critical reality that questions of structural change, and the role of industrial policy in influencing economic viability must relate to the strategic decisions of individual firms.

The extent of ignorance about the manner in which policy choices affect strategy, combined with the inherent uncertainty of future events, should temper any grandiose plans to use industrial policy to manage the course of structural change. Instead, by recognizing the broader implications of specific policy actions and the critical role of policy in conditioning the manner of strategic decisions made by both U.S.-chartered firms and their foreign competitors, both managers and policymakers can reduce the risk facing individual firms and explicitly acknowledge their part in influencing industrial development. By developing policies that individually are responsive to the myriad ways that they influence strategic thinking, and collectively provide a set of coherent and consistent signals to managers, policymakers can respond intelligently to the complexities of industrial evolution.

While this book has focused on structural change in the U.S. automobile industry, the framework established here should be of more general applicability in addressing the critical concerns of structural change in other sectors. In particular, the importance of recognizing the strategic diversity of individual firms and the dynamic interaction between strategy and policy is critical to the effective formulation of responses to the challenges of structural change.

Appendix: Mathematical Description of the Model

This appendix contains a mathematical description of the computer model, which was coded in FORTRAN.

Basic Notation

The index J is used to denote the five firms modeled:

$J =$
1. U.S. passenger-car operations, General Motors
2. U.S. passenger-car operations, Ford
3. U.S. passenger-car operations, Chrysler
4. European producers
5. Japanese producers

For fuel economy and manufacturing cost analysis, the model employs six vehicle classes defined by K:

$K =$
1. Minicompact
2. Subcompact
3. Compact regular
4. Compact special
5. Large regular
6. Large special

For determining market-clearing price and volume, a more aggregated set of vehicle classes is employed, denoted by i. These vehicle classes will be described in the section with market clearing.

The model is designed to analyze industry performance over the period 1980–1995 on a yearly basis. The model period is indicated by N or NOW alternatively ($N = 80,95$).

Time Structure of the Model

The model is designed to move forward through each period, using last period's results as base values for the current period's calculations.

Because capital spending incurred as a result of fuel-economy improvements in time N is allocated over periods $N-1$ and $N-2$, model results are generated concurrently at each iteration for two time periods, N and $N-2$ (except for the two beginning and two ending periods). Figure A-1 describes this sequencing of calculations. At each iteration:

The scenario conditional upon period N is revealed, plus a policy and market structure defined by period $N-1$.

Demand and supply are set equal through price adjustments, conditional upon each firm's strategy. New fuel economy ratings for each manufacturer's fleet are calculated, and capital investment incurred by these improvements is determined.

This capital investment incurred as a result of events in period N is then allocated to periods $N-1$ and $N-2$.

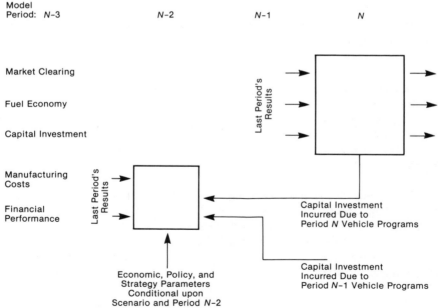

Figure A-1. Structure of the Model over Time

Given the allocation of capital spending incurred as a result of the period N product program to period N–2—and already having calculated sales, price and variable cost information for period N–2—the N–2 period financial performance for each U.S. firm is determined.

The model thus must generate partial results for two additional periods (corresponding to 1996 and 1997) to generate financial results for the 1980–1995 period.

Figure 4–1, chapter 4, describes the structure of the model within each iteration.

Scenario Parameters

Each model run is made conditional upon the choice of scenario, which is jointly defined by the following set of parameters.

Macroeconomic Parameters

1. Inflation rate: annual rate of inflation ($PRINFL$); cumulative change in the overall price level since the beginning of the model ($CUMINF$).
2. Annual real personal-consumption expenditures ($XINCME$).
3. Spending allocated to user-operated transportation: the yearly percentage of personal-consumption expenditures devoted to user-operated transportation in the United States ($FRAUTO$).
4. Automobile-fuel price: the composite price in 1979 dollars per gallon of automotive gasoline and diesel fuels ($GASPR$).

Domestic-Policy Parameters

1. Quotas or voluntary export restraints: minimum and maximum constraints on the unit volume of Japanese sales in the United States, either uniformly or by vehicle class ($TGTMIN, TGTMAX$).
2. Tariffs: ad valorum tariff imposed either uniformly or by vehicle class upon Japanese vehicles ($TARIFF$).
3. Subsidies: the cost of capital funds for U.S. firms ($XINT$) (also a financial parameter). Setting equal to 0 corresponds to a government provision of capital funds or a subsidy on their costs.
4. Fuel economy: fleet-weighted fuel economy for each manufacturer ($AVFUEL$).

Foreign-Firm-Strategy Parameters

1. Japanese production costs: per-unit real total cost of manufacturing and transporting each class of Japanese vehicles to the United States (*COSTJP*).
2. Degree of future market capture. *d*UNTPFT* is the present value of the stream of future profits tied to a current sale, with *d* the discount factor and *UNTPFT* the current cash profit from a sale of that vehicle class.
3. Sales penetration: the targeted Japanese unit sales volume in the U.S. market, expressed both as an upper and lower boundary constraint (*TGTMIN, TGTMAX*).

Fuel Economy

This module updates the following variables for each period based upon each U.S. manufacturer's fuel-economy-improvement program.

BFUEL(J,K): composite-vehicle fuel economy is miles per gallon for manufacturer *J*, vehicle-class *K*.

WGHT(J,K): curb weight in pounds for vehicle-class *K*, manufacturer *J*.

CFUEL(J,K): last period's vehicle-class fuel economy.

PWGHT(J,K): last period's vehicle-class weight.

The following parameters define each U.S. manufacturer's fuel-economy-improvement program:

YRDWN(J,K,I): the year for round *I* of downsizing vehicle-class *K* of manufacturer *J*.

YRMTS(J,K,I): the year for round *I* of material substitution for vehicle-class *K* of manufacturer *J*.

YRFWD(J,K): the year for front-wheel-drive conversion for vehicle-class *K*, manufacturer *J*.

TECHOP(J,ITO): the penetration of technology *ITO* into manufacturer *J*'s fleet in the current year.

PTECOP(J,ITO): last year's penetration of technology into manufacturer *J*'s fleet.

The fuel-economy subroutine starts off with the manufacturer's values for last year's fuel economy ($BFUEL(J,K)$ and curb weight ($WGHT$ (J,K)). It then updates these values based upon any changes in the vehicle specifications as determined by the fuel-economy-policy variables $YRDWN$, $YRMTS$, $YRFWD$, and $TECHOP$.

Vehicle curb weight ($WGHT(J,K)$) for manufacturer J, vehicle-class K, in time period NOW, is a function of the percentage weight reduction due to round I of downsizing ($WRDWN(I)$), material substitution ($WRMTS(I)$), and front-wheel drive ($WRFWD$).

$$WGHT'(J,K) \quad = \; WGHT(J,K)*(1 \; - \; WRDWN(I))$$
$$\text{if } YRDWN(J,K,I) \; = \; NOW$$

$$= \; WGHT(J,K) \text{ otherwise}$$

$$WGHT''(J,K) \quad = \; WGHT'(J,K)*(1 \; - \; WRMTS(I))$$
$$\text{if } YRMTS(J,K,I) \; = \; NOW$$

$$= \; WGHT'(J,K) \text{ otherwise}$$

$$WGHT'''(J,K) \quad = \; WGHT''(J,K)*(1 \; - \; WRFWD(I))$$
$$\text{if } YRFWD(J,K) \; = \; NOW$$

$$= \; WGHT''(J,K) \text{ otherwise}$$

for each J,K,I.

Fuel-economy values reflecting reduced weight are given by the following relation:

$$BFUEL(J,K) \; =$$

$$CFUEL(J,K) \left[\frac{0.575}{\left(\dfrac{WGHT \; + \; 300}{PWGHT \; + \; 300}\right)^{0.471}} \; + \; \frac{0.425}{\left(\dfrac{WGHT \; + \; 300}{PWGHT \; + \; 300}\right)^{0.320}} \right]$$

This relationship is based upon empirical studies done by NHTSA and is an approximation of the relationship between vehicle inertial weight and fuel economy found in the Wharton Automobile Model.[1] Improvement in fuel economy resulting from improved efficiency is given by the increased penetration of technology *ITO* in the manufacturer's fleet this year times the percentage fuel-economy improvement resulting from that technology:

$$BFUEL(J,K) = \sum_{ITO} (BFUEL(J,K)*(TECHOP(J,ITO)$$
$$- PTECHOP(J,ITO))*FUELGA(ITO))$$

This approach treats fuel-economy gains through weight reduction and improved efficiency as cumulative. The final result is new curb weights and fuel economies for each vehicle class for each U.S. manufacturer.

For Japanese and European producers there is insufficient information to specify a schedule for fuel-economy improvement. Accordingly, the percentage improvement in vehicle-class fuel economy for foreign manufacturers is set equal to the corresponding improvement in fuel economy for General Motors.

$$BFUEL(J,K) = (BFUEL(1,K)/CFUEL(1,K))*(BFUEL(J,K)$$
$$J = 4,5; K = 2,5$$

In the case of minicompacts, for which there is no domestic production, the percentage improvement in fuel economy is set equal to the corresponding improvement in subcompact cars.

Market Clearing

The model distinguishes between market-clearing price and quantity and corporate sales and selling price. Each period, conditional upon the scenario and the previous period's market results, the market is cleared.

Market-Clearing Variables

1. *CPRICE(i)*: Market clearing price for vehicle-class *i* (described below), which is defined in terms of the present value of life-cycle costs.
2. *TSALE(i)*: Unit sales of vehicle-class *i*.

Corporate Sales and Price Variables

1. *PRICE(J,K)*: manufacturer selling price for vehicle-class *K*, manufacturer *J*.

2. *SALE(J,K)*: unit sales in current model period of vehicle-class *K*, manufacturer *J*.

The first section below will describe the calculation of market-clearing variables. The second section will then describe how corporate sales and price variables are linked to the market-clearing variables.

Structure of the Market-Clearing Approach

The market clearing model has equations for demand, supply, and competitive price setting, in addition to a set of relationships linking the results of the market clearing with individual-firm sales.

Demand

A partial-equilibrium linear-demand system is employed. Cross elasticities of demand between new autos and other sectors of the economy are ignored. Further, it is assumed that demand curves are linear in price and income. A linear specification allows demand elasticities to vary with volume. This linear specification is felt to be important in this formulation because of the large volume variations that the model deals with. An alternative formulation using a constant-elasticity specification lacks this desirable property.

Let $i = 1,6$, where

$$i = 1: JAPANESE\ SMALL\ BASIC\ CARS$$

$$2: JAPANESE\ SMALL\ LUXURY\ CARS$$

$$3: U.S.\text{-}EUROPEAN\ SMALL\ BASIC\ CARS$$

$$4: U.S.\text{-}EUROPEAN\ SMALL\ LUXURY\ CARS$$

$$5: U.S.\text{-}EUROPEAN\ LARGE\ BASIC\ CARS$$

$$6: U.S.\text{-}EUROPEAN\ LARGE\ LUXURY\ CARS$$

Define:

$Q_d(i)$ = quantity demanded of vehicle-class i during time t. (called *TSALE(i)* elsewhere in the analysis).

$P(i)$ = consumer price of vehicle-class i during time t. (called *CPRICE(i)* elsewhere in the analysis).

$P(i)$ is defined as a measure of the consumer cost of vehicle purchase, and includes an operating-cost component.

$Y =$ spending allocated to user-operated transportation in the United States in the current model period.

    $= XINCME*FRAUTO$

Let $P'(i)$, $Q'(i)$ be the corresponding variables for time-1 and similarly for all other variables.

By definition, the elasticity of $Q(i)$ with respect to $P(j)$ is given by

$$E(i,j) = (P'(j)/Q'(i)) \; \frac{\partial Q(i)}{\partial P(j)}$$

$$= (P'(j)/Q'(i)) \quad d(i,j)$$

where $d(i,j)$ is a constant. Two conditions are imposed upon $d(i,j)$. First, all classes of automobiles are substitutes to some degree of each other. This substitutability means that $d(i,j) \geq 0 \; i \neq j$. Second, the demand for a given class of vehicle falls as its own price rises, so $d(i,i) < 0 \; \forall \quad i$.

The elasticity of demand with respect to income is given by

$$\eta(i) = (Y'/Q'(i)) \; \frac{\partial Q(i)}{\partial Y}$$

$$= (Y'/Q'(i)) \quad a(i)$$

where $a(i)$ is a constant and Y is a consumer income for vehicle purchase and operation. Since there is no clear evidence as to how income elasticities vary between vehicle classes, equal income elasticities for all classes are assumed.

This partial-equilibrium demand system is given by

$$
\begin{bmatrix}
Q_d(1)-Q'(1) \\
Q_d(2)-Q'(2) \\
Q_d(3)-Q'(3) \\
Q_d(4)-Q'(4) \\
Q_d(5)-Q'(5) \\
Q_d(6)-Q'(6)
\end{bmatrix}
=
\begin{bmatrix}
d(1,1)d(1,2)\ldots d(1,6)a(1) \\
d(2,1)d(2,2)\ldots d(2,6)a(2) \\
d(3,1)d(3,2)\ldots d(3,6)a(3) \\
d(4,1)d(4,2)\ldots d(4,6)a(4) \\
d(5,1)d(5,2)\ldots d(5,6)a(5) \\
d(6,1)d(6,2)\ldots d(6,6)a(6)
\end{bmatrix}
\begin{bmatrix}
P(1)-P'(1) \\
P(2)-P'(2) \\
P(3)-P'(3) \\
P(4)-P'(4) \\
P(5)-P'(5) \\
P(6)-P'(6) \\
Y-Y'
\end{bmatrix}
\quad \text{(A.1)}
$$

Expanding, a demand schedule for vehicle-class i will be:

$$Q(i) = Q'(i) - (\sum_j d(i,j)*P'(j)) + (\sum_j d(i,j)P(j))$$

$$+ a(i)(Y - Y')$$

$$\forall i \tag{A.2}$$

Supply

It is assumed that Japanese producers jointly seek to maximize profit from U.S. sales conditional upon possible sales constraints representing either trade restraints or more complex underlying competitive behavior. Japanese producers set price in the U.S. market and, furthermore, know how U.S. producers will behave in response to shifts in the demand curve.

By assumption, supply curves for U.S.-produced vehicles are linear. Letting $Q(i)$ be the quantity of vehicles supplied in class i, $E(i)$, the supply elasticity for vehicle-class i, is given by:

$$E(i) = (P'(i)/Q'(i))\frac{\partial Q(i)}{\partial P(i)}$$

$$= (P'(i)/Q'(i))e(i)$$

The supply response for U.S. producers is given by:

$$\begin{bmatrix} Q_s(3) - Q'(3) \\ Q_s(4) - Q'(4) \\ Q_s(5) - Q'(5) \\ Q_s(6) - Q'(6) \end{bmatrix} = \begin{bmatrix} e(3)\ e(4)\ e(5)\ e(6) \end{bmatrix} \begin{bmatrix} P(3) - P'(3) \\ P(4) - P'(4) \\ P(5) - P'(5) \\ P(6) - P'(6) \end{bmatrix} \tag{A.3}$$

Under this supply specification, domestic producers do not shift their supply curve in response to actions taken by the Japanese. This specification both avoids the difficulties of modeling oligopoly interaction and allows for the representation of a wide variety of behaviors.

Equilibrium Conditions

The market is cleared when supply equals demand.

$$Q_s(i) = Q_d(i) \ \forall i$$

Expanding gives the following:

For $i = 1,2$ (*JAPANESE PRODUCERS*)

$$Q_d(i) = Q'(i) - (\sum_j d(i,j)*P'(j))$$

$$+ (\sum_j d(i,j)P(j)) + a(i)(Y - Y') \tag{A.4}$$

For $i = 3,6$ (*U.S.-EUROPEAN PRODUCERS*)

$$(Q'(i) - e(i)P'(i)) + e(i)P(i)$$

$$= Q'(i) - (\sum_j d(i,j)*P'(j))$$

$$+ (\sum_j d(i,j)P(j)) + a(i)(Y - Y') \tag{A.5}$$

Solving the System

This system is solved for each period to maximize Japanese profit subject to new economic and market conditions and Japanese volume constraints revealed in each new period.

The solution is computed in two stages. First, a new set of consumer prices is calculated to reflect this period's fuel prices and vehicle fuel efficiencies. A new market equilibrium is determined with these revised prices and the new level of consumer income, using equation A.1. In the second step, conditional upon these new market conditions, the system is solved to reflect Japanese competitive behavior. In other words, producers take into account the altered economic and market conditions of the new period in making competitive decisions.

In the first stage, prices are modified in the following manner. Define:

$$GASCST(i) = (56500*GASPR)/BFUEL(J,K)$$

as the discounted cost of operating vehicle-class i. Because fuel economy is calculated on a less aggregated vehicle classification, only some of the vehicle classes for which *BFUEL* is defined are used to calculate *GASCST*. Then:

$$P(i) = P'(i) - GASCST'(i) + GASCST(i).$$

This equation gives the new consumer price of vehicle-class i adjusted to reflect changes in operating costs but not changes in manufacturer selling price. Substituting the new $P(i)$ and new Y into equation A.1 gives a new set of market demands reflecting this period's changes in fuel prices, income, and fuel efficiency.

The second stage then takes this modified set of demand conditions and generates a new market equilibrium subject to possible constraints on Japanese volume.

The equilibrium conditions for U.S.-European producers (equation A.5) specify a set of four equations in six unknowns, since both quantities supplied and demanded are specified in terms of $P(i)$. These equations can be solved for $P(i)$, $i = 3,6$ in terms of Japanese prices $P(1)$ and $P(2)$. These price equations can then be substituted back into equation A.4 and A.5 to obtain a set of reduced-form market-equilibrium equations in terms of Japanese prices only. The reduced-form equations give the change in $Q(i)$, $i = 1,6$, of a change in $P(j)$, $j = 1,2$, with the intermediate effects on U.S.-European prices taken into account. The effects of Japanese prices on U.S.-European prices will depend upon the U.S.-European supply elasticity (see table 4–6, chapter 4). With a noninfinite supply elasticity, a price hike in one market segment will induce price increases in other segments that feed back and moderate the quantity decline in the original market segment.

Given the system in reduced form, Japanese profit maximization requires choosing $P(1)$ and $P(2)$ so as to maximize profit subject to a minimum and maximum sales constraint.

$$MAX\ \Pi\ =\ P(1)Q_1(P(1),P(2);y)\ +\ P(2)Q_2(P(1),P(2);y)$$
$$-\ C1(Q(1))\ -\ C2(Q(2))$$

subject to:

$$Q(1)\ +\ Q(2)\ \geq\ TGTMIN \text{ (minimum sales target)}$$

$$Q(1)\ +\ Q(2)\ \leq\ TGTMAX \text{ (maximum sales target)}$$

It is assumed that Japanese producers manufacture at constant average and marginal cost, so that

$$Ci(Q(i))\ =\ C(\mathrm{i})^*Q(i)$$

$$=\ COSTJP(i)^*TSALE(i)$$

This system can be solved using Lagrange multipliers for $P(1)$ and $P(2)$. Substituting Japanese prices into the reduced-firm system gives quantities and prices for the entire market. If the sales constraints are not binding, the marginal revenue of the sale of an additional vehicle equals marginal cost. Under volume constraints, marginal revenue for the two classes are equal, but not necessarily equivalent to marginal cost.

Representing Different Policies and Strategies

This market-clearing formulation can be modified to examine several issues of interest. Japanese sales targets *TGTMIN* and *TGTMAX* can represent either uniform quotas or more complex underlying competitive behavior. The model can also be modified to handle sales constraints applying to only one vehicle class. In this instance, marginal revenue from both vehicle classes will no longer be equal.

Changes in *COSTJP* can represent tariffs, changes in the competitive advantage of Japanese industry or in the yen-dollar exchange rate, and local-content regulations, which may alter the manufacturing cost structure.

Dimensions of future market capture are represented by reducing current Japanese vehicle costs by an amount representing the present value of the expected future stream of profits tied to the sale of the current vehicle. The magnitude of this reduction will depend upon vehicle repurchase rates, the time between repurchases, and the amount of profit earned on the vehicle. This analysis treats the expected amount of undiscounted profit earned from a future sale as being equal to that of the current sale. Vehicle repurchase cycle is assumed to be four years, and the discount rate by assumption is 10 percent. The model thus represents dimensions of future market capture in the following fashion:

$$COSTJP(i) = \text{[manufacturing cost]} - \text{[discounted stream of future purchases tied to current sale]}$$

$$= COSTJP(i) - d*UNTPFT(i)$$

where d is the discount factor reflecting the vehicle-repurchase rate, and $UNTPFT(i)$ is the current cash profit from the sale of a vehicle of class i.

Linking Market Equilibrium to Corporate Sales

The market clearing model described so far generates for each period a set of prices and quantities in four vehicle classes (small basic; small luxury; large basic; large luxury) for two sets of producers, the Japanese and the aggregated U.S.-European producers. For use in the rest of the model these results should be in terms of prices and sales for each of the five firms modeled, and using a less aggregated set of vehicle classes.

Let:

$CPRICE(i)$ $= P(i) =$ vehicle sales

$TSALE(i)$ $= Q(i) =$ consumer price

$SALE(J,K)$ $=$ sales by manufacturer J, vehicle-class K

$PRICE(J,K)$ $=$ manufacturer J selling price for vehicle class K

$CSHARE(J,K)$ $=$ manufacturer J's percentage-unit market share of vehicle-class K.

Equations A.6 and A.7 give the set of relations that are used to link market-clearing results with corporate sales. These relations are based on an analysis of the 1979 market, and they are assumed to remain constant through the period of the model.

Equation A.6 shows the relationship between market-clearing variables and individual-firm sales:

$$SALE(J, 1) = (.05* TSALE(3))* CSHARE(J, 1)$$

$$SALE(J, 2) = (.78* TSALE(3) + .22* TSALE(4))*$$
$$CSHARE(J, 2)$$

$$SALE(J, 3) = (.17* TSALE(3) + .46* TSALE(J, 4))*$$
$$CSHARE(J, 3)$$

$$SALE(J, 4) = (.32* TSALE(4))* CSHARE(J, 4)$$

$$SALE(J, 5) = TSALE(5)* CSHARE(J, 5)$$

$$SALE(J, 6) = TSALE(6)* CSHARE(J, 6) \qquad \text{(A.6)}$$

Note that it was not necessary here to break sales down for Japanese and European producers.

Equation A.7 gives the relationship between market-clearing price and individual-firm selling price:

Let $GDUM = 56500* GASPR$

Japanese prices ($J = 5$)

$$PRICE(5,1) = (CPRICE(1) - GDUM/BFUEL(5,1))*.75$$

:minicompact

$$PRICE(5,2) = (CPRICE(1) - GDUM/BFUEL(5,2))$$

:subcompact

$$PRICE(5,3) = 0$$

:compact (regular)

$$PRICE(5,4) = (CPRICE(2) - GDUM/BFUEL(5,4))$$

:compact (special)

General Motors, Ford, Chrysler, European prices ($J = 1,4$)

$$PRICE(J,1) = (CPRICE(3) - GDUM/BFUEL(J,2))*.75$$

:minicompact

$$PRICE(J,2) = (CPRICE(3) - GDUM/BFUEL(J,2))$$

:subcompact

$$PRICE(J,3) = 1.26*PRICE(J,2)$$

:compact (regular)

$$PRICE(J,4) = (CPRICE(4) - GDUM/BFUEL(J,4))$$

:compact (special)

$$PRICE(J,5) = (CPRICE(5) - GDUM/BFUEL(J,5))$$

:large regular auto

$$PRICE(J,6) = (CPRICE(6) - GDUM/BFUEL(J,6))$$

:large special auto   (A.7)

Attempts using linear regression to relate historic share changes for U.S. producers to changes in price and vehicle characteristics were unsuccessful. Other researchers have apparently also had a similar lack of success,[2] although recently the use of logit models in explaining the share of branded goods has proven useful.[3,4]

This approach was rejected here because of the greater level of aggregation used in the model and the lack of confidence in the parameters.

Variable Manufacturing Costs

The calculation of $TMCOST(J,K)$, the variable manufacturing cost in 1979 dollars of vehicle-class K by U.S.-manufacturer J, reflects vehicle programs for improved fuel economy, productivity improvements, and scale economies. The following are among the principal parameters used to calculate $TMCOST$ each period:

1. Base variable production costs—$VCBASE(J,K)$: the variable cost of production in 1979 dollars for vehicle-class K, manufacturer J. This cost corresponds to estimates by industry experts of production costs for the 1979 baseline fleet (see table 4–8, chapter 4).
2. Variable cost of material substitution—$VCMTS(I)$: the additional variable cost per unit of round I of material substitution (assumed equal across all vehicle classes).
3. Variable cost of front-wheel drive—$VCFWD$: the change in per-unit variable cost due to front-wheel-drive conversion, uniform across manufacturers and vehicle classes.
4. Variable cost of downsizing—$VCDWN$: the per-unit variable cost resulting from round I of downsizing.
5. Variable cost of technology—$VCTEC(ITO)$: the per-unit variable cost of implementing each efficiency-improving technology.
6. Relative-factor proportions of capital and labor—$SHRLBR$, $1 - SHRLBR$: the proportion of total variable cost accruing to each factor of production. Used in determining the effects of productivity changes.

The calculation of $TMCOST$ for each U.S. manufacturer is done in three steps. First, variable costs are altered to reflect the current period's fuel-economy-improvement program. In other words, if this period's vehicle-class K of manufacturer J incorporates one or more fuel-economy improvements, the variable cost of these measures must be included in the total per-unit variable cost.

For each J,K:

$$TVCDWN = VCDWN(I) \text{ if } YRDWN(J,K,I) \leq NOW$$

$$\text{and } YRDWN(J,K,I + 1) \geq NOW$$

$$= 0 \text{ otherwise}$$

$$TVCMTS = VCMTS(I) \text{ if } YRMTS(J,K,I) \leq NOW$$

$$\text{and } YRMTS(J,K,I + 1) \geq NOW$$

$$= 0 \text{ otherwise}$$

$$TVCFWD = VCFWD \text{ if } YRFWD(J,K) \leq NOW$$

$$= 0 \text{ otherwise}$$

$$TVCTEC = VCTEC(ITO)*TECHOP(ITO)$$

$$TMCOST(J,K) = TVCDWN + TVCMTS + TVCFWD$$
$$+ TVCTEC + VCBASE(J,K)$$

This value of *TMCOST* is then altered to reflect capital (*CUMPRO* (*C*)) and labor productivity advances (*CUMPRO*(*L*)) and scale economies (*SCALE*). Productivity advances are handled by breaking *TMCOST* into, respectively, a capital component (1 − *SHRLBR*) and a labor component (*SHRLBR*) and multiplying each component by its respective change in productivity given by *CUMPRO*. The division of total variable cost into capital and labor components is assumed to be the same as estimated shares of these factors of production in 1979 (table A–1).

$$TMCOST(J,K) = (TMCOST(J,K)*SHRLBR*CUMPRO(L)) +$$
$$(TMCOST(J,K)*(1 - SHRLBR)*CUMPRO(C))$$

Scale-economy effects are estimated using a piecewise linear approximation of table 2–7, chapter 2, as given in table A–2. Scale economies are calculated on the basis of *platforms* rather than individual vehicle types:

Table A–1
Labor Share of Total Variable Production Cost

Vehicle Type	Labor Cost Proportion
Subcompact	.585
Compact regular	.57
Compact special	.578
Large regular	.44
Large special	.49

Source: Author's calculations based upon 1979 manufacturing structure.

Table A–2
Piecewise Linear Approximation to Production Scale Economies

Platform	Platform Volume	Scale Effect
Subcompact platform	> 400,000	1.00
	200,000–400,000	$1.159 - (VOLUME - 200000)*7.55E - 7$
	< 200,000	$2.35 - (VOLUME)*6.51E - 6$
Compact platform	> 400,000	1.00
	200,000–400,000	$1.0937 - (VOLUME - 200000)*4.7E - 7$
	< 200,000	$2.126*(VOLUME)*5.156E - 6$
Large platform	> 400,000	1.00
	200,000–400,000	1.00
	< 200,000	$1.656 - (VOLUME)*3.23E - 6$

thus, specialty and regular classes, which share common platforms and are differentiated basically by their level of luxury, are aggregated. Production is treated as being equal to sales; based upon the level of sales, the parameter *SCALE* is defined on the curve (see table A–2).

$$TMCOST(J,K) = TMCOST(J,K)*SCALE$$

$$SCALE \geq 1.0$$

Japanese production costs $(COSTJP(i))$ are supplied exogeneously to represent different states of the Japanese industry. European variable production costs are not calculated.

Capital Investment

Capital investment in real terms for U.S. manufacturer J for year N $(CAPINV(J,N))$ is the sum of two components.

1. Fuel-economy-related capital investment—$CAPFE(N + 1)$, $CAPFE$ $(N + 2)$: capital investment incurred as a result of the manufacturer-fuel-economy vehicle programs for periods $N + 1$ and $N + 2$.
2. Nonfuel-economy-related capital investment. This spending represents investment required to maintain the overall competitiveness and market appeal of the product line independent of fuel-economy improvements. Following an assumption by NHTSA, nonfuel-economy-related capital spending is assumed constant in real terms. It consists of three components.

ANNLNB: annual real investment in land and buildings.

ANNMNE: annual real investment in machinery and equipment.

ANNTOL: annual real investment in tooling.

The calculation of *CAPFE(N)* requires defining the following model parameters:

1. Per-vehicle capital cost of downsizing—*CDWN(I)*. Uniform across all manufacturers and vehicle classes (this is true for all capital cost parameters).
2. Per-vehicle capital cost of front-wheel-drive conversion—*CFWD*.
3. Per-vehicle capital cost of material substitution—*CMTS(I)*.
4. Per-vehicle capital costs of vehicle-efficiency technologies—*CTECH (ITO)*.
5. Preexisting manufacturer's production capacity in downsizing—*CPTDWN(J,K,I)*: the highest previous level of production (equivalent to sales) for that manufacturer-vehicle-technology combination. Similarly defined for material substitution (*CPTMTS(J,K,I)*, front-wheel drive (*CPTFWD(J,K,I)*, and vehicle-efficiency technologies (*CPTTEC(J,ITO)*).

The capital costs of a fuel-economy-improvement program are calculated by multiplying the number of cars produced with a technology configuration, minus the preexisting manufacturing capacity to produce those vehicles, times the per-vehicle capital cost of those measures.

$$CCTEC \;=\; \sum_{ITO} (TECHOP(J,ITO)*SALE(J,K) - CPTTEC(J,ITO))$$

$$*CTECH(ITO) \text{ if } \geq 0$$

$$= 0 \text{ otherwise}$$

$$CCDWN \;=\; CDWN(I)*SALE(J,K) \text{ if } YRDWN(J,K,I) = NOW$$

$$= CDWN(I)*(SALE(J,K) - CPTDWN(J,K,I))$$

$$\text{if } YRDWN(J,K,I) < NOW$$

$$\text{and } YRDWN(J,K,I + 1) > NOW$$

$$= 0 \text{ otherwise}$$

$$CCMTS, CCFWD \text{ defined similarly to } CCDWN$$

$$CAPFE(J) = CCTEC + CCDWN + CCMTS + CCFWD$$

$CAPFE(N)$ is then allocated over the previous two years' capital-investment spending: 60 percent in the preceeding year and 40 percent in the year before that. This allocation accords with industry practice.[5] Total real capital-investment spending for each model period, including both fuel-economy- and nonfuel-economy-related capital spending, is given by the following expression:

$$CAPINV(J) = (.6 * CAPFE(N + 1) + .4 * CAPFE(N + 2)$$

$$+ ANNLNB(J) + ANNMNE(J)$$

$$+ ANNTOL(J))$$

Capital investment by foreign-based firms is not calculated.

Financial Statements

Using the previously generated model values for corporate sales, prices, capital investment, and variable cost, the model generates detailed financial statements for each domestic producer for each model period. The following financial parameters defined for each domestic firm are used:

Cost of capital—*RATINT:* the inflation-adjusted cost of capital-firm J, consisting of a real underlying rate plus an inflation premium. For surplus funds, this parameter defines the return earned on investments elsewhere.

Depreciation rates for land and buildings—*DEPLNB:* the straightline depreciation rate, based on historical analysis.

Depreciation rate for machinery and equipment—*DEPMNE,* straight-line.

Amortization rate for tooling—*AMOPER,* straightline.

For each domestic firm, assets are divided into four categories: land and buildings $(BVLNB(J))$, machinery and equipment $(BVMNE(J))$, tooling

($BVTOOL$), and other capital ($OTHCAP$). Book value for the first three of these asset categories is calculated in the following fashion.

First, that period's capital-investment spending is allocated among them according to shares based on historic analysis. The effects of inflation are introduced here ($CUMINF(N)$):

$$BLVNB(J) = BVLNB(J) + (.05*(.6*CAPFE(J,N+1)$$
$$+ 0.4*CAPFE(J,N + 2)) + ANNLNB(J))*CUMINF$$

$$BVMNE(J) = BVMNE(J) + (.35*(.6*CAPFE(J,N + 1)$$
$$+ 0.4*CAPFE(J,N + 2)) + ANNMNE(J))*CUMINF$$

$$BVTOOL(J) = BVTOOL(J) + (.6*(.6*CAPFE(J,N + 1)$$
$$+ 0.4*CAPFE(J,N + 2)) + ANNTOL(J))*CUMINF$$

Depreciation (DEP) and amortization ($AMORT$) charges for that period are then calculated:

$$DEP = DEPLNB(J)*BVLNB(J) + DEPMNE(J)*$$
$$BVMNE(J)$$

$$AMORT = AMOPER(J)*BVTOOL$$

Finally, new book values of these assets are determined:

$$BVLNB(J) = BVLNB(J)*(1.0 - DEPLNB(J))$$

$$BVMNE(J) = BVMNE(J)*(1.0 - DEPMNE(J))$$

$$BVTOOL(J) = BVTOOL(J)*(1.0 - AMOPER(J))$$

Book values for $OTHCAP$ are altered to reflect inflation but are otherwise constant.

The calculation of other financial variables is straightforward. Sales revenue for each domestic firm is given by the expression:

$$REVNUE(J) = \sum_{K}(PRICE(J,K)*.85*SALES(J,K)*CUMINF)$$

The .85 represents the dealer discount. Total variable production costs are determined by:

$$TWARCO(J) = \sum_{K}(TMCOST(J,K)*SALE(J,K)*CUMINF(N))$$

Table A–3
Pro-Forma Income-Statement Relationships

Firm	A0	A1	R^2	F Statistic	Degrees of Freedom	Durbin-Watson
General Motors						
Selling and administration	1.155E9	.01536	.643	19.8	11	1.69
Maintenance, repair, and replacement	1.240E9	.02157	.707	14.5	6	2.38
Research and development	.919E9	.00526	.494	8.8	9	.81
Nonincome taxes	.489E9	.02120	.856	41.7	7	1.77
Ford						
Selling and administration	.697E9	.01522	.424	2.9	4	.86
Maintenance, repair and replacement	.407E9	.00880	.395	5.2	8	1.19
Research and development	.259E9	.01770	.850	45.3	8	1.12
Nonincome taxes	−1.338E9	.02920	.887	79.2	10	1.03
Chrysler						
Selling and administration	−.292E8	.0442	.631	6.8	4	2.96
Maintenance, repair, and replacement	−.890E8	.0353	.718	20.4	8	1.34
Research and development	.239E8	.0162	.478	7.3	8	1.94
Nonincome taxes	−1.102E8	.0279	.776	13.9	4	1.85

Note: Parameters estimated in terms of 1979 constant dollars.
General form: dependent variable = $A0 + A1*$ (sales revenue).

The values for other income-statement items—selling and administration ($SNA(J)$), maintenance, repair, and replacement ($XMRR(J)$), research and development ($RND(J)$), and nonincome taxes ($OTHTAX(J)$) are determined through linear-regression relationships on sales revenue (see table A-3). Pension costs ($RET(J)$) are constant in real terms.

The calculation of an income statement, balance sheet, and sources and uses of funds statement is a straightforward application of accounting identities.

Notes

1. Stephen P. Bradley and Annel G. Karnani, *Automotive Manufacturer Risk Analysis: Meeting the Automotive Fuel Economy Standards,* Report prepared for the Department of Transportation-Transportation Systems Center (Bedford, Mass: HH Aerospace Design Co., [1978]), p. 40.

2. Eric J. Toder, *Trade Policy and the U.S. Automobile Industry,* pp. 116, 44, 46.

3. K. Cowling and A.J. Raynor, "Price, Quality, and Market Share," *Journal of Political Economy* 78 (November–December 1970):1292–1309.

4. Jack E. Triplett and Keith Cowling, "A Quality Adjusted Model for Determining Market Shares in an Oligopoly," U.S. Department of Labor, Bureau of Labor Statistics, Working Paper no. 4 (Washington, D.C.: December 1971).

5. Statement of Chrysler Corporation, *Government Regulation of the Automobile Industry,* p. 220.

Index

Abernathy, William, 4
Administrative guidance, 73, 89; in trade policy, 86
Advertising, 32
American Motors Corporation, 15–62, 98; alliance with Renault, 30, 50; multinational strategy of, 38; in simulation model, 98
Antitrust, 216
Automobile fleet. *See* Vehicle mix
Automobile industry, concentration in U.S., 21; history of U.S., 15–62; importance of, 3; role in Japan, 87

Barriers to entry, dealer network as, 33
Baughman, M.L., 4
Bradley, Stephen P., 4
Brayton engine, 180

CAFE. *See* Corporate Average Fuel Economy
Capacity, domestic, 27–28; Japanese, 82–83, 85–86; quotas and, 175; small cars and, 27
Capital cost, 136, 209
Capital investment, 23, 24, 43, 54–61; Japanese, 89; projected, 139, 185–186; simulation model and, 96, 115–116
Captive imports, 98
Cartelization, 175
Chrysler, 15–62 passim, 74, 78–79, 98, 140–148, 151, 156, 164, 174, 185, 190–195, 198, 202, 205, 214, 215, 216, 218–220, 223, 226–227, 230, 231, 232; component sourcing, 31; demand and, 141–142, 144, 145, 146–148, 232; manufacturing strategy and, 30; merger with Ford, 218–220, 230; Mitsubishi and, 38–40, 51; multinational strategy of, 38–40; oil prices and, 194–195, 205; Peugeot and, 38–40, 51; product strategy, 50–51; subsidies and, 214–215
Clean Air Act, 7, 19, 220
Comparative advantage, international, 26
Competition, basis of, 57; multinational, 84–88
Competitive advantage, Japanese, 69, 79–82, 88, 228; shifts in 83–84, 169–174
Component suppliers, 103, 136; European, 80; Japanese, 80; U.S., 31, 80
Congressional Budget Office, 180, 183, 186

Consolidation, of domestic industry, 19–21; 218–220, 229–230; of Japanese industry, 69–70, 77, 89, 170
Consumer loyalty, 45, 112–113. *See also* Quality
Consumer repurchase. *See* Consumer loyalty; Quality
Consumption expenditures, and automobile demand, 16, 100; real personal, 129–130
Corporate links, Chrysler-Mitsubishi, 37, 40, 74; Chrysler-Peugeot, 37, 40; Ford-Toyo Kogyo, 37, 43, 74, 78; GM-Isuzu, 41, 74, 78; Honda-BL, 89; Nissan-Motor Iberica, 89; Nissan-Peugeot, 89; Nissan-Alfa Romeo, 89; Renault-American Motors, 27, 30, 33, 37, 50
Corporate Average Fuel Economy (CAFE), 7, 45, 46, 57, 61, 226, 227; non-U.S. capital investment and, 43; risk and, 8. *See also* Fuel economy
Corporate strategy. *See* Strategy
Cost, capital, 136, 209; Japanese manufacturing, 79–80, 83, 136, 169–174, 228; manufacturing, 23, 27–29, 61, 215–218, 229; productivity improvements and, 133, 136; simulation model and, 96, 113–119

Data Resources Inc., 129, 184
Decline, economic, 2, 3
Demand, consumer spending and, 100; domestic, 15–18; European, 67, 82; fuel prices and, 16, 17, 100, 186–189; Japanese, 68, 70, 82–83, 87–88; projections, 65, 67–68, 137; risk exposure and, 231–232; structural change and, 226. *See also* Market clearing; Risk exposure
Department of Transportation, U.S., capital investment projection, 139
Diesel engine, post-1985, 180; restrictions on, 19, 220–223, 227, 232
Downsizing, 52, 179; in simulation model, 96
Dumping, 170
Durability, 79, 80. *See also* Quality

Elasticities, demand, 109–110; income, 110–111; supply, 111–112
Electric car, 180
Electronics, in Japanese automobiles, 88

Emissions, 19; competitive effects, 61, 88; Japanese regulations on, 73. *See also* Diesel engine

Energy policy, 57, 202–205; risk exposure and, 233, 234

Environment, exogenous, in simulation model, 99–100. *See also* Scenarios

Equity, 226–233, 235

Europe, Japanese imports to, 88–89; in simulation model, 98. *See also* Demand

European automakers, 44

Exchange rate, 83–84, 88, 170

Expectations, trade policy and, 87, 229. *See also* Rational expectations

Exports, Japanese, 84–85, 86, 88; Japanese government policy, and, 86–87, 91; U.S. market and, 90

Extensive demand, 7, 108

Financial performance, Japanese, 75; in simulation model, 98, 113–119; U.S. industry, 21, 45

Financial strategies, 54–57

Fleet mix. *See* Vehicle mix

Ford, 15–62 passim, 68, 74, 78–79, 98, 140–148, 151, 156, 164, 174, 185, 190–195, 198, 202, 205, 214, 215, 218–220, 223, 226, 227, 230, 231, 232; component sourcing, 29, 31; demand and, 141–142, 144, 145, 146–148, 231–232; financial strength, 56–57; Japanese competitive advantage and, 174; manufacturing strategy and, 30; merger with Chrysler, 218–220, 230; multinational, 37, 43–44, 88; product strategy, 52–53; oil prices and, 194–195, 205; subsidy and, 214–215; Toyo Kogyo and, 37, 43, 74, 78; trade policy and, 164, 174, 231

Foreign content, 31, 120. *See also* Local content

Foreign exchange rate. *See* Exchange rate

France, trade barriers, 86

Fuel economy, 19, 88, 226–227; capital investment and, 103, 115–116, 140, 185–186; diesel engines and, 221; projected improvements in, 139, 179, 180, 185, 194–195, 205; risk exposure and, 184–197; in simulation model, 96, 101–105, 114–115; variable cost and, 103. *See also* Technology; Corporate Average Fuel Economy

Fuel prices, 65, 129–130, 179, 183–184, 221, 227. *See also* Oil

Front-wheel-drive, 96

General Motors, 15–62 passim, 68, 74, 78–79, 98, 140–147, 151, 156, 164, 169,

174, 185, 188–189, 190–195, 198, 202–203, 205, 214, 218, 221, 223, 225, 226, 227, 230, 231, 232, 234; component sourcing, 31; demand and, 141–142, 144–145, 146–148, 231; diesel engine restrictions and, 221–223; Isuzu Motors and, 41, 74, 78; manufacturing strategy and, 30; multinational, 40–41, 88; oil prices and, 189, 194–195, 205; post-1985 fuel economy and, 230; product strategy, 51–52; risk hedging, 234; trade policy and, 202

Government policy, antitrust, 216; competitive implications of, 2, 6–8, 9, 57–61, 198, 209, 215, 223–224, 227, 231, 235; capital investment and, 23, 43, 54–57, 61, 185–186; cost reductions and, 215–216, 229; effects on Japanese, 165–169, 170, 174–176, 227–229, 232–233; energy policy, 202–205; Ford-Chrysler merger, 218–220; historical, 18–19; Japanese, 69–73, 80, 86–87, 89–91, 174–175; less-developed countries, 68, 84–85; in simulation model, 100; subsidies, 209–215; value-added tax, 216. *See also* Strategy; Fuel economy; Energy policy; Safety; Emissions; Risk exposure; Risk hedging; Trade policy; Subsidies

Hartman, Raymond S., 4

Honda, 27, 53, 74, 77–78, 89

Industrial policy, 3, 10, 232–237; Japanese, 88. *See also* Government policy

Inflation, 100

Innovation, 15; trickle-down, 6, 81

Intensive demand, 7, 108, 191

International comparative advantage. *See* Comparative advantage

Internationalization, forces for, 65; U.S. market and, 19–21, 33–37

Isuzu, 41, 74, 78–79, 163

Japan, auto industry, 69–91

Japan, Inc., 90

Japanese automakers, 19, 21, 26, 32–33, 43–44, 53–54, 69–91, 151, 163–164, 176, 228, 229, 232; price setting in U.S., 108–109, 119–120

JEEP, 50. *See also* American Motors Corporation

Joskow, P.L., 4

Karnani, Annel, 4

Labor, content of auto, 136; Japanese, 80, 83, 87, 88, 169–170; U.S., 29, 136, 215

Leone, Robert A., 4
Less-developed-countries, autos and, 66–69;
    competing in, 88–89; government
    policies, 68; Japanese exports to, 84
Life-cycle costs, 107. *See also* Price
Local content, 170, 174, 175, 228;
    European firms and, 26–27; Ford and,
    231; Honda and, 27, 78; Japanese firms
    and, 85, 89. *See also* Trade policy
Loyalty. *See* Quality; Consumer loyalty

Manufacturing cost. *See* Cost
Manufacturing strategy, Japanese, 30, 66,
    69; multinational, 37, 66; restructuring,
    27, 29–30. *See also* Cost
Market clearing, in simulation model,
    105–113
Marketing, in Japan, 80–82; in U.S., 32–33
Market segmentation. *See* Vehicle mix
Market share, import, 65, 131, 152–153,
    164–165, 170, 176, 188; Japanese
    domestic, 74–75; simulation model and,
    108, 205; U.S. historical, 19–21; world,
    34–35
Material substitution, 96, 180
Mazda. *See* Toyo Kogyo
Mellon Institute, 103
Merger, Ford-Chrysler, 218–220, 230, 232
Methodolgy, 10–11, 95–128. *See also*
    Simulation model
Minicar, 88
Ministry of International Trade and
    Industry (Japan), 70, 86, 87, 89, 90, 175
MITI. *See* Ministry of International Trade
    and Industry
Mitsubishi, 37, 40, 74, 78
Multinational strategy, 10, 29, 33–44, 65,
    66–69, 77–80, 228–229

National Highway Traffic Safety
    Administration (NHTSA), 19, 103
Nissan, 21, 74, 75–77, 89
Nontariff trade barriers. *See* Trade policy;
    Trade barriers; Government policy
Normative issues, analysis and, 9, 12, 231;
    in simulation model, 99

Oil, price fluctuations, 179, 183–184, 232;
    strategic risk and, 190–195; vehicle mix
    and, 188, 200. *See also* Fuel economy;
    Fuel prices; Risk exposure
OMA. *See* Orderly Marketing Agreement
OPEC, 183, 202
Orderly Marketing Agreement (OMA),
    86–87, 174–175. *See also* Trade policy;
    Quota; Voluntary Restraint Agreement

Parts, automotive. *See* Component
    suppliers
Personal-consumption expenditures. *See*
    Consumption expenditures
Petroleum. *See* Oil
Politics. *See* Government policy; Industrial
    policy; Quota; Risk exposure; Trade
    policy
Porter, Michael, 4
Positive issues, analysis and, 9
Price, 16, 70; setting, 108–109, 119–120,
    136; simulation model and, 96, 105–113
Product-development cycle, 23, 44, 45, 191,
    232
Productivity, 133, 136, 215; in simulation
    model, 96; Japanese, 80
Product strategies, 44–54, 70, 73, 88, 132,
    180

Quality, 120, 170, 228; competitive effects
    of, 29, 152–157, 176, 230; Japanese, 73,
    80. *See also* Consumer loyalty
Quota, 7, 157–163, 169, 174, 228; effect on
    Japanese, 168–169, 200; Ford and, 231;
    indirect effects of, 174–175; oil price
    fluctuations and, 198–202, 205–206, 227,
    233

Rational expectations, 4, 121
Regulation. *See* Government policy
Renault, 27, 30, 33, 37, 50
Replacement demand, 16. *See also* Demand
Repurchase loyalty. *See* Consumer loyalty;
    Quality
Risk exposure, 8, 57, 190, 195, 223–224,
    230–235; cost reductions and, 229–230;
    demand and, 226; diesel engine
    restrictions and, 221–223; fuel economy
    and, 226–227; government policy and, 8,
    206, 209, 218–220, 236; multinational,
    66–69; oil prices and, 205; subsidies and,
    215
Risk hedging, 233–235
Robotics, 30, 80

Safety, 19, 61; in Japan, 73
Scale economies, 23, 25, 61, 169; in small
    cars, 25, 65; component communality
    and, 25; in design and development,
    25–26, 66; internationalization and, 35,
    65–66; in simulation model, 96,
    114–115; Japanese, 79
Scenarios, 96, 99–100; nominal, 129–130;
    oil-price-reduction, 184; oil-shock, 183;
    optimistic, 130; pessimistic, 130
Simulation model, 12–13, 95–126;
    advantages, 11, 95; assumptions
    underlying, 119–121; decision structure,

121; financial performance, 113–119; firms in, 98; fuel economy and, 105; market clearing in, 105–113; strategy in, 96; structure of, 95–98
Small cars, 26, 27, 188–189. *See also* Scale economies
Spence, A. Michael, 4
Steel industry, 2, 10
Stirling engine, 180
Strategic planning, 3. *See also* Strategy
Strategy, of automakers, 23–62, 70, 73, 88, 132, 180; definition of, 5–6; momentum, 8, 234; political environment and, 237; in simulation model, 96, 99, 100; timing and, 61–62. *See also* Risk exposure; Government policy
Structural change, as generic problem, 1; auto industry and, 3, 11, 141–142, 144, 145, 147–148, 225, 230–237; definition of, 6; industrial policy and, 3–5, 236–237; internationalization and, 5, 10; Japanese auto industry and, 82–86, 89, 163–165, 170; methodology and, 3–5, 10–12, 95–98. *See also* Risk exposure; Government policy; Industrial policy; Strategy
Subsidies, 209–215, 230–231; risk exposure of, 232
Supply and demand, in simulation model, 96. *See also* Market clearing; Simulation model
Suzuki, 74, 78

Tariff, 157–163, 228; oil price fluctuations and, 198–202; projected impact on Japanese, 168–169. *See also* Trade policy
Technology, as competitive dimension, 88, 89; fuel-economy related, 96, 101, 103–105, 179–182
Textile industry, 2, 10

Toyo Kogyo, 37, 43, 74, 78
Toyota, 21, 74, 75; manufacturing strategy, 37; product strategy, 53
Trade barriers, 68; against Japan, 84–86; Japanese, 73, 80
Trade policy, 86–87, 91; expectations about, 229; corporate strategies and, 91, 156–163, 169, 176, 227–229; oil price fluctuations and, 198–202; politics and, 91, 175; risk exposure of, 198, 227. *See also* Government policy; Voluntary Restraint Agreement; Orderly Marketing Agreement
Transition pressures, 62

Uncertainty, and risk hedging, 234–235
United Kingdom, 86

Validation, of simulation model, 121–125
Value-added tax, 216
Variable production costs, 113–115. *See also* Costs
Vehicle mix, 16–18, 44–45, 70, 169, 175; projected shifts in, 132, 137–138, 159, 165, 168, 180, 183, 188, 202; simulation model and, 101, 102, 107
Vertical integration, 8. *See also* Component suppliers
Volkswagen, 19, 21, 32–33, 53, 68; U.S. local content and, 26–27
Volkswagen of America, in simulation model, 99
Voluntary Restraint Agreement (VRA), 86; indirect effects of, 174–175. *See also* Trade policy; Orderly Marketing Agreement; Quota
Volvo, 78; product strategy, 45–46
VRA. *See* Voluntary Restraint Agreement

World-car, 66

About the Author

Jeffrey Allen Hunker, formerly a research associate at the Harvard Business School, is now a consultant with the Boston Consulting Group. His specialty is international competition in technology-intensive sectors. He holds the A.B. from Harvard College and the D.B.A. from the Harvard Business School. Dr. Hunker's work encompasses international strategic planning, government policy and regulatory impacts, and the management of technological innovation. In addition to articles in management journals, he is coauthor of *Regulation and Technological Innovation in the Automobile Industry,* prepared for the Office of Technology Assessment.

338.47 6292
H937

116 084